Living Well

Carole Lewis

General Editor

Regal

From Gospel Light
Ventura, California, U.S.A.

Regal

PUBLISHED BY REGAL BOOKS
FROM GOSPEL LIGHT
VENTURA, CALIFORNIA, U.S.A.
PRINTED IN THE U.S.A.

Regal Books is a ministry of Gospel Light, a Christian publisher dedicated to serving the local church. We believe God's vision for Gospel Light is to provide church leaders with biblical, user-friendly materials that will help them evangelize, disciple and minister to children, youth and families.

It is our prayer that this Regal book will help you discover biblical truth for your own life and help you meet the needs of others. May God richly bless you.

For a free catalog of resources from Regal Books/Gospel Light, please call your Christian supplier or contact us at 1-800-4-GOSPEL *or* www.regalbooks.com.

Library of Congress Cataloging-in-Publication Data
Living well / Carole Lewis, general editor.
    p. cm.
  Includes bibliographical references.
  ISBN 0-8307-4290-5 (hard cover)
  1. Devotional calendars. I. Lewis, Carole, 1942-
  BV4810.L58 2006
  242'.2—dc22   2006025210

1   2   3   4   5   6   7   8   9   10   /   10   09   08   07

Rights for publishing this book in other languages are contracted by Gospel Light Worldwide, the international nonprofit ministry of Gospel Light. For additional information, visit www.gospel lightworldwide.org; write to Gospel Light Worldwide, P.O. Box 3875, Ventura, CA 93006; or send an e-mail to info@gospellightworldwide.org.

Contents

Section Two: Begin Again

Key Scripture Verse: Micah 6:8

February 25	Keep It Simple
February 26	The Mission Field
February 27	Divine Dress Code
February 28	The Golden Rule
March 1	Walking the Talk

Key Scripture Verse: 2 Corinthians 12:9

March 2	Identify Your Weakness
March 3	Transforming Limitations
March 4	Who Needs Old Bootstraps?
March 5	Speak Grace

Key Scripture Verse: Philippians 1:6

March 6	When Change Comes
March 7	God's Mysterious Ways
March 8	First Things First
March 9	Don't Say, "Never Surrender"!
March 10	Redeeming Our Bad Choices

Key Scripture Verse: Colossians 3:23

March 11	God's Day-Timer
March 12	It's Not About Me
March 13	Working for the Lord
March 14	For His Glory

Key Scripture Verse: John 1:16

March 15	God's Got You Covered
March 16	Trusting God with the Outcome
March 17	Saved!
March 18	Claim the Blessings

Key Scripture Verse: Philippians 2:10-11

March 19	The Power of Jesus' Name
March 20	Prayer Walking
March 21	Service as Worship
March 22	In Training

Key Scripture Verse: Joshua 1:5

March 23	Fearless or Faithless?
March 24	When We Are the Prodigal One
March 25	Jesus, Our Light
March 26	Unfailing Love

Key Scripture Verse: Isaiah 40:31

| March 27 | Carried Across the Finish Line |
| March 28 | Gift of Encouragement |

Section Three: Living in Grace

Key Scripture Verse: 2 Corinthians 3:17

Key Scripture Verse: Psalm 139:13-14

Key Scripture Verse: Galatians 2:21

Key Scripture Verse: Hebrews 3:12-13

Key Scripture Verse: Romans 3:22-24

Key Scripture Verse: John 15:5

Key Scripture Verse: Proverbs 18:10

Key Scripture Verse: Colossians 2:6-7

Key Scripture Verse: Colossians 3:17

Key Scripture Verse: Matthew 28:19-20

Section Four: A New Creation

Key Scripture Verse: Romans 6:4

Key Scripture Verse: Psalm 37:4

Key Scripture Verse: Colossians 3:1-2

Key Scripture Verse: Isaiah 41:13

May 30	*Baby Steps*
May 31	*Letting Go of Fear*
June 1	*Healthy Pregnancy, Happy Heart*
June 2	*Gym Phobia*
June 3	*In God's View*

Key Scripture Verse: Deuteronomy 20:4

June 4	*Leave the Fighting to God*
June 5	*Spiritual Warfare*
June 6	*V.I.C.T.O.R.Y.*
June 7	*Quiet Time: The Ultimate Weapon*
June 8	*View from the Top*

Key Scripture Verse: Hebrews 4:16

June 9	*Approach the Throne with Confidence*
June 10	*Awesome Invitation*
June 11	*Enter In!*
June 12	*With Humble Boldness*

Key Scripture Verse: Ephesians 2:10

June 13	*Amazing Calling*
June 14	*God Doesn't Waste a Thing!*
June 15	*Living Beyond Our Weaknesses*
June 16	*Forget the* Mona Lisa
June 17	*Make Him Proud*

Key Scripture Verse: Zephaniah 3:17

June 18	*Love Songs*
June 19	*You Are Loved!*
June 20	*The Blessing*
June 21	*It's All About You!*
June 22	*Put a Song in God's Heart*

Key Scripture Verse: 2 Corinthians 10:5

June 23	*To Love God More*
June 24	*Escaping Bondage*
June 25	*To Arms!*
June 26	*Pulling the Weeds*

Key Scripture Verse: 2 Corinthians 3:18

June 27	*Radiant*
June 28	*Seek His Presence*
June 29	*Transformation Takes Time*
June 30	*Reflecting His Glory*
July 1	*Shining Through*

Section Five: Healthy Boundaries

Key Scripture Verse: John 8:32

July 2	*Starting Point*
July 3	*F.E.A.R.*
July 4	*Obedience to Truth*
July 5	*Coming into the Light*

Key Scripture Verse: Isaiah 59:1

July 6	*God's Favorite Child*
July 7	*Keeping Vigil*
July 8	*Loving Discipline*
July 9	*Holding Back a Flood*

Key Scripture Verse: Proverbs 25:28

July 10	*Tried God Lately?*
July 11	*Boundary Rebuilding*
July 12	*Reality Check*
July 13	*Keep Your Defenses Up*

Key Scripture Verse: Psalm 3:3

July 14	*Hope Restored*
July 15	*Safe from Doubt*
July 16	*Shielded by His Love*
July 17	*Trusting His Timing*
July 18	*Transparency with God*

Key Scripture Verse: 1 Peter 5:6

July 19	*Giving Over Control to God*
July 20	*The Good Shepherd*
July 21	*He Is Faithful*
July 22	*Humility, Not Humiliation*
July 23	*Living in His Will*

Key Scripture Verse: Colossians 4:2

July 24	*Praying in the Midst of Change*
July 25	*Prayer as Work*
July 26	*Past, Present, Future*
July 27	*Conversations with God*

Key Scripture Verse: Galatians 5:7

July 28	*Only You!*
July 29	*Staying on Track*
July 30	*Leave the Past Behind*
July 31	*Battling for Balance*
August 1	*Master of Deception and Distraction*

Key Scripture Verse: Romans 12:11

Key Scripture Verse: Proverbs 4:23

Key Scripture Verse: Mark 9:7

Section Six: Choosing Thankfulness

Key Scripture Verse: Psalm 136:1

Key Scripture Verse: Luke 1:49

Key Scripture Verse: Psalm 18:19

Key Scripture Verse: John 14:26

September 1	Seeking the Holy Spirit
September 2	Relying on the Holy Spirit
September 3	God's Power Source

Key Scripture Verse: Deuteronomy 4:7

September 4	Angelic Aid
September 5	Interactive Relationship
September 6	Just Do It!
September 7	My Prayer Journal

Key Scripture Verse: Psalm 18:28

September 8	Living in the Light
September 9	Ask the Right Questions
September 10	Trimming the Lamp
September 11	Facing Dark Days
September 12	Take Aim and Pray

Key Scripture Verse: Psalm 119:14

September 13	Trust in God, Not in Riches
September 14	What Money Can't Buy
September 15	Trusting God with Our Finances
September 16	Rich in the Lord

Key Scripture Verse: Romans 8:32

September 17	Forgiven and Restored
September 18	The Rest of the Story
September 19	The Heart of the Matter
September 20	Will There Be Enough?
September 21	Unfathomable Love

Key Scripture Verse: Hebrews 12:28

September 22	Teachable Moments
September 23	Unconditional
September 24	Three Cs
September 25	Glimpses of Kingdom Beauty

Key Scripture Verse: Ephesians 5:20

September 26	Failing the Test
September 27	Lifestyle of Thankfulness
September 28	Thanking God—In Advance
September 29	Always a Reason for Thanks
September 30	God Things

Section Seven: Celebrating Victory

Key Scripture Verse: Psalm 115:1

October 1	*It's All About God*
October 2	*He'll Take It from Here*
October 3	*Sing His Praises*
October 4	*Look to the Lord*
October 5	*Source of Our Significance*

Key Scripture Verse: 1 Corinthians 10:31

October 6	*Losing It*
October 7	*Potluck Pitfall*
October 8	*What's Your Motivation*
October 9	*You're Being Watched!*
October 10	*Quoting Chapter and Verse*

Key Scripture Verse: 1 Peter 3:8

October 11	*Only Through His Power*
October 12	*Gift of Self*
October 13	*Tears of Joy and Sorrow*
October 14	*Loving When It's Tough*

Key Scripture Verse: Psalm 133:1

October 15	*Behaving Like Adults*
October 16	*Pleasing God, Not Men*
October 17	*Conflict and Food*
October 18	*An Unforgiving Heart*

Key Scripture Verse: Numbers 35:34

October 19	*Personal Pollution*
October 20	*A Pleasing Aroma*
October 21	*Lord, Close My Lips*
October 22	*God's Cleanup Crew*
October 23	*Letting Go of Chocolate*

Key Scripture Verse: Psalm 95:6

October 24	*Come as You Are*
October 25	*Worshiping God by Caring for Our Bodies*
October 26	*Worship—It's About Him!*
October 27	*Bow Down in Spirit*

Key Scripture Verse: Ephesians 5:19

October 28	*Consolation of His Word*
October 29	*Careful Speech*
October 30	*Written on Your Heart*
October 31	*A Radical Commitment Record*

Key Scripture Verse: 1 Corinthians 15:57

November 1	*In Times of Trouble*
November 2	*Symbol of Victory*
November 3	*A Daily Deal*
November 4	*Victorious Finish*
November 5	*Learning Perseverance*

Key Scripture Verse: Psalm 126:3

November 6	*God Is at Work*
November 7	*Discovering Hidden Places*
November 8	*Putting the Scale in Its Place*
November 9	*Attitude of Gratitude*
November 10	*Wear Your Joy*

Key Scripture Verse: 1 Peter 4:7

November 11	*Every Day Is a Gift*
November 12	*Preoccupied with Food*
November 13	*Be Prepared*
November 14	*Making Excuses*
November 15	*Moment by Moment*

Section Eight: Start Living

Key Scripture Verse: Revelation 1:3

November 16	*Stop It!*
November 17	*Reading Out Loud*
November 18	*Keep Your Eyes on Jesus*
November 19	*Heart Knowledge*
November 20	*Listening with the Heart*

Key Scripture Verse: Revelation 3:20

November 21	*Welcome Jesus Inside*
November 22	*Will You Answer the Door?*
November 23	*He Chose You*
November 24	*Only a Prayer Away*
November 25	*"Jesus with Skin On"*

Key Scripture Verse: James 1:22

November 26	*The Bible Is Talking to You!*
November 27	*A Listening Problem*
November 28	*Don't Just Stand There*
November 29	*Out of the Word, Into the World*
November 30	*Do What It Says!*

Key Scripture Verse: Hebrews 3:15

Key Scripture Verse: Psalm 32:9

Key Scripture Verse: Ephesians 6:17

Key Scripture Verse: Proverbs 6:27-28

Key Scripture Verse: Proverbs 23:20

Key Scripture Verse: Hebrews 13:7

Key Scripture Verse: Matthew 26:41

Preface

In some ways, writing this devotional book was easier than writing the first one in 2002, because our First Place people were eager to contribute their stories after seeing the first devotional in print. They were so eager, in fact, that the devotionals came in quickly and we received many more contributions than we were able to use.

But in other ways, writing this devotional was more difficult. The hard part, as usual, involved me. As the general editor of the project, my job was to write at least one devotional for each of the 80 verses covered in the book. During the writing of the first devotional, *Today Is the First Day*, it had been only 6 weeks since our daughter Shari was killed by a drunk driver. I was completely undone. But God miraculously wrote all of my 80-plus devotionals in 8 short days. Of course, He used my brain and hands; but as I look back, I can see that it was really quite easy because I had to completely depend on His strength at a time when I had none of my own. As I sat in front of my computer each morning during those 8 days, the stories flew into my brain and out onto paper.

Now, when my life is relatively trauma free, I didn't count on the fact that I had to get out of the way before I was able to write a single word that made sense. What a lesson this has been! God does His best work when we have no strength of our own—when we are finally willing to move over and let Him drive!

The first devotional book covered First Place Bible Studies 1 through 8 and the 80 verses from those studies. This devotional book covers Bible Studies 9 through 16, using the 80 verses from those studies. First Place now has 160 memory verses that are an integral part of finding balance in all four areas of life—the physical, the mental, the emotional and the spiritual. Can you imagine the power that would radiate from us if we memorized all 160 verses?! Not a bad challenge to accept.

My prayer is that this book will bless you in the reading of it just as much as it has blessed those of us who have written it. Learning to live the life of balance that Jesus Christ offers is truly what living well is all about!

Carole Lewis
First Place National Director

How to Use This Book

This 365-day devotional book has been designed for use by anyone seeking inspiration and growth through a daily time of fellowship with God.

The book is divided into eight sections, one section for each of the last eight Bible Studies released by First Place. The writings are based around 80 key Scripture verses—10 verses within each section. To help you absorb and meditate on each verse before moving to a new one, we have offered several devotionals around a single verse, exploring it from different angles. The verses have been carefully selected to encourage and inspire a closer walk with the Lord, especially when the verses are committed to memory. Each new verse is identified by an open-Bible icon.

If you're not participating in a First Place group but would like additional help with Scripture memorization, Bible Studies 9 through 12 (to which the first four sections in this book correspond) include CDs with memory verses set to music. These CDs have an exercise tempo and are great to use when exercising or just listening to while driving in the car. The memory verses in section five of *Living Well* are from the Bible Study *Healthy Boundaries*. This study includes a DVD that explains more about the nine commitments of First Place and the concept of balance. The two Bible Studies corresponding to sections six and seven of *Living Well* include First Place exercise DVDs. The last Bible study, *Start Living*, includes a CD with 10 motivational messages from Carole Lewis, National Director of First Place.

If you are a member of a First Place group, you may want to start this devotional by reading the section that corresponds to the Bible study you are currently using. This will help you in several ways:

- Using the devotionals that correspond to the memory verse you are memorizing will help impress the truths of that particular verse on your mind.
- Since there are four or five reflective readings for each verse, you will be able to meditate on that verse each day as you pray and as you journal.
- The verses will take on a fresh meaning as you read personal accounts of how God has used the verses in the lives of First Place members.

If you are not a member of a First Place group, you will still benefit from the wisdom and encouragement found in this devotional. *Living Well* is for anyone wishing to gain inspiration and strength in the following areas:

- Weight loss
- Prayer
- Journaling

You will notice throughout the devotional that contributors mention terms that may be unfamiliar to you, such as "CR" (Commitment Record), "Live-It plan" and so on. These are descriptions of some of the nine commitments of First Place. The purpose of these commitments is to help people draw closer to the Lord and become stronger and healthier in every area of life—mental, physical, emotional and spiritual. For those of you who are not participating in a First Place group, here is a complete list of the nine commitments:

- Attendance—Choosing to show up
- Encouragement—Choosing to reach out to others
- Prayer—Choosing to pray
- Bible reading—Choosing to read God's Word
- Scripture memory verse—Choosing to memorize God's Word
- Bible study—Choosing to study the Bible
- Live-It plan—Choosing to eat right
- Commitment Record (CR)—Choosing to be accountable
- Exercise—Choosing to exercise

Many blessings to you, as you allow the scriptural principles contained in this book to strengthen you, and as you allow the words of personal wisdom gained from God's Word and His Holy Spirit to inspire you.

Living well comes from living a life of balance.

Making Wise Choices

Introduction

Living well is about making wise choices. We all make many choices throughout our lives. The daily choices are fairly easy: what to wear, what to eat, what kind of car to drive. Other choices have the ability, if poorly made, to result in horrific consequences, not only for us but for future generations as well. These choices involve who we marry, what type of profession we pursue, how we raise our children and whether we have a personal relationship with Jesus Christ.

Making wise choices means learning to do the right thing every time we are faced with a decision. Although we are flawed human beings, the more we make wise choices, the more we learn what it means to live well.

June Chapko, the writer of the First Place Bible study *Making Wise Choices*, graciously agreed to write a devotional for each of the 10 Scripture memory verses she chose for that study. June has been a First Place Leader for many years and is presently the Women's Ministry Director at her church in San Antonio, Texas. You will find June's devotionals following mine in this first section.

For me, and for thousands of First Place members across the world, the wisest choice any of us has ever made is the decision to accept Jesus as our Savior. As we begin to grow in Christ, we discover that giving Him first place in every area of life—spiritual, mental, emotional and physical—is what living well is all about.

It's About Choosing Life

*This day I call heaven and earth as witnesses against you that I have
set before you life and death, blessings and curses. Now choose life,
so that you and your children may live.*

Deuteronomy 30:19

Each new day brings decisions about whether to choose life or death, blessings or curses. When our family heard the tragic words, "Shari didn't make it," on Thanksgiving night, 2001, we had a decision to make in the spiritual realm: Would we choose death or would we choose life? As Johnny and I stood in the hospital hall, reeling from the news that our daughter had been killed by a drunk driver, I heard Shari's husband, Jeff, tell their three daughters, "Girls, tomorrow we will believe the same thing about God that we believed this morning." At that moment, I knew that Jeff had chosen life.

Choosing life always means choosing God. When we choose life, we choose to believe that God is good, even when our present circumstances are not. It really doesn't matter what our situation looks like today; the remedy is always going to be found in giving our circumstances to God. Do you need to lose a lot of weight? Give the problem to God. Is your marriage in a mess? Give the problem to God. Are your finances a disaster? Give them to God.

God's way is to bless His children, not curse them. As we learn to give Christ first place in everything that concerns us, He gives us blessing upon blessing, and abundant life becomes ours. This book is the seventh that God has written through me since Shari's death in 2001. God has used a terrible tragedy to help and heal countless others. Choose life today. You won't be sorry!

PRAYER

*Father, I want to choose life when I make decisions about what to eat or what to say.
I want to choose life so that I may become a life-giver to everyone I know.*

Journal: List some areas in which you need to choose life today, and ask God to help you.

—Carole Lewis

Leaving Your Children an Inheritance

*This day I call heaven and earth as witnesses against you that I have
set before you life and death, blessings and curses. Now choose life,
so that you and your children may live.*
Deuteronomy 30:19

I was only 21 when my mama died in 1967. Mama smoked most of her adult life, and even when she developed lung cancer, she refused to stop. Her death haunts me even today because I wonder if I will see her in heaven. God has used Deuteronomy 30:19 to help me understand the value He places on making the right choices in life while there is still time. When Mama died, I quit smoking. It was a choice I made to lengthen my life. Because of that choice, the chain of smoking ended with me.

After I became a Christian in 1974, I learned the importance of taking care of my body because it is His temple. When I began the First Place journey many years later, that lesson became real to me. The Lord taught me that I can choose to take care of my temple—or not. I can choose the blessing of life or the curses brought about by death without Jesus in my heart. God urges us to choose life so that we and our children may live.

Though my children are all grown and have families, they know the Lord. They too will know the blessings that come with making the right choices, and they will see their mother in heaven one day! I am so grateful that God has helped me choose life over death, for His sake and the sake of my children.

PRAYER

*Father, help me make wise choices throughout my life, especially as I continue
my weight-loss journey. Help me make choices that encourage my children to
improve the quality of their lives and honor You.*

Journal: Whose life may be affected by the choices *you* make today?

—June Chapko

His Will over Self-Will

*This day I call heaven and earth as witnesses against you that I have
set before you life and death, blessings and curses. Now choose life,
so that you and your children may live.*
Deuteronomy 30:19

As a research project, a nurse friend of mine interviewed former critical care patients who had been placed on a respirator to aid breathing as a temporary measure. Consistently, the former patients recalled a struggle to synchronize with the rhythm of the breathing machine when they began to awaken. In each story, patients told of wanting to breathe on their own. In their efforts to self-will the rate and depth of their breaths, they could not fully benefit from the oxygen the respirator could deliver to their lungs. The patients also spoke of a moment when they realized that they had to let go and let the machine do the breathing for them.

Daily I make decisions that can take me closer and more into the perfect plan God has for me, or I can make decisions that distance me from God's plan. Each day, I must choose to spend time with Him. I must choose to give Christ first place. Why would I want to place myself at risk for a spiritual, emotional, mental or physical crisis?

Just as the critical care patients had to choose to let go and let the machine do the breathing for them, I too must give up my self-will every day and choose to follow God's leadership in all decisions, synchronized to His will and direction.

PRAYER
*Thank You, heavenly Father, for setting before me life and death.
Thank You for giving me the wisdom to choose life,
and thank You for loving me when I have not always chosen life.
I claim the blessings You have for me, in Your Name.*

Journal: Is there consistency in the way you make decisions for daily living? Are your actions decisions for life?

—Sybil D. Smith

Receiving the Blessing

*This day I call heaven and earth as witnesses against you that I have
set before you life and death, blessings and curses. Now choose life,
so that you and your children may live.*

DEUTERONOMY 30:19

I'm a single mom. Not long ago, my First Place leader invited my daughter and me to go to the fair. Weighing in at 364 pounds, I dreaded going because I knew I wouldn't fit on any of the rides. But for the sake of my five-year-old daughter, Kaitlyn, I went.

Kaitlyn had never been to the fair because I was so large. When we got there, I didn't think she would want to ride any of the rides, but she wanted to ride everything. She couldn't ride alone; and since I couldn't fit, my First Place leader rode the rides with her. At first I was grateful, but once they got on the first ride and I saw Kaitlyn laughing with glee and having so much fun, my world fell apart! I thought, *That should be me riding with my daughter and sharing that moment.*

I have now stopped all the excuses. I have started making better choices for myself and Kaitlyn. This is my fourth session in First Place, but now I'm doing it with my whole heart. Each step I take, I'm taking a step with Jesus. I pray harder and work harder because I know that by the time the fair comes to town next year, I will be the one riding rides and laughing with my daughter. Next year I will *fit*!

PRAYER

*Lord, help me to be true to the life choice I have chosen
for myself and my child today.
I choose today to serve You and live a healthier life.*

Journal: List a new blessing that has fallen on you since you chose a healthier lifestyle.

—LaWanda DeLoach

Eating Healthy—
A Life-Giving Choice

*This day I call heaven and earth as witnesses against you that I have
set before you life and death, blessings and curses. Now choose life,
so that you and your children may live.*
Deuteronomy 30:19

I make it a point to observe the eating habits of those who have no problem with their weight, and I have come to the realization that making excuses for my eating habits is the root of my struggle with food.

One beautiful morning after my workout at our city lake, I stopped by the Cracker Barrel for a delicious French toast breakfast. I justified eating the French toast by applying sugar-free syrup and ordering turkey sausage. While I waited on my "sugar free" French toast, a man and woman came in and sat at the table beside me and I overheard them placing their order. They each ordered oatmeal, one piece of toast and orange juice. I couldn't believe they ordered oatmeal. Why would you go to Cracker Barrel only to order oatmeal?!

I ate my three pieces of "diet" French toast and left feeling overstuffed. I noticed the oatmeal couple didn't seem to feel deprived—and they left with a healthy skip to their steps. As I questioned their choice in my mind, the Spirit of the Lord told me that my excuses kept me in bondage, while their choices kept them healthy. I used sugar-free syrup and a good workout to rationalize my French toast choice when it's exactly that type of excuse that keeps me in the struggle mode. I began to pray that the Lord would change my food choices from "diet choices" to healthy choices.

PRAYER

*O Father, please help me to think healthy food thoughts and get out of the diet food men-
tality. Help me, Lord, to choose food that will give me a good, healthy life.*

Journal: List some of the changes you need to make in your food choices to make your life healthier.

—Beverly Henson

A Balanced Life

*Jesus grew in wisdom and stature, and in favor
with God and man.*
Luke 2:52

When I joined First Place in 1981, I had no idea what it meant to live a balanced life. I began First Place like I began everything else at that time, deciding which of the nine commitments I would or would not do. I later realized that the key to the balanced life was learning to practice all of the nine commitments, which affect all areas of life. Luke 2:25 tells us that even Jesus, God's Son, had to grow in all the mental, the physical, the emotional and the spiritual! He was sent to live on Earth and to be tempted in all things just as we are. But He was without sin.

The commitments work together to bring balance to life. The first two—Attendance and Encouragement—help us stay balanced emotionally. The next four—Scripture reading, Scripture memory, Bible study and Prayer—keep us balanced spiritually. The last three—the Live-It plan, Commitment Record and Exercise—keep us balanced physically. When we consistently practice the commitments, our thinking stays in line with what is true and right.

I am so thankful that Jesus walks this path with us and has shown us how to live well.

PRAYER
*Dear Lord, thank You for the First Place program that
brings balance into my life. Thank You most of all
for Jesus, the One who makes balance possible.*

Journal: Write down the areas in which you lack balance in your life, and ask God to give you wisdom and help you to change.

—Carole Lewis

Being Faithful

Jesus grew in wisdom and stature, and in favor
with God and man.
Luke 2:52

I am a Sanguine. That means my personality is all about having fun. So having balance is not one of the strong points of my nature. I've always wanted to be where people are enjoying themselves . . . not at home cleaning, studying or doing whatever non-Sanguine people do!

Even after I called on Jesus to save me in 1974, I still didn't have a clue that the way I was living needed to change, that God wanted me to find balance.

It wasn't until 1983 that I allowed Jesus to begin balancing my life. He worked slowly through a precious friend, Evie, who over the years discipled me through audiocassettes containing recorded Scripture verses and prayers. And she shared nutritious recipes and simple exercises. When I memorized Luke 2:52, I praised God for having sent this friend into my life. She pointed me to Jesus!

Today this verse reminds me that if I am to have balance in my life, I must seek God's wisdom, aim for good health, spend more time with the Lord and treat others with love. Now I begin the day with Jesus, asking Him to show me His plan for my day. When I am faithful to do my part, my life is in balance.

PRAYER
Lord, You have brought a sense of balance into my life. You have made order out
of chaos. Even on days when I feel like a failure, You keep me moving forward.
Help me to become balanced each day by keeping my focus on You.

Journal: Has God used a friend or someone in your life to help you find balance? Write about it in your journal, and then write a prayer, thanking God for using that person in your life.

—June Chapko

Favor with God and Man

Jesus grew in wisdom and stature, and in favor
with God and man.
Luke 2:52

"Dear Lord, give me favor in this interview," I prayed as I drove to the next town for an interview. I had only been out of nurse's training for a short time and wanted to work in a large hospital before I settled down in our small town facility. My prayer was answered, and I was hired to work in the emergency room, where I found favor with the doctors. Though I was new to nursing, they had respect for my years of experience caring for my children. I tried my best to love my coworkers and patients with the love of the Lord and to work hard and with integrity.

A year had passed when the hospital administration had to lay off those of us who had been on the job fewer than five years. My director called me into her office and in tears told me she had to let me go. I felt bad for her, but I knew that God had put me there for a purpose, and I was in His hands. I prayed with her and told her I would be fine.

In the years since, I have gone on many medical missions to other countries, all because I found favor with the doctors and nurses at that first hospital.

PRAYER
Dear Lord, help me trust You wherever You lead me.
And help me treat others with love and respect and
do my very best in everything.

Journal: List some areas in which you desire God's favor; then write a prayer asking for His blessing and the strength to do your best in those areas.

—Bev Schwind

Being About His Business

Jesus grew in wisdom and stature, and in favor
with God and man.
Luke 2:52

This verse in the Bible is about Jesus when He was a 12-year-old boy. His mother and father found Him in the Temple court, sitting among the teachers and asking and answering questions. The Bible doesn't describe Jesus' next 18 years. But we can be sure that although Jesus was unique, He went through the same things we do. He grew physically and mentally, related to other people, had friends—and we know that He loved God.

Jesus grew in wisdom—He matured mentally. He studied the Scriptures, because He was able to quote verses from memory to answer Satan's temptations (see Matthew 4:1-10). Certainly carpentry was physically taxing work and we know Jesus walked long miles during His ministry, so no doubt He was physically fit. Jesus also grew spiritually, as He loved God and spent many hours in prayer talking with His heavenly Father. God said of Jesus, "This is My Son, whom I love; with Him I am well pleased" (Matthew 3:17). He grew emotionally (and socially) as He grew up in his hometown of Nazareth. He related well to other people—we only need to read the Gospel accounts to see that.

It is important to me that I strive with God's help to be more like Jesus as I grow and mature in my Christian walk. This means that I need to learn to put Christ first in every area of my life and love Him with all my heart.

PRAYER

Heavenly Father, I pray that I can continue to grow in every area of my
life to be more like Christ. Thank You, precious Lord, for Your example
of how we are to grow more like You.

Journal: During your prayer time today, ask God to show you areas to work on in your life. How can you cooperate with Him to become more Christlike?

—Janet Kirkhart

Getting Spiritual Nourishment

Jesus grew in wisdom and stature, and in favor
with God and man.

Luke 2:52

There was never a point in time when I made a conscious decision to not feed myself spiritually. However, when we decided to remodel our home, I did make the conscious decision to return to work full-time to pay for the new furnishings. I became so tired from work and the long commute that I cut back on family gatherings and social events. Soon I was too tired to attend midweek prayer service, and I often spent Sunday nights getting a head start on Mondays.

Failure to nurture the spiritual life leads to unanswered questions and confusion. In the healthcare world, "atrophy" is a term used to indicate a wasting away of body tissue or a failure to grow from lack of nutrition. Little did I realize my faith was in a state of atrophy. I certainly was not following the path Jesus had laid out for me—He lived a balanced life physically, emotionally and mentally while fulfilling His spiritual mission.

My out-of-balance life in an overweight body brought me to a point of brokenness. In my brokenness I asked, "Where is God in all of this?" Through a desert experience, I found the healing that comes from living a life utterly dependent on the Sovereign Triune God of this universe. I no longer suffer from the faith atrophy that my misplaced priorities brought about. Now I accept the boundaries He places on my life, and I choose to give Him first place each day.

PRAYER

Thank You, Lord, for the healing You bring in the brokenness of our lives.
Thank You for Your power that provides the opportunity to reverse faith atrophy.
Thank You, Jesus, for Your example of a balanced life.

Journal: Is your reliance on self out of balance? Is your spiritual life being neglected as you take care of things yourself? Do you have questions that long for an answer? Write God a letter today asking for His help.

—Sybil D. Smith

Obedience as Strength

Be strong and very courageous. Be careful to obey all the law my servant
Moses gave you; do not turn from it to the right or to the left that you
may be successful wherever you go.

Joshua 1:7

This verse has three commands followed by a promise. The commands are for me to be strong, courageous and obedient. God's promise is to give me success wherever I go, so long as I keep my part of the bargain.

Most of us desire to have success in life. We want to have a successful marriage, raise successful children, succeed at our jobs, have financial success, and succeed at losing weight and keeping it off. Isn't it great to know that success is God's promise? We are not responsible for successful outcomes—that's God's job! We are responsible for following these three commands.

Being strong, courageous and obedient are tightly intertwined. I become strong as I am obedient. As I gain strength, I become courageous. On the other hand, when I practice disobedience, I become weak and afraid. I believe the key to this verse is the word "obey." Just as children become strong and courageous as they obey their earthly parents, we too become strong as we learn to obey God.

I am learning that obedience is God's love language and that as I practice obedience to the laws and commandments found in the Bible, God's will is for me to be successful. Giving Christ first place in our lives is simply learning to obey Him.

PRAYER
Help me to obey You, my God. I want to have success wherever I go
today and I know that my obedience is the key to success.

Journal: List areas of weakness and fear in your journal, asking God to show you how obedience in these areas will give you success.

—Carole Lewis

Follow the Arrows

Be strong and very courageous. Be careful to obey all the law my servant
Moses gave you; do not turn from it to the right or to the left that you
may be successful wherever you go.
J o s h u a   1 : 7

In one of my First Place classes, I asked everyone to form a line facing the door. I then shut off the lights and led them into the hall. At the far end was a lighted sign that said "EXIT" and an arrow pointed to the right. I carried a flashlight and walked in front of them toward the sign. I told them to be careful to obey all my instructions and not turn to the left or the right unless told to do so.

It was quite dark and took courage for some to do what they were told. When we reached the sign and followed the arrow outside, I congratulated them and explained that they were successful, because they didn't allow other doorways to lead them in the wrong direction.

In our spiritual walks, our weight-loss journeys or any other roads we take in life, when we remain strong and courageous—obeying all that God tells us to do—we will be successful. Our problems arise when we obey *part* of what God commands, thinking we are being obedient. Partial obedience is disobedience, and disobedience to God is sin.

God's Word provides a path for us to follow, and God has lighted signs posted everywhere. If we will simply look for them and follow the arrows, we will be successful wherever we go.

PRAYER
God, help me to be strong and courageous. Total obedience is what You require of me,
but my flesh weakens in the face of temptation. Help me to not turn toward the doors
that lead me out of Your light, but instead to stay close to You.

Journal: What doors have you slipped through that have moved you away from the path God has marked out for you?

—June Chapko

Called out of Our Comfort Zones

Be strong and very courageous. Be careful to obey all the law my servant
Moses gave you; do not turn from it to the right or to the left that you
may be successful wherever you go.

Joshua 1:7

I led a First Place group at the church I had attended for many years when circumstances demanded that I leave that church and move on. I shed many tears over leaving the group I had learned to love dearly! I did not believe in my heart that I could love another group as much as the one I was leaving and doubted that I'd even find a church where I could lead a new First Place group.

But God was in control and led me to a church that was begging for a First Place group but had no one willing to lead. In my former group there were several members who were equipped and willing to lead, but this church had no one.

I knew this was what the Lord wanted me to do. I started a group and such a lovely group of women joined me. I enjoy them so much, and they have really been an encouragement to me. I thank the Lord for His wisdom in leading me where I was needed and where I needed to be.

There is really no need to fear any of life's challenges if we obey God. He will bring joy to our lives as we obey Him.

PRAYER
Dear Lord, help me be strong and courageous as I face the challenges
of today. As I obey Your voice and Your Word, help me not to be
afraid of what lies ahead. You are with me!

Journal: Write about something going on in your life that requires you to be strong, courageous and obedient.

—Joe Ann Winkler

Taste the Goodness

Be strong and very courageous. Be careful to obey all the law my servant
Moses gave you; do not turn from it to the right or to the left that you
may be successful wherever you go.

Joshua 1:7

The Lord loves me and has given me His law to follow in order to guide and protect me from evil. Through the First Place program, I have learned to rely on God's law to be strong and courageous and to face the truth about tempting foods. They are just not good for me, regardless of how good I used to think they tasted or looked.

Today I choose not to eat them. Each day that I refuse to give in to temptation, I experience how truly good being at a healthy weight feels. Nothing tastes as good as that!

When it comes to my food plan, I no longer diet, but choose to Live It as the First Place program taught me. There are simply foods that are good for me to eat and foods that are not beneficial for my body. Following my Live-It food plan requires me to not turn to the right or to the left; if I start eating certain foods that I know have given me trouble in the past, I know I have begun to veer off course. One bite of these items is too much, because due to my sinful nature, a thousand bites of it will never be enough. One bite grows from a taste, to a sliver, to a slice, to a slab—and before you know it, I have eaten it all just so that gnawing emptiness will go away!

But when I remember that God's Spirit is the only One who can fill me, I can turn away from unhealthy foods and taste His goodness.

PRAYER

Lord, thank You for granting me the courage and strength to make changes in my life.
Help me to recognize that veering just a little bit to the right or left leads to the same old
path. Thank You, Lord, for showing me a new way, a way that works—Your way, Lord!

Journal: What are some foods you should avoid completely? Choose today not to eat them, and write your commitment in your journal.

—Roberta Wasserman

Taking Action Against Temptation

Therefore, prepare your minds for action; be self-controlled; set your hope
fully on the grace to be given you when Jesus Christ is revealed.
1 Peter 1:13

My last session of First Place was a good one for me. Being the leader of the group doesn't always mean that I have a good weight loss myself, but this time was different. The session ended and I had lost 15 pounds! I was thrilled and determined that the Christmas holidays would not find me gaining any of the weight back that I had worked so hard to lose.

This verse from 1 Peter was an important one as I planned for success. You see, for the last three years I had received a gift in the mail in mid-December: four pounds of pecans. Every year, I had gotten into trouble with this gift. It always started innocently enough—I'd think, *I'll just open one of the bags and have a little taste.* But before I knew it, I was off and running, sampling all the different flavors.

But this year, as I prepared my mind for action, I told our First Place staff that when the box came, I wanted them to take it down to our pastor and give it to him for Christmas. After a few years of giving away those pecans, my name was removed from the list and the tempting nuts didn't even arrive, all because I prepared my mind to be self-controlled before that December rolled around!

PRAYER
Thank You that when I prepare my mind for action and
practice self-control, Your grace surrounds me and
You reveal Yourself to me.

Journal: Explain how you will prepare your mind for action today and how you will practice self-control when temptations arise.

—Carole Lewis

Back to Basics

Therefore, prepare your minds for action; be self-controlled; set your hope
fully on the grace to be given you when Jesus Christ is revealed.
1 Peter 1:13

One year in November, my friend and I decided to do the "Triple Dare" from *Back on Track*, Carole Lewis's 16-week First Place challenge. Our goal was to emerge 20 pounds lighter in February! We began excitedly, following the Live-It plan, exercise routine and other commitments. I checked off each day's activities, but when I weighed in after the first week, I discovered I had only lost one pound. The second week, I was dismayed to find that I had gained one and a quarter!

I was heartsick. How could this be? Then this memory verse stared back at me from my Bible study: "Prepare your minds for action . . ." Had I truly prepared my mind? Or had I simply begun without stretching and asking God to teach me the basics? God reminded me that I should be transformed by the renewing of my mind (see Romans 12:2). He wanted to transform me, one week at a time, helping me to learn new biblical truths about His grace.

This memory verse also says, "be self-controlled . . ." When I was honest with myself about my lack of self-control, I realized the full meaning of this verse: If I am to be successful, I must focus on Jesus. He alone can help me prepare my mind and be self-controlled. My obedience to His commands will see me through the 16-week challenge, but even more, it will see me through my life's journey until I see Him face to face.

PRAYER

Lord, forgive me for plunging in without preparing my mind. Many times I have drawn up a plan and asked You to bless it, rather than calling on You to design a plan for me to follow. Help me get out of Your way and allow You to reveal Your perfect plan for me.

Journal: Spend quality time with God today, asking for His plan for you regarding your weight-loss journey. Allow Him to reveal to you *His* action steps that you are to follow. Commit them to your heart, write them in your journal, and begin today to be transformed.

—June Chapko

Escaping Hindrances, Embracing Truth

Therefore, prepare your minds for action; be self-controlled; set your hope fully on the grace to be given you when Jesus Christ is revealed.

1 Peter 1:13

"Prepare your minds for action" literally means to rein in all the loose ends of our thinking, or to put it another way, to put a girdle around our minds. When we put a girdle around our minds, we refuse to let them run off in any and all directions. We force ourselves to reject the false beliefs and the lies that are so familiar—even comfortable—and we focus on the truth as revealed in God's Word. We believe it, we receive it, we embrace it, and we listen and heed the Holy Spirit as He declares our true identity in Christ.

Preparing our minds for action also means we act. We develop a strategy for victory by making plans and putting them into practice. Scheduling our Bible study time, prioritizing our exercise time and preplanning our meals are a few ways we can ensure we are not caught off guard. We are fighting for our lives and our Savior's glory is at stake, so we steel ourselves to act against the hindrances that try to rob us of health and wholeness. Some of those hindrances are external, such as the fries at McDonald's, the Frosty at Wendy's, the Whopper at Burger King. Other hindrances are internal, such as emotional eating or a stubborn and rebellious spirit, but they are just as destructive. We must prepare our minds and ask the Spirit for self-control so that we can act with determination, setting our hope fully on the grace of Jesus.

PRAYER

Today, Lord, please help me rein in my mind. You already know every hindrance and distraction I will encounter today. Keep me girded and belted to Your truth, reminding me moment by moment that You have a plan for my victory, and it will succeed if I submit to You.

Journal: What hindrances, whether internal or external, have tripped you up in the past? How can you brace yourself against them today?

—Eulalia King

Only the Bread of Heaven Satisfies

*Therefore, prepare your minds for action; be self-controlled; set your hope
fully on the grace to be given you when Jesus Christ is revealed.*

1 Peter 1:13

I was alone at home one morning dealing with a disappointment, and as in times gone by, I heard my refrigerator start calling out to me. Over and over again my mind went to the comfort I might find in the refrigerator. Finally, I went to scope out the fridge, not noticing the eight-inch red "STOP" sign I had posted on the door. However, when my hand touched the handle, my ears were flooded with continuous repetitions of one line from the gospel song "Fill My Cup, Lord": "Bread of Heaven feed me till I want no more." My hand released the refrigerator door as though it were a hot coal.

What a dramatic rescue! My journey to the refrigerator could have become a highway to destruction. However, an exit ramp had been in the making for some time in the form of Scripture memorization, Bible study, prayer and reflection. Because I had prepared my mind, I realized in that moment that I was hungering for more than physical food could satisfy. The sweet music from heaven sent me to the Bread of Heaven for a time of praise and thanksgiving. My cup was filled to overflowing. God was faithful to do what He promised.

Only the Bread of Heaven can satisfy us in times of disappointment. I do not always hear the music when I touch a refrigerator door today, but that experience always comes to mind when thoughts of a refrigerator-foraging expedition begin to beckon!

PRAYER
*Thank You, Lord, for preparing my mind in advance for daily temptations that I might face.
Thank You for intervening with Your grace and mercy and providing a way of escape. Thank
You for Your faithfulness that will keep me on the road to finding balance in my life.*

Journal: What preparations have you made for today's journey? Is today's journey about God's work? Is your spirit flexible so that it can be taught and shaped freely? Are there any pockets of resistance?

—Sybil D. Smith

Feast on His Word

*Therefore, prepare your minds for action; be self-controlled; set your hope
fully on the grace to be given you when Jesus Christ is revealed.*
1 Peter 1:13

After years of failed attempts to lose weight, I wanted to give up. However, the Lord just would not give up on me. He led me to First Place. Through studying His Holy Word, I learned that God wanted to renew my mind. I realized in examining my past that all my failed attempts to lose weight truly started in my mind, whether it was the idea that I could take just one bite of a tempting food, or the self-incriminating thoughts that plagued my mind when I seemed to fail *again*! I also learned that in order to have victory over a lifetime of doing the same thing (overeating) and getting the same unwanted results (being overweight), I needed God's help to renew my mind.

Preparing my mind involved feasting on God's Word and staying connected to those supportive people who reminded me of my goal to obtain a healthy weight and maintain it. With my mind prepared by being aware of my thoughts and the messages I was feeding myself, I could face temptation without getting discouraged. I recalled that Satan tempted Eve in the Garden and she was taken in by his lies. He also assailed Jesus in the wilderness, but the Lord answered and resisted the temptations with God's Word. Clearly my mind was a battleground, but with God's grace and the example of Jesus, I could be prepared to fight.

PRAYER

*Heavenly Father, thank You for helping me to prepare my mind. Thank You for giving
me self-control, a fruit of the Spirit, to keep the enemy from sabotaging my goals.
Thank You for granting me awareness to discern between Your truths and Satan's lies.*

Journal: Are you willing to be open to new ideas and new ways of thinking? Are you willing to renew your mind and challenge the enemy? Be honest with yourself about your thought patterns and write a prayer asking God to renew your mind.

—Roberta Wasserman

Being Attentive to His Voice

So give your servant a discerning heart to govern your people and
to distinguish between right and wrong.

1 Kings 3:9

As the director of First Place, I pray every day for a discerning heart and to be able to distinguish between right and wrong so that I can serve God and our First Place members to the best of my ability. Over the years, I have noticed that I do my best listening to God and best work for God in the early morning hours. If I am preparing to speak or writing a book, God seems to always awaken me in the middle of the night with His ideas and thoughts on what I need to say.

I have learned that if I ignore His voice and roll over and go back to sleep, the thoughts are no longer with me when I wake up again.

God works with each of His children individually, and this may not be the time He speaks to you at all. He knows us so well that He knows when our most productive time of the day will be, and His voice is the clearest during the time, if we will listen and then obey.

Learning to have a discerning heart is nothing more than listening to God and doing what He says. In my flesh I have no power to govern even myself or to distinguish between right and wrong, but the power of the Holy Spirit living inside of me has great power, if I will only listen and obey.

PRAYER
Lord, I want to have a discerning heart so that I might distinguish
between right and wrong choices today.

Journal: Write down the time of day when God speaks to you best. Ask God's help in learning to spend time with Him during your best time so that you might be able to listen and obey.

—Carole Lewis

Growing in Wisdom as You Lead

So give your servant a discerning heart to govern your people and
to distinguish between right and wrong.
1 Kings 3:9

Being a First Place leader brings with it a great responsibility. We are dealing with people's lives: helping them uncover hidden hurts, get rid of old habits and learn a new way of living. When I felt God call me to lead a group for the first time, I was more than a little nervous. I rather felt like Moses did when he brazenly questioned God, "Who am I, that I should go?" (Exodus 3:11).

I began to pray earnestly for God to give me a discerning heart to govern His people, but even more, to distinguish between right and wrong. I wanted my own life to be an example to others in the choices I made. I needed the wisdom to lead members of my groups into making wise choices that would enable them to lose weight and maintain a healthy lifestyle. God's answer to me was the same one He gave to Moses in Exodus 3:12, "And God said, 'I will be with you.'"

We are all leaders—we all mentor other people: children we raise, employees we supervise, friends and acquaintances that we communicate and grow in relationship with. So we all need a discerning heart. When we pray, asking God to give us that leadership quality, He will. The wisdom and discernment that come from God are vital to success in whatever we are involved in. Whether leading First Place, preaching to a congregation, heading up a women's ministry or conducting a vacation Bible school, discernment from God is necessary for success.

PRAYER

Lord God, as Your servant, I need a discerning heart. I don't want to use my own knowledge to lead those whom You send across my path. My limited view of things cannot compare with the depth of Your wisdom. Help me as I involve myself in the lives of others, to make wise choices and to distinguish between right and wrong.

Journal: What group or relationship are you involved in that requires a discerning heart?

—June Chapko

Bringing God to Work

So give your servant a discerning heart to govern your people
and to distinguish between right and wrong.

1 Kings 3:9

Praying in the car is part of my morning drive to work. I ask God to give me discernment as I work in the hospital emergency room. I have learned to look in my patients' eyes as they tell me why they are there, and then listen to what the Lord might tell me about them.

One day a young teenage boy came in with his mother. They were on vacation at a local campground where the boy had fallen hard off his bike going down a hill. When I saw the boy, an inner voice told me he was sicker that we realized. The doctor checked the boy and we monitored his vital signs, looking for a head trauma or any other visual signs of injury. The boy did not complain, and the mother sat by his side working on her knitting, very relaxed. The doctor had told us to discharge the boy in an hour if there was no change in his vital signs, but I was not comfortable about a discharge, and the doctor agreed to keep him all night.

Later that night, the boy was in grave danger from a rupturing spleen. He was immediately rushed to the operating room for surgery. The family was very grateful and knew if we had allowed the boy to return to the campground some 20 miles away, he would not have made it back to the hospital in time. God answered my prayer for discernment, and I am so thankful I listened to His voice.

PRAYER

Father, I thank You for the gift of discernment. Help me to use it in every
situation so that I may make the right decisions.

Journal: Have you heard an inner voice or had a feeling about something and ignored it, only to find that you should have listened? How can you improve in this area of your life?

—Bev Schwind

A Time to Weep, a Time to Let Go

*So give your servant a discerning heart to govern your people and
to distinguish between right and wrong.*

1 Kings 3:9

In the middle of a deep, sound sleep in the wee hours of the morning, I was awakened by God speaking to me. He told me of news that He knew would sadden me. I didn't want to believe the information, and I shook my head in disbelief as I wept into my pillow. I just wanted to go back to sleep and pretend it was a dream.

The next day at the church office where I supported the youth pastor, the news did come to pass. The youth pastor told me of plans to leave his current ministry and to plant a new church. God had prepared my discerning heart beforehand, and therefore my response was one of joy instead of sadness. I was able to distinguish between a right and wrong reaction. It would have been wrong for me to be bitter—to fail to be supportive as he sought to answer God's call on his life.

When we feed on the Scriptures and study the depths of their meaning, we begin to see life from a different perspective and our hearts are transformed, becoming discerning and understanding. The commitments we make to First Place are commitments we make to ourselves and to God. They will help us distinguish between right and wrong choices, reactions and behaviors. God will send His Holy Spirit to guide us and lead us. We have to be willing to "weep into our pillow" to be submissive, to let go and to let God move.

PRAYER

Father God, thank You for a discerning heart. Thank You that You teach me how to distinguish between right and wrong. I trust in You for my needs of today. In Jesus' sweet name I humbly pray. Amen.

Journal: Write about a challenge you are facing that requires discernment from the Lord.

—Patty Miller

When Food Becomes Your Master

"Everything is permissible for me"—but not everything is beneficial. "Everything is permissible for me"—but I will not be mastered by anything.

1 Corinthians 6:12

I have been involved with First Place for over 25 years, so it is hard to believe that God is still teaching me about myself in the area of food. Food is such an integral part of our daily life that it will probably be a lifetime learning process if we are to gain victory over our weight.

I have learned that there is one type of food that sends me into a downward spiral: anything sweet and creamy. As long as I stay away from sweet and creamy foods, I am able to stay on the Live-It plan. When I begin eating anything sweet and creamy, all my good intentions fly out the window. Since sweet and creamy foods want to become my master, I have a decision to make: I can stay away from those foods that want to master me, or I can give in and never reach my weight goal.

How about you? Is there a certain food that wants to master you? It might be sweet and creamy or salty and crunchy, but every time you eat it, you get off track and start a downward spiral. The food is permissible—that is, it's not "evil"—but it's just not beneficial for you. Would you be willing to give it up to have victory in losing weight? Will you refuse to be mastered by that food?

PRAYER
Teach me, O God, which foods are not beneficial for me and help me stay away from them.

Journal: Make a list of the foods that, when you eat them, send you off track. Begin praying about whether you need to give up these foods for a while so that they no longer master you.

—Carole Lewis

What's Right for *Me?*

"Everything is permissible for me"—but not everything is beneficial. "Everything is permissible for me"—but I will not be mastered by anything.

1 Corinthians 6:12

When I quit working some years ago, I was finally able to enjoy not having to get up early and rush out the door to be at my desk at 8:00 A.M. The problem was that I was used to rising early and automatically woke up. This early hour allowed me to spend time with God before the day got busy. One morning my husband remarked, "I don't know why you're up so early; if I didn't have to go to the shop, I wouldn't be awake so early!"

After he left, I thought about his statement and Satan said, "He's right! You don't have to be up early. You worked hard those many years, and you deserve to sleep in." So, the next day I did not get up. This went on for two weeks. My time with the Lord became shorter, and my plan for morning exercises never materialized.

When I saw this Scripture, I knew I had "permission" to sleep late, stay in bed or order my day the way I wanted; but, even though it was permissible, it wasn't beneficial. It was God's blessing that enabled me to quit my job and be available during the day to help in our family business when needed. If I wasn't careful, sluggardly ways would master me. This Scripture helped me get back to what I knew was right for me. I made the wise choice to rise early and spend time with God before beginning my day.

PRAYER

Thank You, Lord, for enabling me to have more hours to accomplish all that You have called me to do. Help me to remember that while everything is permissible for me, I also have the freedom to say no to what is not beneficial for me.

Journal: In your own life, what is something that is permissible that you have said no to? How has saying no benefited you in your weight-loss journey? In your spiritual growth?

—June Chapko

When Self-Control Fails

"Everything is permissible for me"—but not everything is beneficial. "Everything is permissible for me"—but I will not be mastered by anything.
1 Corinthians 6:12

With the bountiful food supply in First Place comes satisfaction—except for those of us who are "Baggers," who can't stop until they eat their way to the bottom of the bag. Even though I read labels and assign an exchange value to count on the Live-It plan, I still have a problem with gluttony.

Our food industry feeds on any dietary need: low fat, low calorie, low sugar and so on. Baggers excitedly rush to buy, because now it's permissible—we can! These bags become our master; for when we fail to use prayer control, portion control and self-control before opening them, we set ourselves up for a fall. These bagged goodies (like ice cream bars, cookies, chips, candies) are offered to us not by grocers but by Satan's hand. We know before we carry them home we have no self-control in ourselves.

In order to gain control, Baggers must follow these three steps:

1. Prayer control—Before you do anything, pray! *Lord, may I honor You as I eat this item of food.*
2. Portion control—Before eating, measure out individual portions and rebag them in snack bags. Date them for later.
3. Self-control—First record the exchange on your CR, pray again, and then *gratefully enjoy it*, knowing that tomorrow will bring more.

PRAYER
Lord, may I honor You today in my choices. So many things are permissible for me, but I have no control without You. Help me recognize gluttony in any area of my life. Give me the grace to repent and turn that area of my life over to You.

Journal: With what areas of gluttony do you struggle today? Why is gluttony so hard to recognize? If you tend to have no control, what steps can you take to honor God with your eating?

—Judy Marshall

Choosing the Good
(Instead of the Good-Tasting)

"Everything is permissible for me"—but not everything is beneficial. "Everything is permissible for me"—but I will not be mastered by anything.

1 Corinthians 6:12

Before First Place, my past experiences with attempting weight loss were based on a deprivation mind-set. As a young girl of eight, I had gone to a formal weight-loss program with my mother. At that time, I remember that I could not even have ketchup! It was a very strict program. I believe this approach set me up for future binge eating. It was like I had to make up for lost time or something once I started eating those forbidden items!

While doing my First Place Bible Study, I vividly recall an actual renewal of my mind with this Scripture from Corinthians: I began to give myself permission to eat anything I wanted. Nothing was forbidden to me. However, the key to this permissive stance was that this freedom eventually brought me to the place of choosing what was beneficial for me. Once I was no longer tempted by the seemingly forbidden fruit—having given myself permission—I was actually free to make the right and best choice for me.

This is so much like our relationship with the Lord. He does not make any of us choose Him. He does not force His will upon us or put us in a place of bondage. Instead, He approaches us with unconditional love and free will, and in time, we learn to choose Him and His will, because we have discovered at last what is truly good for us.

PRAYER

Oh my Lord, Your ways are not my ways. Your ways of thinking are so different from mine. Thank You for showing me the way to freedom, by granting me the freedom to choose.

Journal: Have you begun to accept that God's will is better for you than your own? Are you willing to give yourself permission to eat whatever you want, trusting that if you truly receive God's love, you will eventually learn to love yourself and choose what is best for you?

—Roberta Wasserman

The Master Builder

Unless the LORD builds the house, its builders labor in vain.
Psalm 127:1

When we purchased our present home on Galveston Bay, we wanted to build a master bedroom, bath and utility room on the water side. God led us to a local man who knew what he was doing, and he designed a beautiful addition to our home and supervised the laborers who built the addition. Even today, I am amazed at how perfectly the job was done.

In any building process, there are those who supervise and those who do the hard labor. God is the Master Builder of our bodies and we are the laborers. My greatest problem in losing weight has always been that I don't want to do the hard work it will take to build a beautiful body for God. Sometimes I want to supervise while *He* does the hard work!

The nine commitments of First Place all work together to build a body that is balanced in all four areas: emotional, spiritual, mental and physical. The Lord, our Master Builder, is the only one who knows what needs to happen first. We might need emotional healing before we begin losing weight, or we might need to let go of some sin that we've been holding on to.

Let the Master Builder determine what needs to happen first; you won't be sorry. The job will be perfect when you do the hard work to carry out His designs.

PRAYER
*Forgive me, Lord, for forgetting that You are the Master Builder and that
I am only a laborer, doing what You tell me to do. Help me do the hard work
needed for success in losing weight.*

Journal: Write down some of the ways you have tried to take over God's job of building a body that brings honor and glory to Him.

—Carole Lewis

Only God Can Craft the Perfect Body

Unless the LORD builds the house, its builders labor in vain.

Psalm 127:1

My husband used to build homes and often dealt with architects and blueprints. He took great care to build each home as it had been planned and drawn. It was of utmost importance that the blueprints be accurate. If not, then all the labor that he and the subcontractors put into that house would be useless. Knowing the design, measurements and finished picture, an architect draws up plans so that builders can transform it into a dream home. If the foundation is wrong or the framing is off, the house will be out of square and not up to code. Materials need to be of good quality and knowledgeable subcontractors must be employed.

My body (my house) was designed by the Lord, the Great Architect. He designed me to be a unique individual. My physical body makeup is what God intended it to be. Before finding First Place, I often tried to take over as supervisor of the building and remodeling of my body. As a result, everything I did was in vain. I was so impatient that I tried fad diets, pills, powders and more. I caused my body to be out of plumb with God's design.

This verse helped me to relinquish my supervisor position, returning it to the Lord. When He builds, it will be done right. Day by day, changes are made and my body responds to God's craftsmanship. I've learned that leaving God out of the building process produces futile efforts on my part.

PRAYER

*Lord, forgive my impatience over the years. I don't know why I thought
I could build a better house on my own. Years of roller-coaster dieting
have taught me that I am not an architect. Thank You for
being the builder of my temple.*

Journal: What part do you perform in the rebuilding of your temple? Do you need to stop supervising and start laboring?

—June Chapko

Letting Go of the "Diet Plan"

Unless the LORD builds the house, its builders labor in vain.

Psalm 127:1

I was a diet-aholic, using various sound (and some not-so-sound) diet plans—always losing weight only to regain it, plus some. I never made a permanent change. Sound familiar?

Drawn to fad diets for decades, I found myself laboring in vain. The problem with these plans was that God was not their builder, so through them lives could not be changed completely as He desires. The one piece of the building plan missing from all other diets is the reason First Place works: God is our Master Builder and has individual plans in mind for each of us.

God is rebuilding this "house" for Himself, and it is not according to *my* plan, but His. We are co-laborers in His new project—a new *me*. The work is no longer laborious, but actually a pleasure when I allow God to do the work. Asking Him for the time, energy and discipline it takes to follow all nine commitments in First Place, I am blessed by His faithfulness in answering that prayer. Brick by brick—one commitment at a time—I work alongside Him to rebuild a healthy temple that brings honor to Him. When I allow Him to continually rebuild all four areas of my life—physical, mental, spiritual, emotional—He is always willing and more than able to make my house beautiful, whole and livable again.

No more laboring in vain for me! With the Lord as my First Place Builder, today is all about tomorrow with Him.

PRAYER

Lord, today I come to You, the Master Builder, asking for help that only You can give. Thank You for allowing me the privilege to join You in rebuilding this temple according to Your plans. And thank You for Your willingness to make my house beautiful, whole and livable again so that I may bring honor to You today.

Journal: Ask yourself, *What can I turn over to God so that He can begin the rebuilding process today?* Post this list on the fridge or some other prominent place as a reminder to you as you work hand in hand with Him to rebuild.

—Judy Marshall

Getting Fit from the Inside Out

Unless the LORD builds the house, its builders labor in vain.
PSALM 127:1

When I came to the First Place program, my only goal was to lose weight. My reasons for weight loss were tied very closely to a poor self-image. For me, being worthy equated to being thin, a false message I had received since childhood.

When I came to know the Lord and discovered Him through the First Place Bible Study, I began to receive different messages. It took me a long time to believe these truths that were so new to me. I read a statement with scriptural evidence that I was a worthwhile human being of magnificent worth. I remember going to pastors and asking them if the basis to this awesome claim was valid. They reassured me that it was based on the truth about the unconditional love of a holy God who could not lie.

As I began to receive this new message, my desire to be thin for the wrong reasons was replaced with a desire to eat healthy for the right reason. I wanted to begin to eat to live—and to no longer live to eat. My life began to have meaning and purpose of different kinds, and the web of deception tied to my self-image and weight was swept away. I began to be rebuilt from the inside out, and—like an old house that has been gutted and restored—I began to appear outwardly like the new creation I had become. The Lord was now the foundation of my life, and Jesus Christ was the Chief Cornerstone—and it showed!

PRAYER
Oh Jesus, thank You for tearing down the old house and rebuilding it on a strong and firm foundation. Thank You for loving me just the way I am, because You know who I truly need to be. Thank You for leading me and guiding me to Your truth that is changing me.

Journal: What is the internal dialog about your worth telling you? Where did these ideas originate from, and are they based on the truth of God's Holy Word? What is your motive for weight loss? Is it to stand on a false foundation the world tries to sell you, or is it a response to the One who created you in His image?

—Roberta Wasserman

Finding Freedom from the Quick Fix

Unless the LORD builds the house, its builders labor in vain.
PSALM 127:1

My dad was a builder—well, that's an understatement! During my childhood, besides the houses he built for his customers, he built four houses for our family. We were a small family—just Mom, Dad and me. Every few years, Mom would say, "Let's paint the bathroom or kitchen" and Dad would say, "Oh, let's build a new house." Dad did the main construction tasks, but Mom and I helped in whatever ways we could. We always moved into the houses before they were finished and spent the next year or two living in the work-in-progress, only to start the project over again on another house, just when we were almost done.

This pattern seems so similar to our approach to dieting and healthy living. When we decide that it is time to remodel our body, we start a new diet. When we grow tired of that diet, we move on to another, and another, and yet another new craze. We never quite finish the task.

As members of First Place, we learn to recognize that we are under construction from within as well as from without. By putting Christ first and following the nine commitments, we no longer labor in vain—and we have the freedom to follow through, working on and living in the bodies the Master Builder has created and is re-creating. Over the long-haul, our "houses" will become beautiful dwellings for God, but only as we labor under His love.

PRAYER
Lord, I know that You are not finished with me. I am truly a work-in-progress.
Help me to stay focused on Your plan so that I am not laboring in vain.

Journal: Are you still looking for the quick fix? Have you really committed your labor to the Lord? Is it time to give it to God?

—Kathy Geehreng

Humility Is Key

Who is wise and understanding among you? Let him show it by his good life,
by deeds done in the humility that comes from wisdom.

James 3:13

Recently, I attended the funeral of Carloss Morris, one of the founders of Stewart Title Company. Carloss was a member of my church in Houston, and I had known him most of my life. He was one of the most humble men I have ever known. When anyone met Carloss, they would never have dreamed that he owned a hugely successful nationwide title company.

As I sat and listened to person after person giving testimony to the wisdom of Carloss Morris, I was reminded that those who are wise usually don't know it. Every speaker said, "I never heard Carloss say an unkind word about anyone."

What a wise man Carloss had become! He had learned to never speak unkind words about another human being, and he understood that a wise life was full of goodness done to others. I was convicted as I listened that I still have a long way to go.

True wisdom will produce a good life full of good deeds done in deep humility.

PRAYER

Dear Lord, I want to be remembered as a wise person when I die.
Help me today to live a life pleasing to You, full of good deeds
done in humility, never speaking unkindly of any of Your children.
Help me to be more like You, Jesus.

Journal: Ask God to show you where you lack humility. Write down areas that He shows you, and begin praying that God will give you the wisdom to change.

—Carole Lewis

Our "Wisdom" Is Foolishness

Who is wise and understanding among you? Let him show it by his good life,
by deeds done in the humility that comes from wisdom.

James 3:13

Many years ago, before First Place, I was determined to lose weight quickly. I chose an 800-calorie-a-day diet plan. While most healthy diets promote no fewer than 1,400 calories a day for women, I wanted to lose weight quickly. And I did! In 5 months I lost 72 pounds. The foolishness of my choice would do severe damage to my body's metabolic rate and nutritional balance for years to come. When I tired of the severity of the diet I was using, the weight returned, and along with it, extra pounds. I fell into depression, feeling unloved—and definitely disliking myself. I saw myself as a failure.

During my 800-calorie-per-day diet, I thought myself wise, but God saw my foolishness. I looked gaunt and anorexic. My energy level plummeted, and I constantly complained of aches and pains. My decision to limit my body to 800 calories each day was selfish and motivated by pride. I wanted to look good fast, but worse than that, I wanted to be able to say, "I did it!"

Now, as I work on making my body as fit and healthy as possible, I do so in the humility that comes from wisdom. That wisdom comes from God, not me. I'm not always wise and understanding, but I strive to do what God tells me. When I use heavenly wisdom, I feel better about myself—and it shows in how I live and how I pursue a healthy weight.

PRAYER

Lord, thank You for Your wisdom. Help me use it consistently and show it by the wise
choices I make in taking care of my body. I don't want to be prideful, so humble me
from the inside. Show me my foolishness before I act it out.

Journal: Does your life show that you are wise? In what area(s) do you need God's intervention?

—June Chapko

What Story Does Your Life Tell?

Who is wise and understanding among you? Let him show it by his good life,
by deeds done in the humility that comes from wisdom.

James 3:13

My grandmother made quilts. Not the machine-made variety available in stores today, but hand-stitched quilts made from the very fabric of my grandmother's life. I can still hear her telling me her quilt story. As she ran her hand across each small square, she would say, "I made the dress your mother wore the day she started school from this cloth," or "My kitchen curtains were this design," or "This was taken from my daddy's casket lining."

My grandmother also liked to look at quilts others had made, and she said she could tell what was going on in the life of the quilter by looking at how the quilts had been put together. Were the stitches neat and even, or were they hurried and broken? Were the patterns bright, cheerful and creative, or did dull colors tell stories of sadness and hard times? To my grandmother, these details were the life story of a quilter, told through her quilt.

James tells me that my life is just like my grandmother's quilts. All the various pieces, some joyous and some sad, must be carefully sewn together with wisdom and humility so that they display God's power working in me. When others observe my life and the deeds that flow from it, do they see a pattern of wisdom and humility? Is the love of Jesus woven into every event? Is His name embroidered on my work? Today I pray the pieces of my life are stitched together in a way that displays His love, mercy and grace.

PRAYER

My Lord God, I thank You that I can be confident that You are weaving all the events of my life into a pattern that tells the story of Your awesome power at work in my life.

Journal: Write a "quilt story" about your life by stitching events together in a way that displays the Lord at work in you.

—Elizabeth Crews

A Mother's Example

Who is wise and understanding among you? Let him show it by his good life,
by deeds done in the humility that comes from wisdom.

James 3:13

I was amazed to see all the weeds in my mother's garden. She had kept a show garden for years, but since Dad died, Mother was having a difficult time keeping up with things. She rose from her kneeling position in the garden using the hoe handle as a support and said, "I believe God is telling me it is time to let my garden go and transplant myself to a smaller home." She gave me her usual smile, and we began to discuss what we would do.

Her humility and wisdom made things easier for my brother and me. She was 88 years old when we went through the upstairs to help her get ready to move. She lovingly kept some of the mementos of her past—and laughed and tossed out others. It was hard for her to leave, but she was confident she would bloom in her apartment, which had a window box.

She was 90 years old when she said she might as well give up her car, as we seemed to drive her wherever she needed to go. Her wisdom through the years continued as she moved out of state to live with me, and today at the age of 96 she sits in her chair in our home and reads her favorite book, the Bible. Her wise humility in realizing when it's time to give up things and make a change has not always been easy, but she has done it. As a result, she is still blooming where she is planted.

PRAYER

Thank You, Lord, for the seasons of my life. Help me as I go from season to season to show wisdom and not let pride interfere with my decisions.

Journal: Ask the Lord to help you make wise choices and to give you humility to face whatever challenge lies ahead.

—Bev Schwind

The *Only* One to Trust

Some trust in chariots and some in horses, but we trust in
the name of the LORD our God.
Psalm 20:7

There is a saying today, "Those with the most toys wins." We are constantly tempted to trust in cars, boats, four wheelers and all kinds of "toys" that have no eternal value. If our happiness is determined by the things we possess, we are in big trouble.

Last fall when Hurricane Rita was approaching, we said good-bye to our home when we left, knowing that if the hurricane came into Galveston, our home would have 20 feet of water over the top of it. We left knowing that the lifetime of "stuff" we had accumulated was just that: stuff.

We were grateful when we were spared the wrath of the storm, but were grieved that so many of our neighbors to the east lost everything they owned. Our Christian friends who survived Hurricanes Katrina and Rita are living proof that God is the only one we can trust. I know in the days to come there will be wonderful testimonies of God's sufficiency and grace in their lives.

The nine commitments of First Place teach us how to trust only in God. We learn to pray before we make foolish purchases. We memorize Scriptures that help us to trust God and make wise choices when we eat. If we trust in Him, He is faithful to His promises. We don't need stuff when we have the strength of the Lord on our side!

PRAYER
Dear Lord, help me trust only in You and not in the
possessions You have given me.

Journal: Are there things you don't think you could live without? Ask God to help you hold loosely the horses and chariots of this world.

—Carole Lewis

Chariots Break Down, Horses Get Tired

*Some trust in chariots and some in horses, but we trust in
the name of the LORD our God.*

Psalm 20:7

I, like so many others, am spoiled by modern technology and the equipment we have come to expect will provide instant answers. It seems difficult to wait when we have fax machines, computers, cell phones, digital cameras and photo printers. I remember when I had to wait seven days (or pay extra) to get photos developed. Now I view them instantly on my digital, load them on the computer and can even print them on a small photo printer in a matter of seconds.

There are weeks when I have been faithful to do all my First Place commitments, but when I get on the scale, I haven't lost weight—or at times I've even gained a little in spite of my faithfulness. Times like that I get impatient and want to jump on a chariot (some fad diet), pulled by swift horses (my own power), because God is taking too long to get me where I want to go. In times like those, I must remember that God has been teaching me truths I need to learn in order to be successful.

One important truth He has taught me is about patience, which is grown by trusting God. Chariots break down and horses have limited strength, but God's power goes on forever! Fad diets fade away, and willpower gives out in due time. We must trust in the name of the Lord our God to give us success.

PRAYER
*Forgive me, God, for trusting in anything or anyone but You.
Help me learn all You have to teach me and to use that knowledge consistently.
Teach me to trust You and grow in patience.*

Journal: What chariots have you boarded in your quest to obtain faster solutions to your struggles? Where have those chariots taken you?

—June Chapko

The *Real* "Real Thing"

Some trust in chariots and some in horses, but we trust in
the name of the LORD our God.
Psalm 20:7

In 1969, Coca-Cola started their "It's the Real Thing" ad campaign. In 1990, they changed it slightly to "You Can't Beat the Real Thing." (Since Diet Dr. Pepper is my drink of choice, I have to admit I am not in agreement with Coke's claims.)

This world (chariots and horses) many times offers success and victory, but supplies only disappointments and disillusionments—definitely not the real thing! Just when we think we can bank on something, it changes.

The only thing we can know for sure is that our God does not change, and we can trust in His name. He is the same yesterday, today and forever. He never leaves us nor forsakes us. He will be with us always until the end of the age. He never slumbers or sleeps. He is the beginning and the end. He is our Rock, our Anchor, our Strong Tower, our Shelter, our Savior, our Comforter and our Prince of Peace. He is the Real Thing, and He can't be beat.

So whether you drink Coca-Cola or Diet Dr. Pepper or something else, remember that only our Lord is the *Real* Real Thing. Trust in Him.

PRAYER
Heavenly Father, thank You for Your trustworthiness and for being there for
me when I need You. Thank You for Your unchanging and unconditional love.
You are my Shelter I run to in the storms of this life. You are the Anchor that holds me
in place in stormy circumstances. You are the Rock I can stand on in the shifting sands
of this world. You are my Savior and the One and Only Real Thing. I know that
I can trust in Your name, my Lord and my God.

Journal: If you have faced some disappointments and disillusionments in your life and are dealing with some real trust issues, write in your journal exactly what you are feeling. Then list all the wonderful attributes of God that will see you through whatever is coming your way. You can trust God, and He will give you peace and comfort beyond measure.

—Mary Etta Jackson

Leaning on His Strength

Some trust in chariots and some in horses, but we trust in
the name of the LORD our God.
Psalm 20:7

Every time I began a new weight-loss program, I was filled with enthusiasm and hope for my future success. I would throw myself into the new program and strive to do it perfectly. My hope was firmly placed on this new plan for weight loss, regardless of the details. Each time, I just knew that *this* was the answer, that *this* plan would work. However, after repeated failures, I was left each time feeling worse about myself, and the initial weight loss was all regained in a vicious repeating cycle.

When I came to the First Place program, I began to see that I had been placing my hope and trust in a diet program instead of trusting in an amazing God—the only One who had a permanent solution to my weight and lifestyle issues. I discovered that the almighty God cared about my weight problems, as insignificant as they felt to me next to a magnificent Lord. Over time, I began to let go of my trust in temporary programs. God offered me a new way of life, a new way of living and a new way of being.

It was an internal transformation that led to an external and eventually obvious change. I have maintained my weight loss for over 10 years now, along with my continued relationship with a living God who always wanted me to choose life. Today, my trust is in *Him*.

PRAYER

Oh my precious Lord, You have given me life. You have granted me
freedom to stop trusting in diets and scales and to trust in You,
the living God who showed me a new way. Yes, Lord, by Your grace
I live it one day at a time. Thank You, Jesus, thank You.

Journal: Are you ready and willing to try a new way of life? A new way of living—one that our trustworthy Lord has designed? Write a prayer of readiness today.

—Roberta Wasserman

Don't Look to a Guru—Look to God

Some trust in chariots and some in horses, but we trust in
the name of the LORD our God.

Psalm 20:7

"Try this; try that!" "Buy our new product." "Listen to the latest guru." "Get more stuff and you'll be satisfied!" This, that, or the other thing—whatever that thing is always promises to bring us comfort, peace of mind and an ever-elusive false sense of happiness. Sometimes, when attempting to navigate the rough waters in my life, I am tempted to look for quick fixes or temporary solutions. Although fame, fortune and wealth appear highly desirable, they never can guarantee personal satisfaction. No person, place or thing of this world can—and they're not supposed to.

Our ancestors trusted in chariots, horses and an array of false idols. We, too, have trusted in money, food, relationships, cars, careers, most anything to meet our unfulfilled needs. Today, I understand this is pure foolishness. Yet even armed with this knowledge, I still occasionally succumb to the false hope that someday the magic weight-loss pill will appear on the horizon like a bright beacon of light. Thank goodness, I've learned that by relying on God, making healthier food choices and exercising more frequently, I can achieve my goals for a healthier body. Stated simply, I've learned on a deeper level the difference between wise and foolish choices.

Every day, we have the opportunity to choose God's way or the way of the world. God or a shiny chariot—who or what will you choose? Be wise. Choose life! Trust in the Lord. You'll be thankful you did.

PRAYER
Dear Lord, today I choose to trust in You. The things of this fallen world always leave me
hungering and thirsting for more. Give me a heart that beats for You alone and a mind
that quickly recognizes wisdom from folly. Thank You, Jesus, for Your truth and love,
which are the perfect ingredients for lasting change.

Journal: Take a moment and ask God to help you identify any false substitutes you might be trusting in today, and then list them in your journal.

—Carol Van Atta

2011
*Dad Baehr went
to Greenpoint to
live.*

God's Part, Our Part

*For God so loved the world that he gave his one and only Son,
that whoever believes in Him shall not perish, but have eternal life.*
John 3:16

There are two parts to this verse: God's part and our part. God's part was to give—He gave His one and only Son, Jesus, so that we might have eternal life. Our part is to believe—when we believe that Jesus came to Earth, died for our sins and rose again, we receive eternal life.

Being born again is the greatest gift we could ever receive, but this experience is only the starting point for each of us.

I believe that one of the many gifts God gives us are the people He places in our lives: our families, friends, coworkers and people we meet along the way. If we believe that God loves these people (because He loves *the whole world*) and places them in our lives, then surely He desires that we love them as well.

I've heard it said, "I could do this job if it wasn't for the people." Our world is made of the people in it! God sent Jesus for us but also for everyone else in our world. Our part is to continue believing God and sharing His love with people we know.

PRAYER

*Dear Lord, I want to share Your love today with everyone I come in contact with.
Help me believe that You gave me these people
and that my job is to love them unconditionally as You love me.*

Journal: Is there someone you have trouble loving? Write that person's name in your journal and ask God to love that person through you.

—Carole Lewis

God's Sacrifice

For God so loved the world that he gave his one and only Son,
that whoever believes in Him shall not perish, but have eternal life.
John 3:16

I love my three children beyond words and would do most anything to help them. I would never consider sacrificing one of them for anyone or anything. When I memorized this verse many years ago, I found it difficult to imagine how God could give up His one and only Son for anyone. My mind could not comprehend the depth of that kind of love.

I carried each of my children in my womb for nine months and gave birth to them. I tended to them through illness, agonizing over their pain and suffering. I helped each of them through childhood diseases, peer pressures, temper tantrums and driver's education. I cried with and for them when they were discouraged and prayed for their souls. I rejoiced when each came to know the Lord and wept when they strayed. No, I could not fathom how a parent could sacrifice his or her child for anyone.

By studying God's Word, I have come to understand more about His willingness and desire to do whatever it takes to make sure no one perishes. He wants all to know Him and His love. God hasn't asked me to sacrifice my loved ones. He has shown me that the love I have for them is nothing compared to the love He has for me and for everyone. Because of His sacrifice, I will spend eternity in heaven.

PRAYER
God, Your love is beyond my ability to understand. I only have to accept it.
I am thankful that You provided salvation through Your Son, Jesus.
It must have been painful for You to send Your Son to the cross.
Thank You for Your ever-reaching love.

Journal: Have you accepted God's Son? If so, what does that mean to you? If not, read the book of 1 John and journal about God's love.

—June Chapko

Belief Is What Matters

For God so loved the world that he gave his one and only Son,
that whoever believes in Him shall not perish, but have eternal life.

John 3:16

When I weighed in at 310 pounds, I felt so undesirable. I couldn't see how anyone could love me. I didn't love myself very much, so how could someone else love me? I stayed away from people because I felt like they didn't really want to be around me. I even wondered if God would love me more if I lost weight.

Revelation came while I was meditating on John 3:16. The spirit of the Lord revealed to me there is no weight requirement to *believe*. To God our Father, all His children are a size six! First Samuel 16:7 tells us that "God looks on the heart," not at our dress size. With God, size doesn't matter—belief in His Son is what gives us eternal life, not our toned abs.

I loved the Lord when I weighed 310 pounds, but when I got a true revelation of how much He loves *me*, I was freed to move on spiritually. When I feel undesirable, God desires that I bask in His love for me. Not because I had a good day with my diet and workout or because I met my goal weight and have been on maintenance for seven years—but because I believe!

PRAYER
I thank You, Father, that You love so much.
I am so glad You look at my heart and not my dress size!

Journal: Write a love letter to the Lord and let Him know how glad you are that He loves you.

—Beverly Henson

Christ Can Do

For God so loved the world that he gave his one and only Son,
that whoever believes in Him shall not perish, but have eternal life.

J o h n   3 : 1 6

Believing in Jesus is about much more than the initial salvation experience. Believing that He is God's Son who died on the cross and shed His precious blood so that we can spend eternity with Him in heaven is only the beginning. We must expand our belief in Christ from believing only that He is who He says He is, to believing that He can do what He says He can do in our lives.

When I came to First Place, I had been on so many diets. I had no idea that Jesus could help me with my weight. I didn't realize that part of my belief in Him included believing that He paid the price for my victory over food addiction.

One day as I was walking my two-mile walk, I became aware that I had been seeking to be thin instead of seeking Jesus. I told the Lord that I believed He had the keys to unlock the doors that would set me free from my food addiction so that I could focus on Him. I had to believe that Jesus could do what He says He could do in my life.

That simple step of faith carried my initial salvation experience to a deeper relationship with my Lord Jesus Christ.

PRAYER
Thank You, Lord, for a new belief system.
I believe that You already paid the price for my sinful nature.
I believe that Your blood has set me free.
I believe that You are who You say You are and can do what You say You can do.

Journal: Write your thoughts about some of the areas of your weight loss for which you need the Lord to give you a new belief system and increase your faith in Him.

—Beverly Henson

Begin Again

Introduction

The verses from this section of *Living Well* all relate to beginning again. All the verses point to Jesus, our source of strength and power to start over when we've failed or when life's circumstances have knocked us down. Beginning again is a very real part of life, and learning the secret of beginning again is at the core of *Living Well*.

Beginning again is the heart of my book *The Divine Diet*. I believe that three things must happen if we are to learn how to begin again. These three things are:

- **Accept Where You Are**. A friend of mine has a saying: "Wherever you go, there you are!" Even though it sounds funny, it bears a lot of truth. Before we can begin again, we must accept the fact of where we are right now. Poor choices of our own or of someone else's might necessitate the need to begin again. Whatever the reason, we can never begin again until we take a long, hard look at where we are right here, right now. And remember, most people who are in the top 10 percent of anything were once in the bottom 10 percent. It's okay to be where you are right now, just not okay to stay there.

- **Be Willing to Change**. Before we can begin again, we must be willing to change. Change can take many forms. It may be changing our lifestyle to lose weight and get healthy. It may mean changing our emotional life by forgiving past hurts and letting go of bitterness. It may mean changing spiritually by adding time each day to spend with God. It might even mean changing the way we think so that we think changing is possible for us.

- **Call on God**. The words of Jeremiah 33:3 tell us, "Call to me and I will answer you and tell you great and unsearchable things you do not know." Beginning again will fail every time unless we call on God for help. As we call out to Him, He will show us the way and help us when we fall. As we meditate on and memorize the verses in this section of *Living Well*, we will learn more of what it means to begin again.

Martha Rogers, the writer of the First Place Bible study *Begin Again*, wrote one devotional for each of the memory verses she chose when writing the study. You will enjoy getting to know Martha as you read her devotions found right after mine for each of the 10 verses. Martha makes her home in Houston, Texas, and is a retired school teacher who now devotes her spare time to writing. She wrote all the revisions for the first eight First Place Bible studies and continues to lead a First Place group each session.

Grace to you as you learn what it means to begin again. Beginning again is one of the tools for living well.

Making *All* Things New

Therefore, if anyone is in Christ, he is a new creation;
the old has gone, the new has come!
2 Corinthians 5:17

I'll never forget the day we were saying this memory verse in our First Place class. One of the members, after she recited the verse, said, "Out with the old, in with the new." I have never forgotten the paraphrase used that day because this is the essence of our new life in Christ.

Since we are new creations in Christ, God desires to make all things new in our lives. God desires for our minds to be made new, for us to think new thoughts that are pure, lovely, admirable, excellent and praiseworthy (see Philippians 4:8). God desires for our bodies to be made new; and this might mean losing weight and becoming physically fit. God desires emotional health for us, so this might mean we need to be healed of past hurts and pain. Finally, God desires for us to be new creations spiritually, and this happens as we toss out many of our old habits and learn to read, study and memorize God's Word.

Prayer is the tool God uses to accomplish the newness He desires for us. As we learn to talk to God and listen to God, we become entirely new creations. Being "in Christ" is all about relationship, and that relationship is established through prayer.

PRAYER
Dear Lord, I desire to be a new creation in Christ, so I ask You to
get rid of the old and bring in the new today.

Journal: List some of the old things that God might want to replace in your life.

—Carole Lewis

The Forgiven

Therefore, if anyone is in Christ, he is a new creation;
the old has gone, the new has come!
2 Corinthians 5:17

For many years my brother was dead to me. He had been in and out of prison for various drug-related crimes, and I no longer wanted to claim him as my brother. When my mother called me to tell me of yet another arrest and jail sentence, I didn't want to hear it. I had my own life to live, and he wasn't a part of it.

One winter morning, Mother called again to tell me that Johnny, my brother, had accepted Christ in jail. I refused to believe her and told her so. She said, "Martha, Johnny has changed, and he loves you. Why can't you love him?" I couldn't answer her and quickly ended the call. When I started my Bible study, I found 2 Corinthians 5:17 in the reading for the day. If Johnny had accepted Christ, he was a new creation. Could it be true? Could God make him new? Of course He could. He had made me a new creature when I had accepted Him. The more I pondered this verse, the more I began to realize I had to forgive Johnny just as our Savior had done.

I wrote Johnny a letter begging his forgiveness and telling him I had forgiven him for all the hurt he had caused in my life. His letter in return confirmed that, indeed, he was a new creation in Christ. My brother is still in prison, but he is God's child, and I love him.

PRAYER
Father God, help us forgive others even as You have forgiven us.
Help us to see the new creation You bring forth
with Your love and forgiveness.

Journal: Call to mind anyone in your life who has hurt you or wronged you and needs your forgiveness. Pray for that person today and then make an effort to make things right between the two of you.

—Martha Rogers

A Fresh Start

Therefore, if anyone is in Christ, he is a new creation;
the old has gone, the new has come!
2 Corinthians 5:17

As a volunteer chaplain, I ministered to victims of Hurricane Katrina on the Mississippi Gulf Coast. In the physical sense, many of these people had lost all their worldly possessions, and even friends and family members. In a spiritual sense, their world was turned upside down and their faith shaken.

On my first visit (during the second week after the storm), I often heard the question, Why did God let this happen? We know that God did not let this happen! He allows us to choose where we live, the lifestyle we lead and where we place our priorities; however, He has compassion and even weeps with us when we are hurting.

On my second visit (six weeks after the storm), I was struck by the way God was healing His natural world. What a stark difference compared to the miles and miles of rubble left by man-made structures.

It is the same for us. When we follow Christ, we are a new creation. Even though we will surely have our crises, we too can experience natural healing as part of His creation.

PRAYER
Father God, thank You for saving me and making me a new creation.
Help me to realize that You are always with me,
especially when I am hurting. Amen.

Journal: Are you ready to become a new creation by seeking the Lord's help in all ways?

—Jack Dorn

Spread Your Wings!

Therefore, if anyone is in Christ, he is a new creation;
the old has gone, the new has come!
2 Corinthians 5:17

The butterfly has emerged from the chrysalis; its wings folded to its body. I watch it move so that it would have room to hang upside down by its legs from the top of the container. The butterfly then swallows air that causes the fluid to be pumped into the veins of its wings. It remains still until the wings have hardened enough to fly.

My daughter watches this whole amazing process unfolding. When the wings are moving and the butterfly is ready, she sets it free to be what God created it to be. We have been traveling, and she has had to bring the hatching butterflies along so that she can release them at the proper time.

The sun is also necessary to the butterfly, as its body temperature needs to be 85 degrees or more before it can fly well. A butterfly hatched on a cloudy day can be seen lying on a flower trying to catch any of the sunrays that may come through. It basks in the sun. The sun gives it energy to be able to fulfill its purpose.

We need the Son, Jesus, in our life. We need to bask in His Word and seek Him in prayer. The butterfly swallows air so that it can fly. God breathes into us the breath of life!

PRAYER
Thank You, Father, that You have created such a beautiful
winged butterfly from a crawling creature. Thank You for changing
a lowly sinner like me into one of Your children.

Journal: Have you been afraid to spread your wings and do what you need to do? What does the butterfly's journey teach you?

—Bev Schwind

The Ultimate Makeover

Therefore, if anyone is in Christ, he is a new creation;
the old has gone, the new has come!
2 Corinthians 5:17

I was flipping through the television channels one afternoon when I spotted those two words that always catch my eye: "extreme makeover." Then I saw him—the victim. He was the grandfather of a young woman who would soon be married. She loved her grandpa, but she was embarrassed by the bushy gray hair that covered his whole head and face; the cheap plastic glasses stuck on his nose at a weird angle; the pair of tight, worn, dirty overalls that were his daily attire. I found myself thinking, *That guy is a mess!*

Ten Hollywood minutes later, out walked a man in a perfectly fitted black tuxedo. He had short, well-trimmed blonde hair and an angelic face. With clear, wrinkle-free skin and bright white teeth, he was downright handsome! The change was remarkable!

When I first came to First Place, I would have paid a lot of money to have someone do an extreme makeover on my physical body. It took a lot of Bible study, sharing and praying, but then one day it dawned on me that the physical makeover I had watched on TV was nothing compared to the spiritual transformation that had taken place in me the day I asked Jesus to be my Lord and Savior. I can imagine the heavenly host watching, stunned at the change, saying, "I can't believe it! Before Jesus, that woman was a mess!"

PRAYER
Lord, thank You for the makeover that has released my old,
sinful nature and made me a new creation.
Let all people see You in the new me!

Journal: Do you let your appearance keep you from doing the things God has planned for you? Make a list of the changes you have seen in your life as a result of Christ's presence. Are those changes more important than thinner thighs?

—Barb Lee

God's Good Plan

And we know that in all things God works for the good of those
who love him, who have been called according to his purpose.
Romans 8:28

As we were nearing year's end, I received two pieces of devastating news on the same day at the same time. First, I found out that my husband, Johnny, would no longer be on my health insurance because my work was going to an HMO. Second, I heard that Kay Smith, my 17-year associate and long-time friend, would no longer be able to work for First Place from her home in Roscoe, Texas. All full-time employees would now be required to work in the Houston office.

Years ago, I would have been reeling from two such upsetting blows, but because of my history with a God who loves me with an everlasting love, I was sad but undaunted. I knew that God had a plan and that Romans 8:28 is still true.

Johnny is going to go on Medicare with a supplemental policy, allowing us to keep our doctor in California. And just this week we found that our new Medicare prescription plan carries every drug that Johnny takes. Great news for today!

And Kay has found a job in Roscoe at their local bank and will be training to move into a marketing position with the bank. We will miss her terribly, but we know that God knows what He is doing in this situation too. We serve a good God who works for our good.

PRAYER

I praise You, Jesus, that You are working all my circumstances into good because I love You and I'm called according to Your purpose. Help me to trust more and more, even in the face of distressing situations that I can't understand.

Journal: Write down some challenging circumstances you are faced with right now, and thank God that He is already working them out for your good.

—Carole Lewis

The Valley and the Mountaintop

*And we know that in all things God works for the good of those
who love him, who have been called according to his purpose.*

ROMANS 8:28

After revising seven of the original Bible studies for First Place, I had the opportunity to write an original study about beginning again after we slip and fall. In choosing the Bible verses, I looked for those that had special meaning for me in my spiritual walk. This verse is one I've clung to throughout my life.

For years I questioned God as to why my parents divorced, why my mother tried to commit suicide, why I went through a severe illness, why my brother was a drug addict, and why I suffered two miscarriages while also being able to give birth to three sons. Then God began using my trials as a way of helping my students with their own difficulties. Many times I told them that God could take care of their troubles because He had taken care of mine. Two girls in particular came to know Christ through the bond we developed as I worked with them. My losses were worthwhile when I considered that I reached these girls with the gospel precisely because of my losses.

As I wrote *Begin Again*, I thought back over some of the events and was able to use them as testimonies of God's great faithfulness. Every event was traumatic, but I learned anew that God's timing and His reasons are perfect. When we are called to His service and are obedient to His will, He will take us through the deep valleys and on to the mountaintops.

PRAYER

*Heavenly Father, thank You for being with us every step of the way and working our
lives for good no matter what the circumstances.*

Journal: Think of times when you had a difficult situation or experienced tragedy. How did God's presence help you through crisis? Write down one good thing that may have come from it.

—Martha Rogers

Loving God More Than Food

And we know that in all things God works for the good of those
who love him, who have been called according to his purpose.
Romans 8:28

Growing up with my parents owning a "mom and pop" store had an advantage and a disadvantage. When I was a child, I thought the advantage was bingeing on an unlimited supply of candy, ice cream and soda; and the disadvantage was that I had to work hard at a young age.

As the years passed, I realized that it was really just the opposite!

I struggled for years with my weight, going from diet to diet with no lasting results. For years I prayed that God would help me lose weight, but with so many attempts and failures, I was losing hope.

I realize now that God has worked all the things of my past together for my good. The hard work ethic that I developed early in life has helped me succeed in many areas of my life, including First Place. Today I can say that I am succeeding in the First Place program because I have been willing to work hard at obeying and trusting God—and He has definitely worked for my good. Yes, it has taken a lot of work, but I love God more than food now, and I am free to accomplish His purposes in my life. He is using me to teach young people how to have a balanced life in all areas—imagine that!

PRAYER
Lord, today I choose to believe that You are taking my past failures
and disadvantages and working them all for my good.
I want You to have first place in my heart.

Journal: Are there some disadvantages or failures in your past that you need to trust God with? How does your love for God compare to your love for other things?

—Debbie Norred

Extending Grace

And we know that in all things God works for the good of those
who love him, who have been called according to his purpose.
Romans 8:28

God can and will use anything in our lives that we have done or experienced so that *He can be glorified*! This was brought home to me several weeks ago when I faced a tremendous heartache because someone questioned my faith and character. During the entire process, I *knew* that God had a plan and that He would use this painful experience for good. I didn't ask God, "Why me?" as I dealt with the rejection and hurt. All the while, the Holy Spirit spoke loving truths into my heart that reminded me of who I am—His child.

But I did ask my heavenly Father, "What do You need me to know or learn from this situation?" It wasn't long before He whispered into my spirit that He was a God of second chances. He said, "Love people and trust me."

Soon after, my pastor gave a sermon on loving the unlovable and extending grace and love when wronged. I knew at that moment that God was working for the good in all that I had recently experienced and that I needed to love the person who had challenged me so that God would be glorified and honored.

Our God is a God of second chances, third chances—as many chances as it takes. So rest assured that when you face something difficult, He *will* be there for you. And He will use it for good.

PRAYER

Dear God, help me see that the testimony You write on my heart is a series
of life experiences that have Your fingerprints all over them. Thank You, Jesus,
for showing us over and over how to love and be loved.

Journal: Make a list of things you have experienced in your life that God has used for your good or someone else's good.

—Kelly Shearer

Good All the Time

And we know that in all things God works for the good of those
who love him, who have been called according to his purpose.

ROMANS 8:28

On June 10, 2003, my husband lost his job of 13 years. He was the sole breadwinner for our family as I stayed home to raise our infant son. He searched for a job for a month, submitting hundreds of resumes, and interviewing, but with no leads. It was apparent that I would need to return to work as a junior high school math teacher, and I was devastated to have to leave our son.

That same day my husband lost his job was the first day of our first session of First Place at our church. I knew that I had been called to be a First Place leader, but in the midst of this overwhelming trial, I didn't know how I would cope. During the next month, I continued to lead the group and spend much time writing in my prayer journal, often ranting and raving over the fact that I would have to return to my former job. During this time, God placed one truth on my heart: He was working all things for my family's good—I just couldn't see it yet. It was as if my mind needed to be opened to the possibility that many blessings could come our way if I would just step out of the way and allow God to work.

Two years later, God is still showering us with blessings because of my decision to step out of the way and allow God to work all things for the good of those who love Him.

PRAYER

Lord, today I commit everything to You, knowing that
You promise to work for my good in all things. I praise You for calling me
to a Christ-centered life that conforms to Your purposes.

Journal: What circumstances seem too difficult for God to work out for your good? Ask God today to open your mind to the possible ways that He could bless you though those circumstances.

—Kathlee Coleman

Keep It Simple

He has showed you, O man, what is good.
And what does the LORD require of you? To act justly and to
love mercy and to walk humbly with your God.
Micah 6:8

God's will for us is quite simple, but we try to make it really hard. If we honored the three commands in this verse, our lives would be richer and fuller than we could ever imagine. God's requirements are so different from man's requirements. Let's look at each one:

- *Act justly*: To do the next right thing—all the time. If I do this, I'll be able to accomplish even the things I dislike doing.
- *Love mercy*: To treat others with the same mercy I want from God. This means I treat kindly the rude person at the grocery store or the mouthy person at the gas station.
- *Walk humbly with your God*: God wants to have a relationship with me. He wants to be my friend. He doesn't want me to be prideful about our friendship but humbly show others how they can have the same friendship with God. I will become "just one hungry beggar telling another where to find the bread."

Do the right thing, treat others with kindness, and humbly share my friendship with God. That sounds like a recipe for a beautiful life, doesn't it?

PRAYER
Dear Lord, You have showed me what is good in Your sight. Help me today to do the next right thing, to treat everyone I meet with mercy and to walk in humility with You.

Journal: Write the three phrases from today's Scripture in your journal, and then jot down some areas in which you might need to improve, asking God to help you fulfill His gentle requirements today.

—Carole Lewis

The Mission Field

He has showed you, O man, what is good.
And what does the LORD require of you? To act justly and to
love mercy and to walk humbly with your God.

Micah 6:8

As a teenager, I longed to be a missionary to a foreign country. I committed my life to His service, wherever it might lead. When I went to nursing school, I thought that if I became a nurse, God would call me to a medical mission field, but that door closed when I became ill and had to drop out of school.

Two years later, I still wanted to be a missionary, so I quit my job to enroll in seminary. Still I didn't feel God's call. Finally I prayed that if He didn't want me on the mission field in a foreign country, He would provide a job in Houston. He provided the job, so I dropped my plans for seminary and stayed in Houston.

Decades passed, and I followed God's calling to teach homemaking in high school. After I married, my husband, Rex, and I began working with the teenagers at church. We went on choir trips, missions trips and camps with the teenagers, and loved every minute of it.

When we retired from working with the youth, we received many cards of thanks for our 24 years of service. One of the cards contained the words of Micah 6:8, and I realized that God had answered my prayer to be a missionary. It didn't require going to a foreign country; all He had wanted of me was obedience.

PRAYER

Father God, may I always listen to Your voice and be obedient to Your command to act
justly, love mercy and walk humbly with You in my daily life.

Journal: List some ways that you are following God's commands for your life.

—Martha Rogers

Divine Dress Code

He has showed you, O man, what is good.
And what does the LORD require of you? To act justly and to
love mercy and to walk humbly with your God.
Micah 6:8

Our granddaughters attend a Christian school whose dress code requires them to wear a certain type of shirt—and they are not allowed to wear shorts or T-shirts with slogans on them. They are required to memorize Scripture and do service jobs.

Some workplaces have rules about what the employees should and should not wear to work: no open-toed shoes, no tank tops, no jeans unless it is casual Friday.

Such external requirements are much like our Christian walk: God has told us to clothe ourselves in mercy and kindness and to act justly. These are the requirements from God.

Even when there are people and situations in life that make us lose patience, God says that we are to clothe ourselves in mercy. In my own life, whenever I start to lose patience over some minor issue, I find that by going into my bedroom and asking God to change my attitude, I can come back out and face the situation with a different spirit. The situation has not changed, but God has changed my heart.

PRAYER
Father, I thank You that You have requirements for my life—
that You love me enough to care what I do with my life and are willing to change me.
Help me to clothe myself in mercy and kindness.

Journal: What is your daily "dress code"? And how does it affect your relationships?

—Bev Schwind

The Golden Rule

He has showed you, O man, what is good.
And what does the LORD require of you? To act justly and to
love mercy and to walk humbly with your God.
Micah 6:8

I had been having success with weight loss in First Place, and people had begun to compliment me about the loss. But at one point, I stopped losing weight and was in my third week of a plateau! During this time, I would look at overweight people with criticism and think, *They sure need to lose weight. They are weak and lack self-control.* When overweight folks would notice my weight loss, I was quick to tell them they needed to join First Place.

Little did I realize that my insensitivity was a symptom of my lack of humility. In an early morning time of Scripture reading and prayer, the Holy Spirit broke through my critical attitude and reminded me that God had shown me what He required of me. That meant *me*, not others.

What a powerful lesson! My subtle slip into disobedience became arrogant, unjust behavior as I told others what God required of them. Had I been spending more time in Scripture reading and prayer, I could have accepted the daily challenges of a plateau without trying to hold someone else responsible.

Back when I had a double chin, I didn't need someone to tell me I needed a weight-loss program. What I needed was for someone to see my misery through the eyes of love and mercy. God's Word teaches me that I am to treat others the way I want to be treated.

PRAYER
Forgive me, Lord, for taking my eyes off Your plan for me. Forgive my critical spirit.
Thank You for Your love and mercy toward me—help me to show others that same
mercy and kindness.

Journal: Are you looking critically at the faults of others while overlooking your own? Ask the Lord to help you see the misery of others with the eyes of love and mercy.

—Michael D. Smith

Walking the Talk

He has showed you, O man, what is good.
And what does the LORD require of you? To act justly and to
love mercy and to walk humbly with your God.

Micah 6:8

There are two ways that I can change my way of living and thinking about food. The first way involves learning all of the rules—the foods to eat and the foods to not eat. The rules about what to eat also come with rules for rigorous exercise. The second way to submit myself to God's plan for my life is to live utterly dependent on Him, seeing my body as the temple where the Holy Spirit resides.

If I choose the first way, I can become rigid and legalistic about the rules and become critical of those who do not follow the rules. When the work of doing the rules becomes too difficult, it is easy to just quit. In reality, the first way is change on the outside, which is only temporary.

When I choose the second way, it is about a change on the inside. I enter into a relationship with my Savior and am consumed by my desire to become more intimate with Him. When I change on the inside, I become authentic in my daily living. What I eat becomes an act of worship, and my desires are to please Him in all that I do.

The Lord has been merciful with this wretched man. Scripture reading, Scripture memory, Bible study and prayer are the tools for an inward change in my living and thinking about food.

PRAYER
Thank You, Lord, for showing me the difference in the spiritual discipline of submitting all of living and thinking to You. I want to submit to You more and more every day.

Journal: Is your walk with the Lord what you want it to be? If not, what needs to change?

—Michael D. Smith

Identify Your Weakness

*But he said to me, "My grace is sufficient for you, for my power is
made perfect in weakness." Therefore I will boast all the more gladly
about my weaknesses, so that Christ's power may rest on me.*
2 Corinthians 12:9

There are three reasons we relapse. The first is that we want what we want when we want it, and the second is that we fail to plan.

The third reason is that we refuse to identify the one food that always trips us up. My trigger food is anything sweet and creamy. Whenever I eat anything sweet and creamy, I want to continue eating foods that are not good choices for me. After doing First Place for 25 years, I am always amazed when God teaches me something new, but He always does. I found that during the last session of First Place, I was able to lose 15 pounds by just not eating anything creamy and sweet like ice cream, cheesecake or creamy candy bars.

The food that gets you off track may not be sweet and creamy. It might be crunchy and salty like snack crackers or chips. It might even be a good food such as peanut butter, but every time you eat a little, you want a lot.

Second Corinthians 12:9 tells us that God does His best work in our weakest areas. Our job is to identify the weak areas and then be willing to give up the food or behavior that is keeping us from experiencing victory.

PRAYER
*Dear Lord, help me today to resist the foods that cause me to get
off track, and to call out to You when I am tempted. I know that Your grace is
sufficient for me, and I am no longer in bondage to poor choices!*

Journal: Write down the food or behavior that is keeping you from having success and begin praying that God will help you remove it from your life as you are obedient to Him.

—Carole Lewis

Transforming Limitations

But he said to me, "My grace is sufficient for you, for my power is made perfect in weakness." Therefore I will boast all the more gladly about my weaknesses, so that Christ's power may rest on me.

2 Corinthians 12:9

When I joined First Place, I seriously doubted that it would work. I'd tried many diets through the years, with some success, but the results didn't last. My willpower was nil and I didn't want to give up certain foods. However, I decided that if I planned to do this, I would do it right.

I was satisfied and somewhat smug when I reached my goal weight and kept it off for several years. During that time, I made many new friends in the program and enjoyed leading a group. I learned the verse in 2 Corinthians and knew that God's grace was all I needed to get me through the sacrifices I made to be healthy—at least *I* thought of them as sacrifices!

Then I met a lady who was the personification of this verse. She humbled my spirit and gave me new insight. She perseveres in all the First Place commitments despite her physical limitations. Even with braces on her legs, she walks to keep the exercise commitment rather than using her challenging situation as an excuse. I have listened to her quote all the memory verses and give her testimony, even though speaking in public is not her favorite thing to do.

This new friend has a powerful testimony of what God has done in her life despite her weaknesses. She has made me stronger and is an example of what God can do through our limitations.

PRAYER

Father God, take my weaknesses and limitations and use them to bring glory and honor to You. Your grace is sufficient. May Your power give me strength to do Your will today.

Journal: What are your weaknesses? List them, and then pray for God's grace to give you the power to overcome any limitations.

—Martha Rogers

Who Needs Old Bootstraps?

*But he said to me, "My grace is sufficient for you, for my power is
made perfect in weakness." Therefore I will boast all the more gladly
about my weaknesses, so that Christ's power may rest on me.*
2 Corinthians 12:9

How can I be so weak? How many times do I have to fall before I get it right? Questions like these plagued me for years—many years. As a woman who lived a very addictive lifestyle, I was familiar with failure. In fact, I was so comfortable with it that accepting a gift like God's incredible favor and grace was difficult for me to comprehend, let alone embrace as truth in my life.

When I first read 2 Corinthians 12:9, I was more than a little surprised. God's Word said that when I was weak (and I was, often), His power would work best in me. Wow! What an amazing statement, so contrary to what the world had taught me. We live in a society that says, "Just pull yourself up by your bootstraps. Be strong!" In First Place, learning how Christ could work powerfully through me because of my shortcomings gave me something I hadn't had in a long time—*hope*.

Now I no longer have to pretend to be strong. I can admit my mistakes, mishaps and failures, and I have a God who loves and forgives me anyway. Today is today and tomorrow is a new day, a new beginning, a fresh start. Instead of pulling up our bootstraps when we fall, we can ask for forgiveness and allow our Lord and Savior to pull us up by His grace. After all, it's a gift—shouldn't we accept it?

PRAYER

*Lord, today I start fresh. I am ready to begin again. In my weaknesses You are strong.
When I fall, You so graciously pick me up and set me on Your solid ground, again.
Thank You for Your gift of grace. May I walk in Your strength and power today, one
step at a time. In Jesus' mighty name, I pray. Amen!*

Journal: Reflect on the times when you believed that in order to improve you had to be strong and handle your problems all on your own. Write about a time when in your weakness God proved Himself to be strong and lifted you up to higher ground.

—Carol Van Atta

Speak Grace

But he said to me, "My grace is sufficient for you, for my power is
made perfect in weakness." Therefore I will boast all the more gladly
about my weaknesses, so that Christ's power may rest on me.

2 Corinthians 12:9

In the early hours of the morning, in November 1973, the Ku Klux Klan burned our family's daycare center to the ground. It was a total loss. My parents went home that night thinking all was lost—the daycare center had been our main source of income. But my parents opened their Bible and got on their knees. It was then that the Lord gave them this verse to get through the fire storm. This verse became a permanent fixture over the door of our new daycare center. We are now the largest single site Christian daycare center in the country.

God's grace got us through the fire, and it is sufficient to get me through the weight-loss battle. When I am weak, He is strong.

Zechariah 4:7 (*KJV*) records the words "with shoutings, crying, Grace, grace unto it." When I am struggling with my diet and exercise, I shout, "Grace, grace unto it." In my weakness His grace is truly sufficient for me. To God be the glory, great things He has done and will continue to do.

PRAYER

Father, Your grace is sufficient for me during my weight-loss
journey and my journey into new health. Thank You that You
have changed me. Your grace will give me the power to be a good
steward over my new healthy body.

Journal: Write down the circumstances you have encountered in your weight-loss journey that God's grace has brought you through.

—Beverly Henson

When Change Comes

Being confident of this, that he who began a good work in you
will carry it on to completion until the day of Christ Jesus.
Philippians 1:6

Kay Smith has been one of my best friends for over 20 years, and she worked for First Place for 17 years as the First Place Associate Director. In November 2005, we learned that due to a change in our church policies, Kay could no longer be a full-time staff member unless she worked in Houston. Because a move was not possible for Kay and her husband, she had to resign from her job with First Place.

I never see this verse that I don't think of Kay, because this is her favorite verse. As I grieved the loss of Kay as an employee, God brought this verse to mind to comfort me and show me that He is still in charge of Kay's life and mine too. God still has good plans for Kay and for the First Place program. We are thrilled that Kay has a new job and that God knows right where she is and will carry on the good work that He started in her the day she accepted Christ as Savior. You can be certain that He will also complete the good work He has started in you. We have a great God who always has a plan and a purpose for our lives.

PRAYER
O Lord, give me confidence in no one but You.
Help me learn that even when I am going through trials,
You are still with me, working for my good.

Journal: Write about a trial you are going through right now. Can you be confident that God has a plan to do a good work through this trial?

—Carole Lewis

God's Mysterious Ways

Being confident of this, that he who began a good work in you
will carry it on to completion until the day of Christ Jesus.

PHILIPPIANS 1:6

When my contract for teaching at a private school was not renewed, I was devastated. I felt as though my world had ended. I had taught school for 28 years, and the thought of not returning to the classroom that fall was almost more than I could bear.

As the next few years unfolded, I began to see how God's hand had been at work all the time. He opened up avenues of opportunities I could never have had if I had been teaching full-time.

One of those opportunities was joining First Place. While working full-time, I had no room for another meeting during the week or keeping the commitments of First Place. But now I could participate. One year after joining First Place, I became a leader. I also began teaching at the college level and found I enjoyed it even more than teaching high school.

Then came the opportunity to attend writing conferences and pursue my love of writing. The greatest opportunity came when Carole Lewis approached me about revising the Bible studies for First Place to fit their new format. I jumped at the chance and that led to my writing *Begin Again*.

God instilled in me a love of writing. He knew the desire of my heart and what He wanted me to do with it. The work He began in me as a child is now being carried to completion as I write for Him.

PRAYER
Heavenly Father, thank You for never giving up on us.
Thank You for guiding our lives and leading
us in the path You have set for us.

Journal: Think about the times God has worked out events in your life. Make a list of them in your journal and thank Him for never giving up on you and for His leading.

—Martha Rogers

First Things First

Being confident of this, that he who began a good work in you
will carry it on to completion until the day of Christ Jesus.
Philippians 1:6

My journey to lose weight began a few years ago, after the birth of my third son. I joined a First Place group at my church. I was ready to conquer my weight issues, but I soon learned that there were others things I needed to address before I lost weight.

During the first study, I found out just how broken I was: full of resentment, jealously and a negative attitude. Yes, I was a Christian, but my attitude did not reflect this to others. With each study, God began to peel away these negative attitudes. During the process, God was faithful, because He kept me on track—not losing or gaining weight—while He continued to heal me of these issues.

Now I have been leading a small group of ladies in my home. This past fall, during a Bible study, God said, "Penny, we can now work on your weight." I suddenly received a desire to exercise, eat right and cook healthy meals for my family. I now wake up every day with a renewed purpose. I look for the good in others, as well as myself. Because of God's help, and the support of my First Place group members, I have lost 30 pounds during the study. I am confident that God, who began a good work in me, will carry it on to completion.

PRAYER
Father God, thank You for not giving up on me, even though
I wanted to give up on myself. I know that I am Your work in
progress and that You will complete Your good work
in me within Your timeframe.

Journal: What work does God want to complete in you? Is there anything you need to give to Him in order for Him to work through you?

—Penny Masseau

Don't Say, "Never Surrender"!

Being confident of this, that he who began a good work in you
will carry it on to completion until the day of Christ Jesus.
Philippians 1:6

"Confident" has not always been a word I would use to describe myself. It has taken many good works of God to begin instilling confidence in me—especially when it came to my physical body. I had dreams of being fit and healthy all my life, yet I battled the bulge for more years than I want to admit. However, God began a good work in me by allowing me to go through some trials that brought me to a place of surrender. One night, I said this simple prayer: "God, I can't do this anymore. Please give me peace and strength, in Jesus' name. Amen."

My life has never been the same. I began to pray every day and read the Word faithfully. The good work had begun. However, I became so spiritually minded that I could hardly do any earthly good. God used First Place to begin balancing all areas of my life. I began to realize that He was concerned about my whole person—body, soul, mind and spirit.

God is still teaching me that it takes spiritual, physical, mental and emotional balance to be complete. I work on all of these areas daily, but now I am confident that God will complete the good work He has begun in me. My dream has come true. I have never looked and felt more fit and healthy in my life.

PRAYER
Lord, I believe that You are a faithful God. Continue to do Your good work in my life,
physically, spiritually and emotionally. I give You all the glory and praise.

Journal: Are there areas in your life in which you lack confidence? If you are willing to say a prayer of surrender today, record it in your journal.

—Debbie Norred

Redeeming Our Bad Choices

Being confident of this, that he who began a good work in you
will carry it on to completion until the day of Christ Jesus.

Philippians 1:6

As a college student, I asked the Lord into my life. Then after being out of church for 10 years, the Lord used a Christian counselor and a post-abortion Bible study to draw me back to church. It was at that time that I recommitted my life to the Lord.

My first Easter as a "new" Christian, I attended a Last Supper service. The Children's Chapel was dimly lit; there were seven goblets on the altar alongside the bread. Families came in, shared communion together and left as I sat alone. The church pianist asked me to come to the altar with her family. As she prayed for me, she spoke this verse into my life.

At that very moment, I couldn't comprehend why God would want to do a good work with the mess I had made of my life. Looking back, I see that God took my bad choices, the abortion, the wrong eating habits I had used to cover up my sin, my weight gain—and used them for His good. He allowed me to minister to others as He has moved me to other churches.

This year the Lord nudged me until I began a First Place program at my church. I believe that through First Place, my relationship with the Lord is richer. I am now more confident and trusting in Him. I can honestly say, "Yes, He who began a good work in me will carry it on to completion!"

PRAYER
Dear Lord, I thank You for the forgiveness of my sins—for forgiving the abuse
I have done to my body through my bad choices. Thank You for loving me
enough to continue to do Your good work in my life. Amen.

Journal: If you are covering up the past with abuse of your body by overeating and no exercise, ask the Lord to continue the good work He has started in you and show you the proper path to take.

—Janet Boyles

God's Day-Timer

Whatever you do, work at it with all your heart,
as working for the Lord, not for men.
Colossians 3:23

In January 2006, First Place was one of the features on the TV news show *Geraldo at Large*. The film crew spent all day on Sunday filming the piece to be shown on Tuesday night. I was amazed that my interview had been sent instantly through the telephone lines to New York and that the producer had the text on her Blackberry one hour later. The next morning, as I meditated on all that had transpired the day before, I was struck with the reality that God has always worked this way, and man is still way behind.

When I think about the fact that God knows instantly whatever I do, whatever I say and wherever I go, I am struck by the awesome truth of how much I do and say for man and not for God. What a thought—Day-Timer by God! His plans become my plans and not the other way around. The stresses of our daily life would seem so much lighter if we remembered how instantaneously our prayers reach Him. What if, instead of lashing out in frustration when things go wrong, we spoke kindly because our words are instantly in God's ears?

PRAYER
Dear Lord, forgive me for forgetting that You are
the One I need to please. Help me today to work for You,
and You alone, in all I do and say.

Journal: Is there an area of your life in which you have been trying to please man rather than God? Ask God to help you reverse this by giving God first place today.

—Carole Lewis

It's Not About Me

Whatever you do, work at it with all your heart,
as working for the Lord, not for men.

Colossians 3:23

For 46 years, I have sung in our church choir and participated in all the Christmas programs. This year, however, I had a difficult time. It was taking me a long time to learn all the words to the music, and I just didn't like some of it (although each song had a special message). I was at the point of dropping out and asked several friends for prayer as to what I should do.

That night, I went to choir rehearsal fully expecting to turn in my music and tell them I wouldn't be participating this year. Before we began practice for Sunday's special, our director said he had planned to send us an e-mail the next day to explain the program of music he had selected and why. Just as he was ready to hit the "send" button, he sensed God directing him to read the message aloud to us before rehearsal.

He told us that since we have such a diverse congregation, he wanted the music to appeal to all groups. Our purpose was to present the plan of salvation and God's love to all people in a way they would understand. I felt as though God was tapping me on the shoulder and saying, "This is what it's about. Not you or what you like or what you think others like—it's about Me and how to get My message to My people."

PRAYER

Heavenly Father, help us today to remember how much
You love us. Help us to be our best for You and to not worry
so much about what others may think of us.

Journal: Record your reason for wanting to make healthy life choices. Are you doing everything you can to succeed? If not, seek God's help so that you can do your best for Him.

—Martha Rogers

Working for the Lord

Whatever you do, work at it with all your heart,
as working for the Lord, not for men.
Colossians 3:23

Sometimes I find myself not giving God my personal best. That's because I buy into Satan's line of thinking and get the "who really cares anyway" attitude. I mean really. Who cares if I don't do my best at home or on the job? Who cares if I don't work at my relationships with my husband, friends and family? Who cares if I don't fulfill the commitments of my First Place program? Who really cares, right?

God cares! He charges each of us to give Him our very best in whatever we are doing. So whether we're folding laundry, serving communion or working at our jobs, God wants our best work. Does that mean perfect work? No, it means our personal best. It means living our lives with the sole purpose of bringing honor and glory to our heavenly Father. And that means we may have to confront an attitude or behavior that keeps us from reflecting back to others the very character and nature of Christ.

Our employer is God, and He wants us to shine for Him—all the time.

PRAYER
Dear God, help me to be mindful that it is You I truly work
for in this world. I pray for a spirit of excellence to fill
my heart so that all that I am and all that I do bring glory to You.

Journal: If there are areas in your life in which you are not giving God your best, ask Him for strength and help in overcoming a spirit of mediocrity.

—Kelly Shearer

For His Glory

Whatever you do, work at it with all your heart,
as working for the Lord, not for men.
Colossians 3:23

All of us have things to do that we don't want to do. When my husband, Bob, was younger, his job every night after dinner was to wash the dishes. He is very quick to admit that he didn't like doing dishes. In fact, he hated washing the dishes. When we were first married, he told me he would help me do anything in the house except wash dishes. I soon learned that he wasn't kidding.

One Wednesday evening after fellowship dinner at church, I was talking with some friends when someone came over to me and said, "Bob is having too much fun in the kitchen; I didn't know you could laugh that much washing dishes." This I had to see for myself. I stood in the doorway in utter amazement. There was Bob in a plastic apron, scouring a giant cooking pot and laughing. He lovingly looked at me and said, "I'm doing this for the Lord and for His glory," and then he squirted someone with the sprayer as he walked by. Bob continued to wash dishes for the Lord every other Wednesday for two years.

At home, Bob's formal dishware of preference remains styrofoam or plastic. But I can't deny that he had an amazing attitude when He was working for the Lord. I can only imagine how much fun we could have if we did everything for the Lord and His glory instead of complaining about the task at hand.

PRAYER
Father God, I know there are tasks ahead of me today that I am reluctant to do. But if
my performance is pleasing and acceptable to You, nothing else really matters.

Journal: What have you been putting off doing? Do one task today that you have dreaded, and do it for the Lord and His glory.

—Betty Lacy

God's Got You Covered

From the fullness of his grace we have all received one blessing after another.
John 1:16

Whenever you see me, you will usually see a green bag rolling along behind me. I use it to transport my laptop between office and home, and I take it on trips packed full of anything I might need on the plane.

Recently, I was at the Christian Bookseller's Convention in Denver, Colorado. One evening, I was having dinner with Geni, manager of our church bookstore, and Geni mentioned that she needed a rolling bag like mine. While strolling around after dinner, we walked into a Brighton store that sells silver jewelry, luggage, shoes and other gift items. Geni spotted the most beautiful red bag either of us had ever seen. There was one problem—the $450 price tag! Geni really wanted that bag, but her better sense told her she should pray about it, so we left the store without the bag.

The next day, Geni announced that she had prayed and thought we should go to T. J. Maxx and Ross to see if they had a bag like mine. If they didn't have one, she felt that would mean she should buy the Brighton bag. After dinner, we started our search. At T. J. Maxx there was one red rolling bag that cost $69.95. Geni didn't feel we should buy the first bag we saw, so we went to Ross. Would you believe, there among at least 100 bags was one red rolling bag exactly like mine, and the price was $24.95!

Both of us were thrilled beyond words that God blessed Geni with the red rolling bag she wanted and saved her $425!

PRAYER

Dear Lord, help me remember today that every blessing I receive is because of the fullness of Your grace over my life.

Journal: Write about a blessing you received that was totally God's grace to you.

—Carole Lewis

Trusting God with the Outcome

From the fullness of his grace we have all received one blessing after another.
John 1:16

When our grandson, Robert Mikell, was diagnosed with cystic fibrosis, all of the family was in complete shock. We learned to cope with the medications, breathing treatments and clapping exercises we had to do with him, and we trusted God to take care of him.

Most children with CF have lung problems, but soon the disease attacked our grandson's liver. It wasn't long before he needed a liver transplant. When that finally happened in 2003, we were ecstatic that God had given us a miracle. But God wasn't through with us yet.

Robert developed many complications after the transplant, was in ICU at various points and near death more than once. Each time, God answered our faithful prayers. Members of my First Place class formed a prayer chain and spread the word of Robert's need for prayer throughout their groups of friends. Another friend made green ribbons for people to wear to let us know they were praying for our dear grandson. What a blessing to walk into class and see all those green ribbons!

In the end, Robert's new liver thrived, and the complications caused by his CF were gradually brought under control. Throughout the seven-month ordeal, our faith never wavered. We knew we had to be strong. We knew that if we remained steadfast and trusted God, He would hear and answer our prayers according to His will. We are so grateful that His will included a more normal life for our grandson.

PRAYER

Heavenly Father, thank You for the blessings You have bestowed on us, and we thank You in advance for the blessings You have in store for us today. May we walk with You and experience the closeness of Your presence in our lives.

Journal: List the blessings God bestows on you each day of your life, and write a prayer thanking Him.

—Martha Rogers

Saved!

From the fullness of his grace we have all received one blessing after another.

John 1:16

In the year 2000, I had eliminated church, Christian music, my Bible and daily devotions from my life. I thought my husband no longer appreciated me, so I began constructing an invisible protective wall, working diligently to emotionally remove myself from our marriage. It worked! I lived and acted like a single person. It was all about me! But I came frighteningly close to losing my marriage, my home, my career and my relationship with my children. My attitude was embarrassingly self-serving and ice cold.

My husband begged me to at least go to church on our wedding anniversary. My daughter had been "pestering" me to go to this new church and hear the pastor. I finally said okay. What I was thinking was, *I'll kill three birds with one stone. I'll shut everyone up; it's Christmas Eve, and it's our wedding anniversary.*

That day, after hearing about Christ's easy yoke and His desire for us to be reconciled to Him no matter what we've done, I left the church service completely changed. I pleaded for my family's forgiveness and mercy. They extended only love and graciousness to me. More than that, God freely extended His grace to me in abundance.

He has given me daily blessings that I've recorded in my prayer journal. But I only have to look at my husband and children to be reminded of the innumerable blessings of God.

PRAYER

Father God, thank You for saving me from my destructive self.
Thank You for the love and forgiveness of my family.
Thank You for the blessing of marriage.

Journal: What blessings has God generously bestowed on you that you haven't yet thanked Him for?

—PJ Bahr

Claim the Blessings

From the fullness of his grace we have all received one blessing after another.

John 1:16

Here I am starting over again. Four years ago, I felt satisfied with my progress in First Place and I didn't sign up for the new fall class. I thought I could do a Bible study on my own; after all, I understood the food exchanges.

As the months rolled on, so did the return of my fat. Not to mention the guilt and depression resulting from the weight gain of each Christmas season. Then it became more difficult for me to stay with my walking, because along with the gradual return of the weight was the return of joint pain and discomfort.

Television ads for weight-loss programs abounded—and tempted me. But God was merciful in allowing me to discern that my problem was a spiritual issue that could not be remedied with a quick fix marketed by corporate America. They wanted my money; God wanted my heart.

Once again, I saw God in His grace and mercy, with outreached arms, wooing me back. In disobedience, I had sought shelter far from the bounds of His protection, and in deep sorrow I returned with a desire to once again live the commitments of obedience. It is never too late to return to God's umbrella of protection.

PRAYER

Thank You, Lord, for giving me enough light to see where my pride and disobedience had taken me. I desire for all of my heart to be in Your presence. Renew a steadfast spirit within me.

Journal: Consider if there is any part of your heart not yielded to God's life-giving ways, and ask Him to bring you back under His protection.

—Sybil D. Smith

The Power of Jesus' Name

That at the name of Jesus every knee should bow, in heaven
and on earth and under the earth, and every tongue confess
that Jesus Christ is Lord, to the glory of God the Father.
PHILIPPIANS 2:10-11

There is power in the name of Jesus. Whether we listen to His name on Scripture CDs, read His name in our Bible or speak His name when reciting our First Place memory verse, the name of Jesus has power.

One day I was walking with a friend. We had finished our three miles on the treadmills and went outside to pray together. As we walked and prayed, she commented that I appeared to be full of the Holy Spirit that morning. You see, I had listened to the book of Matthew for an hour on my drive into town that morning. Over and over I heard of Jesus' miracles and the words He said to His followers. His name was spoken into my ears over and over again. How natural that His Spirit would fill me to overflowing because of my time of worship and praise in the car.

We have a choice every day to listen to, read about or memorize verses that use the name of Jesus. One thing is sure: If we do it, the power of Jesus will fill us to overflowing.

PRAYER

Dear Jesus, there is power in Your wonderful name.
I ask You to fill me to overflowing with Your power today
as I give You first place in my life.

Journal: Write today's memory verse in your journal and meditate on the words as you write. Ask Jesus to help you confess Him today with your mouth to someone He sends your way.

—Carole Lewis

Prayer Walking

*That at the name of Jesus every knee should bow, in heaven
and on earth, and under the earth, and every tongue confess
that Jesus Christ is Lord, to the glory of God the Father.*
Philippians 2:10-11

This past year, I began prayer walking. I walk through my neighborhood in the morning and pray as I walk. I pass a junior high school and pray for the students and teachers there in the same way I pray for the teens and teachers at my church.

I've discovered that I can pray as effectively with my eyes open, drinking in the beauty of God's world, as I do with my eyes closed. With the beauty of the heavens above me and the work of His hands surrounding me, I can't help but praise Him with my heart and confess again and again that He is my Lord and Savior.

The meaning of the words "in heaven, and on earth and under the earth" has become very real to me as I walk. The exercise of walking may be good for my physical health, but the communication with and praise of my Lord does more for my spiritual health. With those two commitments fulfilled, the rest of the day becomes easier.

PRAYER
*Heavenly Father, may my heart today be filled with praise
and thanksgiving for Your love and mercy.*

Journal: Write a psalm of praise to God, giving Him honor and glory.

—Martha Rogers

Service as Worship

*That at the name of Jesus every knee should bow, in heaven
and on earth and under the earth, and every tongue confess
that Jesus Christ is Lord, to the glory of God the Father.*
Philippians 2:10-11

I love to put on a worship tape and turn up the volume when I'm home alone. I know the volume, or my dancing about, does not move God, but He enjoys my spending time with Him. And I enjoy spending time with Him. There have been times when I have sat on the porch after midnight and worshiped Him. Yet I not only want to worship Him with my voice, but also with my life. I want my life to reflect a godly example.

We worship God when we volunteer to minister to others. Several years ago, our Bible study group went Christmas caroling. One of the homes we visited was that of a newly retired couple. The husband was very ill with cancer. He wore a respiratory mask to protect himself from other people because his immune system was so weak. We sang for him and prayed for his healing. He struggled to go back into the house when we had finished singing.

Three years later, I played a game of tennis with this man, who used to be a tennis coach, and he gave me instructions on my game. The term "love" is part of tennis, but it was God's love that led us to this person's home, to serve in His name.

PRAYER
*Lord, thank You for receiving my worship. I want it to be like
sweet incense to You. Teach me some ways of worship that I have
never thought of, and keep me fresh and new in You.*

Journal: Spend time in worship and service this week and record how it changes your prayers.

—Bev Schwind

In Training

*That at the name of Jesus every knee should bow, in heaven
and on earth and under the earth, and every tongue confess
that Jesus Christ is Lord, to the glory of God the Father.*
Philippians 2:10-11

I was discussing this verse of Scripture with one of my friends. She is not only a good friend but is also in my First Place group. She has more than 100 pounds to lose. She said that when she hears this verse, all she can think of is getting down on her knees and not being able to get up. I told her that I could remember that time in my life as well, but we agreed it was refreshing to know that when we stand before the Father, there will be no weigh-in and no gravity, and we will be kneeling in a new glorified body. Hallelujah!

All we have to do right now is live a life before others that confesses daily that Jesus Christ is Lord. We need to daily give glory to the Father for the great things He has done in our lives. Remember that each day you live on this earth as a child of the King, you are in training for reigning.

PRAYER
*Lord Jesus, I give You glory for giving me a new life and
a fresh outlook on kneeling. I look forward to the day when I kneel
before the Father and say that I am Yours and You are Lord.*

Journal: Write about the changes you have experienced since you came to First Place—changes for which you can give all the glory to God.

—Beverly Henson

Fearless or Faithless?

No one will be able to stand up against you all the
days of your life. As I was with Moses, so I will be with you;
I will never leave you nor forsake you.

Joshua 1:5

As a believer in Jesus, I have learned the truth of this verse in the midst of the most difficult situations imaginable. Somehow, this verse just doesn't seem to apply as much when things are going great in life. But it comes alive when God's children are up against great difficulties and trials.

I learned the power of this verse when we suffered financial problems and lost most of our material possessions. I learned still more of what it means to never be forsaken by God as Johnny and I have walked through his cancer journey together. When our daughter Shari was killed by a drunk driver on Thanksgiving night in 2001, I began to fully understand the truth of this verse.

Trials have the power to make us fearless or faithless where God is concerned. Because of God's faithfulness to me, never leaving me nor forsaking me during these great trials, I have chosen the fearless path. Today, I sincerely believe that, in all the days of my life, nothing will be able to come against me that God can't get me through in power and victory.

PRAYER
Dear Lord, help me understand the power in this verse today.
This great power that You showed to Moses is available
to me today, if I will only ask.

Journal: Write about a trial you are going through right now, and claim the power of this verse to see you through.

—Carole Lewis

When We Are the Prodigal One

*No one will be able to stand up against you all the
days of your life. As I was with Moses, so I will be with you;
I will never leave you nor forsake you.*

Joshua 1:5

I had an amazing earthly father who reminded me of God's promise many times throughout my life. I chose this verse for *Begin Again* because of Dad.

I remember as though it were yesterday the time when I had drifted away from God. One week, I battled the flu and felt miserable. I decided to fly home to be with my family. Dad met me at the airport. We walked to the parking garage, and he put his arm around my shoulders. He said, "I don't know what is wrong with you besides being sick, and I don't need to know. Just tell the Lord about it and pray. He'll take care of it. And I'll be praying for you too."

I thought about what he said and turned to my Bible. This verse in Joshua spoke to me in a wonderful way. Even though I had not been close to Him, God had never left me. He waited patiently for me to return to Him. I knew what I had to do.

Dad took me back to the airport for my return flight to Houston. I told him I had listened to his advice and now things were right with God. He hugged me and said God had answered his prayers.

The first thing I did upon my arrival in Houston on Sunday evening was take a taxi to the church closest to my apartment. I returned full force to my Lord that night, and He hasn't failed to keep His promise.

PRAYER

*Heavenly Father, Your love never fails us, and we know You will
always be with us to guide, comfort and give hope.*

Journal: Write down the times in your life when you fully depended on God and He sustained you through that time.

—Martha Rogers

Jesus, Our Light

*No one will be able to stand up against you all the
days of your life. As I was with Moses, so I will be with you;
I will never leave you nor forsake you.*

Joshua 1:5

We spent many years living on the shores of Lake Erie in Ohio. The children grew up swimming and boating as a summer ritual. And we would go to the islands and take a picnic, spending the after-work hours relaxing on the other side of the lake.

I recall one night as we were coming back from the island, a fog had settled in before we knew it and visibility was very poor. My husband had a compass on the boat, so I was confident that we were going in the right direction. But we still listened for any other boats that might be dangerously near. Our boat edged in the direction the compass showed us, and it seemed like an eternity as we strained to see in the fog. A shout of joy and relief went up as one of the children spotted the lighthouse.

Many times, Jesus is compared to a lighthouse because He is a beacon of hope and points the way to shore. Just as when we saw the beacon of light, we knew we were safe, so too when we glimpse Jesus, we know we are in safe waters.

God promises us that He will never leave us nor forsake us. If we use the compass of His Word, He will direct us in the right direction.

PRAYER
*Lord, I thank You that Your light can guide me and You will
never leave me nor forsake me. You are my Light, my Shepherd,
my Teacher and my faithful Friend and Father.
Help me to walk in Your light.*

Journal: Write a description of a friend. What is important to you in friendship? Why is Jesus called "my faithful Friend"?

—Bev Schwind

Unfailing Love

*No one will be able to stand up against you all the
days of your life. As I was with Moses, so I will be with you;
I will never leave you nor forsake you.*

Joshua 1:5

I like to think of this verse as saying "no man or thing" will be able to stand up against you all your days. The Lord has allowed many things to come into my life, even a defective hip at birth. For many years, I have been confined to a wheelchair because of multiple sclerosis, but God has been with me. He has allowed me to lead a First Place group in several different churches; and in 2003, He helped me walk up to five miles a day for almost a year.

All through life I have had hard things to deal with, and now in my latter years, I have the thing most people pray that they or their family do not have to cope with: Alzheimer's disease.

The Lord has been with me and has never forsaken me. When I feel as if I just want to give up, He sends along someone with an encouraging word that lifts me up. God's promises are not just Bible verses—they are real. God will be with us all through this journey called life. He takes every step with us, and when we are weary, He is there to hold us up. I could never have handled all the difficulties I've encountered in my life without the Lord and His unfailing love.

PRAYER
*Dear Lord, thank You for staying close by during
the good times and the bad times.*

Journal: List some struggles you have gone through, and then explain how God was there for you.

—Joe Ann Winkler

Carried Across the Finish Line

But those who hope in the LORD will renew their strength.
They will soar on wings like eagles; they will run and not grow weary,
they will walk and not be faint.

Isaiah 40:31

January 15, 2006, was a day like none I have ever experienced. I participated in the Houston Marathon with more than 18,000 men, women and children. There were three events: a 5K, a half marathon and a marathon. I decided that I would walk the half marathon. The only problem was that I never found the time to train properly. I walk/run three miles every day, but that was the extent of my training. Several weeks before the race, I began praying earnestly that God would help me finish and keep me from injuring my weak left knee.

A precious lady in my First Place class, Cheri Lasiter, has severe cerebral palsy, and she walked the 5K (3 miles) that day. Cheri walks with a walker and has braces on both legs. Her mom drove her to the Convention Center where the marathon began, and they walked a long way from their car to the starting point. Melody Lutz, a First Place leader in Cincinnati, Ohio, also participated in the 5K—and Melody is legally blind. I was as concerned for Cheri's and Melody's safety as I was for my own. So as the race started, I began praying for all of us to be able to finish and for God to protect us from harm.

I saw the truth of this verse when at the end of the race, every one of our First Place people finished and no one was injured. Our hope was in the Lord and He renewed our strength and helped us not grow weary and finish our race.

PRAYER
Dear Lord, help me hope in only You today. You have the power to keep
me safe and renew my energy if I will trust in You, and You alone.

Journal: Write about a time when God helped you because you put your trust in Him.

—Carole Lewis

Gift of Encouragement

But those who hope in the LORD will renew their strength.
They will soar on wings like eagles; they will run and not grow weary,
they will walk and not be faint.

Isaiah 40:31

My husband and I were traveling to Waco, Texas, to attend the fortieth homecoming reunion of my class. From there we planned to go on to Dallas to assist with the final move of my father into a nursing home. As the saying goes, "The best laid plans . . ."

On Saturday morning, I took my husband to the emergency room at a hospital in Waco because he was complaining of chest pains. He was diagnosed as having a heart attack and was admitted to the ICU. I had to drive back to Houston and teach on Monday and make arrangements for someone to cover my college classes for the next few days, then go home and pack for Waco.

Everything had happened so quickly that I had no time to call friends and let them know what had happened. But I had several phone messages. One call meant everything to me. A member of my First Place class had my name as prayer partner for the week. She said, "Martha, I don't know why, but the Lord laid you on my heart this morning as needing special prayer and support. I wanted you to know that I've been praying for you all day. Whatever is going on in your life, God will take care of it and you. I appreciate all you do to make our class so good. I'll keep praying for you the rest of the week."

With that encouragement, I could soar on wings like the eagle, run and not be weary, walk and not grow faint.

PRAYER

Father God, thank You for prayer partners who follow through on their commitment and encourage others. May we be more aware of what that commitment may mean to others.

Journal: Make a list of people you need to encourage this week, and send them a card, note or e-mail—or give them a phone call.

—Martha Rogers

Exceeding Expectations

But those who hope in the LORD will renew their strength.
They will soar on wings like eagles; they will run and not grow weary,
they will walk and not be faint.

Isaiah 40:31

Losing weight can be a battle for all of us. Wise food choices, portion control and exercise can create a body that we are proud of, but slow metabolism and heredity can work against our efforts. Willpower through our own efforts is fruitless; but those who hope in the Lord with confidence will exceed their expectations.

Make an effort to read the Bible every day, and ask God to keep you focused and in control. Step away from your plate when you feel full. You will be amazed how satisfied you are by eating smaller portions. Remember that God loves you deeply and He wants you to be happy and healthy.

God will make us new again and restore our bodies through the power of the Holy Spirit. We can rise above and resist food temptation through faith in Jesus Christ, knowing that all things are possible through Him. Advance to first base and expect a miracle.

PRAYER
Father God, enable us to fly with wings of eagles, practicing patience and
courage to accomplish the goals You have set for us.

Journal: Write about how our every hope is in the Lord, the almighty God, who gives us wisdom and the ability to face temptation without fear.

—Karen L. Duffy

Love Is in the Details

But those who hope in the LORD will renew their strength.
They will soar on wings like eagles; they will run and not grow weary,
they will walk and not be faint.

Isaiah 40:31

When I started walking after many years of not walking, I can't say I wasn't fearful. I trembled at the thought of leaving the security of my wheelchair after being in it for more than 20 years because of multiple sclerosis. I knew the Lord wanted me to do the walking, because He kept whispering in my ear to trust Him.

I repeated Isaiah 40:31 as I started out slowly, and it became easier after a while. I did grow weary, but I trusted God completely to keep me from fainting. And you know what? He did just as He said He would. In the beginning I just walked to our mailbox; but each day I was able to do a little more, until finally I was able to walk one lap inside our mall. Little by little, God helped me walk farther and for a longer period of time. On each lap, I prayed for a different group of people. At the end of one year, with God's help, I was walking up to five miles a day. During that year, I had only one major relapse with my MS. I can truly say that without God walking through my legs, I could never have done it.

No matter what we undertake, if it is God's will, He will see us through it. He will not let us fail. His love has no boundaries, and He cares about every little detail of our life. He is a mighty God!

PRAYER
Dear Lord, thank You for being my strength when I am weak.

Journal: Write about a time when you were weak but God was strong.

—Joe Ann Winkler

Meant to Soar

But those who hope in the LORD will renew their strength.
They will soar on wings like eagles; they will run and not grow weary,
they will walk and not be faint.

Isaiah 40:31

Several years ago, as I was vacationing in Gulf Shores, Alabama, I watched gulls spread their white wings and hover in the wind overhead. They were so beautiful. Then I noticed a group of birds walking and pecking on the beach with long ugly noses and gray bodies. I called them sand hens. It wasn't until I saw those sand hens spread their wings and mount the wind that I realized the ugly birds walking around on the beach were actually the beautiful white gulls. The gulls were not all God intended for them to be until they spread their wings to fly.

When I was obese, I was always of the opinion that if I could be thin, I would have it made; I would be who I was supposed to be. Yet there were several occasions when I was very thin, but I found that I wasn't all I was supposed to be. As a result, eventually I put more weight back on.

Through the First Place Bible studies, I came to realize that until I put my hope in the Lord rather than in being thin, I would never be totally renewed and strengthened. You know, I found that I didn't have to be thin to soar like an eagle. I learned to soar while I was still a large woman, but the more I soared with Him, the more I became who He designed me to be.

PRAYER
Teach me, Lord, to soar with You.

Journal: Write a message to the Lord and tell Him how badly you want to be free to soar.

—Beverly Henson

Living in Grace

Introduction

"Grace" has been defined as "God's unmerited favor." His favor means that I don't get judgment and death from God—which I deserve—because I have trusted in the Lord Jesus Christ as my Savior. It also means that I do get blessings and abundant life from God—which I don't deserve—because the Holy Spirit of God is now living inside of me.

Living in grace has two distinct components, and until both components are flourishing in our lives, we are not fully living in grace.

The first component of God's grace is learning how to receive it. I was blessed to have a mom and dad who loved Jesus and showered me with unconditional love. So it is easy for me to receive God's grace. In fact, for years I was so comfortable with the fact of God's grace that I lived as if He loved me so much that He would overlook my sin and willfulness.

Only after coming to the end of myself did I truly learn what grace looks like. After living a carnal Christian life for 42 years, I cried out to God, and He swooped in, cleaned me up and started making something beautiful of my life. I could never take credit for that kind of grace.

The second component of God's grace is learning how to give it. I have a much harder time with this one. I have had to learn that the same grace God has bestowed on me must flow out of me to everyone I meet. It has been said, "It is much easier to give than to receive." Well, where grace is concerned, I find that it is much easier to receive than to give. Much of the time, I expect more from others than God expects from me. Living in grace should be a life characterized by grace flowing in and grace flowing out.

Denise Munton, the writer of the First Place Bible study *Living in Grace* has written a devotional for each of the 10 memory verses she chose for this study. For each verse in this section, her devotionals follow mine.

Living well is living in grace!

Possessing Everything

Now the Lord is the Spirit, and where the Spirit of the Lord is, there is freedom.
2 Corinthians 3:17

I read in the newspaper about a man who, because of DNA testing, was being released from prison after serving 17 years for a crime he didn't commit. I was amazed that when interviewed the man showed no bitterness, although he was glad that he was soon going to be a free man again. I commented to my husband, Johnny, that this man must surely be a Christian, because even in prison he was already free: free from bitterness, from anger and from self-pity.

The most wonderful part of being a Christian is having the Holy Spirit living inside of us. The apostle Paul explained what this really means a few chapters later:

In truthful speech and in the power of God; with weapons of righteousness in the right hand and in the left; through glory and dishonor, bad report and good report; genuine, yet regarded as imposters; known, yet regarded as unknown; dying, yet we live on; beaten, and yet not killed; sorrowful, yet always rejoicing; poor, yet making many rich; having nothing, yet possessing everything (2 Corinthians 6:7-10).

How comforting to know that no matter what we are going through, no matter what we might be struggling with, we need not be held captive by it. The Spirit of God brings freedom and life to even the bleakest situation. So take heart. Recommit yourself to living a balanced life—to living well.

PRAYER
Dear Lord, help me draw on Your power today and walk in freedom and victory in my present situation.

Journal: Is there something holding you prisoner today? The Holy Spirit has the power to set you free. Ask Him to do it.

—Carole Lewis

Cherished

Now the Lord is the Spirit, and where the Spirit of the Lord is, there is freedom.

2 Corinthians 3:17

After only a few months of being involved in a woman's Bible study for the first time, the Holy Spirit gave me a startling revelation. As I was crying out in a desperate moment of emptiness, He lovingly yet point-blank said to my spirit, "Experience My grace." I was stunned. I began to ask Him what that meant. I knew I was saved by grace, but what else was there? Immediately a surge of excitement went through my body. I suddenly had a deep sense that the Lord was about to do something big in my life.

He did! In the months that followed, what He revealed to me about His grace changed me forever. Not only was I experiencing His grace in my heart and mind, but I was also able to extend grace to others.

By diligently studying His Word, He began to reveal to me how loved, cherished and accepted I was by Him. I began to break free from all the guilt and shame from my past and walk in complete assurance of His love and forgiveness. The legalistic mind-set that had been out to deceive me and hinder my intimacy with the Lord was being chipped away. The key, however, was that I *believed* His truth. I chose to believe. And to think that I had wondered what else there could possibly be. Oh, my!

PRAYER
O Father, I desperately desire to experience all that
You have for me. Reveal Your grace to me. Thank You for Your
Holy Spirit and the incredible freedom You give.

Journal: Who do you go to when you're feeling empty or restless inside? Is Jesus your first resort? What is He revealing to you as you study His Word?

—Denise Munton

Free to Choose the Good

Now the Lord is the Spirit, and where the Spirit of the Lord is, there is freedom.
2 Corinthians 3:17

I used to believe the devil's lies that freedom meant the ability to do what I wanted, when I wanted. But giving my flesh freedom only brought destruction to my body and soul.

I have learned to walk in God's freedom daily by letting my waking thoughts be a prayer of surrender as I ask to be filled with His grace and freed to know, love and serve Him that day. By consciously allowing Him to have His freedom reign within me each morning, I allow Him access to my heart. I am freed from the bondages of sin and I am filled with holy desires; therefore, my actions and motives are pure, bringing balance to my life and the Spirit's power to my weight-loss goals.

If we want to live in freedom, each morning we must choose to allow the Spirit to fill and control us, bringing the freedom that Christ died for. If we don't allow the Spirit access to every area of our life, those areas will serve the enemy's purposes, not God's.

PRAYER
Heavenly Father, fill me daily with Your Spirit.
Thank You for the freedom I have in You!
Have Your way with me, I pray.

Journal: Ask God to reveal what may be keeping you under the yoke of slavery (anger, fear, rebellion, unforgiveness, disbelief?). Then ask the Holy Spirit to sweep it away and fill you with Himself.

—Tammy M. Price

Peace

Now the Lord is the Spirit, and where the Spirit of the Lord is, there is freedom.
2 Corinthians 3:17

As I think of what freedom means, I cannot help but think of God's perfect peace. Before I joined First Place, I must admit I was a mess emotionally. I certainly could not say that I felt free or at peace. I worried about many things. I allowed other people and circumstances to rule my life.

As I studied God's Word and developed a closer personal relationship with my Lord, I discovered that it was His desire for me to personally experience His love and amazing grace. In First Place, we learn that God works on every area of our lives (spiritual, physical, emotional and mental). It was the emotional area in particular that God desired me to allow Him to change. My Lord showed me that I was under a yoke of slavery and in bondage to emotional overeating. But I learned that I do not have to live in bondage. The secret is seeking God, learning His Word, spending a quiet time with Him daily and allowing Him to empower me to resist temptation. I cannot begin to tell you the transformation He has accomplished in my life through First Place. He is bringing health and healing to every area of my life.

PRAYER
Lord God, I thank You and praise You for who You are and what You mean to me. You are my everything! Thank You for the price You paid to buy my freedom.

Journal: Ask God to reveal the area or areas of your life that are in bondage. During your prayer time, ask Him to help you give these areas of your life to Him.

—Janet Kirkhart

Truly Wonderfully Made

For you created my inmost being; you knit me together in my
mother's womb. I will praise you because I am fearfully and wonderfully
made; your works are wonderful, I know that full well.

PSALM 139:13-14

At our First Place Leadership Summit in 2003, one of our leaders, Joe Ann Winkler (who has had MS for over 20 years and has been in a wheelchair most of that time), gave a testimony that vividly illustrates this verse.

At the Leadership Summit in 2002, Joe Ann bought my book *Back on Track*. As she began reading the book, she asked God if He would help her begin walking. She specifically asked God, "Walk through my legs." Joe Anne shared how she first walked to the mailbox and back. Then she ventured down the block, her husband hovering close behind. Next she began walking in the mall, praying for a different group of people each time around. Soon she was walking five miles each day.

The most amazing part of Joe Ann's story is that this was the only time she could walk. The rest of the time she was still confined to her wheelchair! As Joe Ann stood before us at the Leadership Summit, I fully understood that nothing is impossible with God. He made us, and He can do absolutely anything He desires, if we will only ask Him for help.

PRAYER
Dear Lord, help me realize that You know everything about this body of mine. I trust
You to help me take care of it today.

Journal: Ask God for help today with some physical challenge you are facing. Is it weight loss you desire, or physical healing of an illness?

—Carole Lewis

Don't Buy the Lies

*For you created my inmost being; you knit me together in my
mother's womb. I will praise you because I am fearfully and wonderfully
made; your works are wonderful, I know that full well.*

Psalm 139:13-14

How often do we have thoughts such as, *God can't love me. I'm worthless. I'll never measure up.* Even after I came to a greater understanding of God's grace and experienced greater freedom, the enemy came against me with those same lies straight from the pit of hell. Over time, I was beaten down and began to question how much God really loved me, because I was ignorant of the battle that was taking place in the spiritual realm. Instead of going to battle with the Word, I cowered under the lies.

However, once I realized that I had believed the enemy's lies, the Spirit of truth rose up inside me. I began to go to battle. I began to confess the truth with my mouth. I took up the sword of the Spirit and broke free. Approximately two months later, I prayed Ephesians 3:17-19. I said, "O God, I pray that I, being rooted and established in love, may have power to grasp how wide and long and high and deep is the love of Christ, and to know this love that surpasses knowledge—that I may be filled to the measure of all the fullness of God." All of a sudden, I realized that I had a deeper sense of assurance than I'd ever had before. I knew it wasn't about warm fuzzies. Rather, I had assurance that God loved me with a love that cannot be penetrated by lies.

PRAYER
*Thank You, Father, for Your true Word! Reveal any lies that
I have believed, and make known to me Your truth. Thank You, Father,
for Your love, Your grace and Your freedom.*

Journal: Write a prayer and pray it out loud every day about believing and trusting that God's Word is accomplishing exactly what it says it will do.

—Denise Munton

Bragging on God

*For you created my inmost being; you knit me together in my
mother's womb. I will praise you because I am fearfully and wonderfully
made; your works are wonderful, I know that full well.*

Psalm 139:13-14

For several years, in keeping our First Place commitment to exercise, my wife, Anita, and I have walked three miles every day. Our walk has provided an excellent time for us to just be together and talk about our day. And we often have some excellent theological discussions.

One afternoon, as we were walking, I said, "Anita, I have struggled for years with how to adequately define 'praise.' I want to praise God in a way that pleases Him, but I'm not really sure exactly what it means. What do you think it means to praise?" We walked on for a few minutes in silence, and then she said, "I think praise simply means to brag on God." The more I thought about her comment, the more excited I became, and the faster I walked!

Bragging on God! You know, that's exactly what He wants us to do! And that's exactly what the psalmist was doing when he wrote the words of Psalm 139. Now I try not to let a day pass without taking some time to simply brag on God for who He is, for what He has done in my life, for what He is doing in my life and for the victories He is giving me in First Place. After all, according to His Word, He is not only worthy of all our bragging, He also inhabits our bragging. To me, that's a thought worth thinking!

PRAYER

Father, You are, indeed, an awesome God, the Creator of all things, majestic, holy, righteous, loving, patient, gentle and forgiving. And yet, in addition to all of this, You care about everything that touches my life. I thank You, and I praise You. Amen.

Journal: What are you praising God for today? For what blessing in your life can you just brag on Him about?

—Jim Clayton

God's Beautiful Children

*For you created my inmost being; you knit me together in my
mother's womb. I will praise you because I am fearfully and wonderfully
made; your works are wonderful, I know that full well.*

Psalm 139:13-14

Do you know that God was smiling down at your birth, rejoicing over His beautiful daughter (or son)? All the angels in heaven were clapping, cheering and celebrating your beautiful birth. You were unique, adorable, special.

Imagine being given the most beautiful silver heart-shaped mirror with these words written on it in fancy script: "God's Beautiful Son" or "God's Beautiful Daughter." Through the words of Psalm 139:13-14, God reminds you that you are special because He created your inmost being—He knit you together in your mother's womb. Your life is His handiwork, and everything that God has created is wonderful.

I shared this lesson with my First Place class as we worked through the *Living in Grace* Bible study. As we came to the memory verses (Psalm 139:13-14), I took out my special heart-shaped mirror and let the ladies experience God's love for them individually as they reflected on the psalmist's words. There was a lot of healing during that session. And for some, it was the first time they had felt loved and accepted.

PRAYER
*Lord, You have created Your people to give them a life of hope,
love and compassion. Bring rejoicing and celebration into our lives because
of what You have done. In Jesus' precious name. Amen.*

Prayer: Let God's love flow through you. Celebrate the life that God has created, because you are a precious gift from God.

—Barbara Lukies

Aging Gracefully

*For you created my inmost being; you knit me together in my
mother's womb. I will praise you because I am fearfully and wonderfully
made; your works are wonderful, I know that full well.*

Psalm 139:13-14

When the leaves began turning their brilliant colors in the fall season, I had decided, with encouragement from my husband, to let my hair enter into the fall season of my life and become the glorious gray my Creator had given me. This was not an easy decision; but the constant dyeing to get my youthful color back was becoming a pain. It seemed that my hair was looking like a bird's nest at the crown more often than not. I was embarrassed to go to the altar on some occasions and kneel.

I did my graying project during the winter season when I could easily wear a hat, and because many of my friends had gone south for months. I would step out of the shower after washing my hair and think I still had soap in my hair as I saw the grayish white head. I was puzzled at the gray hair in my brush and then realized it was mine! I began picking gray hair off my dark sweaters—mine! My husband, who had an occasional gray hair, loved it. I began to appreciate my hair as it is—and I threw the last bottle of dark brown rinse away.

I had enjoyed extending my dark hair for years until I was ready to enjoy the color of my mature years. I still have as much energy and I play the same game of tennis. We are wonderfully made, even if we're prematurely gray or overweight!

PRAYER

*Father, thank You for knowing me from the time I was formed. I thank You
that You have made me fearfully and wonderfully, and I ask forgiveness for
complaints I may have voiced about Your creation.*

Journal: What aspects of your body have you complained about? Do you appreciate that you are God's workmanship and that your body is the temple of the Holy Spirit?

—Bev Schwind

Live by Grace

I do not set aside the grace of God, for if righteousness could be
gained through the law, Christ died for nothing!
Galatians 2:21

Our daughter Lisa is one of the most grace-filled people I know. She has always been the kind of person who lays aside her own comfort for the good of everyone else. Recently, we were preparing for this year's First Place Leadership Summit. On Saturday, the last day of the Summit, Johnny and I always invite the attendees to our home at the Bay for a time of fun and relaxation.

This year, the lady who helps me clean was not feeling well and I asked Lisa if she might be able to come help me clean my house the weekend before the Summit. I told her that I wanted to pay her the same amount I always pay, and she agreed to come. We got up early on Saturday morning, and at the end of the day, I was totally amazed at all we had accomplished.

Saturday night, when it came time for Lisa to go home, I took out my checkbook to reimburse her for a gift she had bought for me the week before and to pay her for all her hard work. Lisa looked at me and said firmly, "You are not going to pay me for working today. I was glad to do it." As I went to sleep that night, I thought, *I should have named her Grace!*

PRAYER
Dear Lord, bless those who extend Your grace to me today, and help me,
in turn, to extend grace to someone else.

Journal: Is there an area of your life that desperately needs the power of God's grace? Ask Him to come in and help. You won't be sorry!

—Carole Lewis

Stand Firm

I do not set aside the grace of God, for if righteousness could be
gained through the law, Christ died for nothing!
Galatians 2:21

Do you live each day in His grace, knowing that what He did on the cross He did for you? Or do you live each day as if His sacrifice was all for nothing? Do you live in freedom from your past? Are you free from thoughts of guilt and condemnation?

Grace is literally a place in which we stand (see Romans 5:1-2). Standing speaks of our progress and that we are pressing forward. It further denotes our perseverance; we stand firmly and safely, upheld by the power of God.

If you are not living in grace and experiencing freedom, you are not standing. Galatians 5:1 reminds us, "It is for freedom that Christ has set us free. Stand firm, then." Jesus made us free. He paid the price. Our debt has been paid. There is nothing we did to earn it. In fact, if we had to earn it, it would never be ours. At the same time, Jesus commands and empowers us to stand as soldiers stand. We have to intentionally press in and stand in truth. We have to consciously and deliberately stand firm to stand in His place of grace.

PRAYER
O God, I thank You that everything Jesus did was all for me.
Thank You for Your freedom. Thank You for Your peace. Thank You for
Your Word of truth that protects me from the evil one.

Journal: What are some ways you have tried to, or are trying to, earn God's favor and love? Write out and pray the Scriptures that speak of your freedom.

—Denise Munton

Progress, Not Perfection

I do not set aside the grace of God, for if righteousness could be
gained through the law, Christ died for nothing!
Galatians 2:21

You can find how-to books on just about anything you want to know more about—how to sell your home, how to lose weight in 10 days, how to love yourself more, how to save more and spend less. Books are written every day suggesting that we can be better if only we follow the book's directions.

Isn't God awesome for giving us an owner's manual for *ourselves*? Reading the Word teaches us about God and how to be His disciples. We learn that no matter how perfect we try to be, it's not our perfection that God longs for. No, He wants our heart. He longs for our attention and devotion.

Our works and deeds will never achieve righteousness. We can be the best of the best or the worst of the worst, and His grace will always be there for the taking. When I fail, His grace is there. When I make good choices, His grace is there. When I make bad choices, His grace is ready and waiting. I just need to ask for it. The hard part is accepting it!

One of the slogans we use in our First Place group is "Progress, Not Perfection." It's about grace, not legalism. It's about freedom, not bondage. It's about *God* and His grace, not about *me* and my achievements!

PRAYER
Dear God, thank You for Your unending supply of grace. Teach me more
about grace so that I can know You better and experience Your presence
in my life in a deeper, more meaningful way. Help me to accept Your grace
and know that nothing I can do will earn me greater favor.

Journal: What does grace mean to you? Do you accept His grace or reject it? Why?

—Kelly Shearer

Resting in His Power

I do not set aside the grace of God, for if righteousness could be
gained through the law, Christ died for nothing!
Galatians 2:21

One of the reasons I came to First Place was because I had tried to lose weight and couldn't. If I did lose 20 pounds, which I did frequently, they came right back on. I could barely stick with one commitment to the fad diets—so I thought there was no way I could keep the First Place commitments without His power! Admitting that I need Him keeps any pride or self-doing at bay.

By God's grace, I have been able to be faithful to the First Place program for the last seven years. The only time I have failed is when I have set aside the grace of God and tried to go back to my old way of doing things. Thankfully, God never gives up on me and has taught me to ask for and rely on His glorious grace. He gives this mother of five, with four children under the age of six, the grace to be faithful daily in all of my commitments, to write Christian women's books and even lead Bible studies. I can only do these things because of His grace and my commitment to leading a healthy, balanced life.

First Place is not a diet; it is a lifestyle and a template for God's grace. He brings me enough time, energy and joy to know Him, please Him, obey Him and glorify Him. Only He could do this. And He can do it for you!

PRAYER
Glorious heavenly Father, thank You for Your gift of grace through
Your Son, Jesus. Forgive any pride and rebellion that occurs when I fail to rely on You.
Your grace is sufficient in all areas, at all times! Amen.

Journal: How might you be trying to rely on yourself, your power or your ways? What do you believe your rebellion stems from?

—Tammy M. Price

Be Wary of Stinking Thinking

I do not set aside the grace of God, for if righteousness could be
gained through the law, Christ died for nothing!
Galatians 2:21

I sat rigidly, attempting to listen to my fellow group members, but my mind kept drifting back to my disappointing trip to the scale before the meeting. They're supposed to get smaller, not larger, right? I had been feeling prideful all week, due to my near perfect performance following the First Place guidelines. All my ducks were in a neat little row. Unfortunately, somewhere, somehow, these particular ducks had taken a swim in the wrong pond—the Pond of Pride.

For the past several days, I had bought into the age-old lie that righteousness could somehow be earned by my actions. After sharing with my group, I discovered the error in my thinking. If I could gain righteousness in my weight-loss process by simply being good enough, why did I need Christ and His grace? The "stinking thinking"—which tells us that all will be well if we simply follow the right rules and do the right things—can easily creep into our thoughts.

What performance on our part would be good enough to meet God's standards? Unfortunately, none of us is capable of perfection. Only His grace is enough to make us righteous. Thank goodness we don't have to earn it. Instead, we need only accept it.

PRAYER
Dear heavenly Father, forgive me for all the times I've tried to
earn Your approval. May I accept Your grace today and live in a way
that demonstrates to the world to whom I belong.

Journal: Have you found yourself trying to earn God's love? How do you respond when you fail to meet the standards you set for yourself?

—Carol Van Atta

Be an Encourager

See to it, brothers, that none of you has a sinful, unbelieving heart that turns away from the living God. But encourage one another daily, as long as it is called Today, so that none of you may be hardened by sin's deceitfulness.

Hebrews 3:12-13

Encouragement is one of the commitments in the First Place program. The commitment is to contact with a note or phone call one person in your class each week. Even though the commitment doesn't take much time, it seems to be one of the hardest to keep. With our busy lives, we sometimes forget how important encouragement is for all of us.

I work out with Becky, a fellow First Place leader, most mornings. Becky is 23 years younger than I am—and obviously in better physical condition. Becky committed to do the half marathon with me and encouraged me so that I could finish. Even though I acted put out by her constant encouragement of "Come on, come on," I couldn't have finished with a 3:45 time without it. All of us need encouragement, and all of us need to give encouragement.

During the race, I looked for others who were struggling and offered encouragement to them. A lady with MS struggled to run. As I came up beside her, I asked her if she had run this race before. She said that she had, and when I told her how great she was doing, she said to me, "Just keep going; you'll finish too." What a great word of encouragement for me that day. I started out to encourage her, but she encouraged me!

PRAYER

Dear Lord, help me encourage everyone I meet today so that I will not be hardened by sin's deceitfulness.

Journal: Is there someone in your life who needs your encouragement? Write down ways you can give encouragement to that person today and then do it.

—Carole Lewis

Eyes on the Cross

See to it, brothers, that none of you has a sinful, unbelieving heart that
turns away from the living God. But encourage one another daily, as long as it is
called Today, so that none of you may be hardened by sin's deceitfulness.
Hebrews 3:12-13

Before I began to understand the Lord's grace, the sin of having a critical spirit was alive and well in me. I had it all figured out, even when I couldn't live up to the standards I set. I just couldn't figure out why other Christians didn't get it. Family, friends, you name it, the standards for Christian living had all been set for us—at least in my mind.

As the Holy Spirit revealed His grace, my heart melted. I immediately recognized my legalistic mind-set that was hardening my heart and hindering my intimacy with the Lord. I had made a list of "don'ts" instead of living in the incredible "dos" the Lord had for me. I stopped looking at other people's splinters and saw the gigantic log in my eye. I was surprised at the freedom that came over me. I didn't have to worry about other people's so-called shortcomings anymore. That was between them and God.

The process of sanctification in a person's heart is very individual. And there was a lot of sanctification that needed to take place in me. All I had to do was allow the Lord to reveal my sin and then allow Him to cleanse me and change me. Instead of harboring a critical spirit that keeps me bound and miserable, I now can keep my eyes on the Cross that keeps me free!

PRAYER
Father, thank You for Your faithfulness and gentleness as You reveal my sin. Help me
keep my eyes on the Cross as I seek to know You more.

Journal: In what areas is God extending freedom to you? In what areas do you need to extend freedom to others?

—Denise Munton

Junk Food and Sin

See to it, brothers, that none of you has a sinful, unbelieving heart that
turns away from the living God. But encourage one another daily, as long as it is
called Today, so that none of you may be hardened by sin's deceitfulness.
Hebrews 3:12-13

I struggled for years with a love for food, particularly junk food, and a desire to be thin. Yet the Lord, through the First Place Bible studies, helped to renew my mind and see that each time I chose a type of food that appealed outwardly and satisfied my cravings for junk food and sweets, I was truly robbing my body of the quality nutrients it required to function. In addition, each time I chose appealing junk food, I was turning away from the Lord who gives life. Repeating this behavior hardened my heart and reinforced a negative habit. Choosing God's will became a decision to choose food that had the ultimate to offer me in terms of nutritional value for my body. Like sin, the junk food was simply an illusion, a moment of instant gratification that in the long run was truly empty.

Today I continue to make food choices that are life-giving. And I encourage others to do the same.

PRAYER
Lord, You have blessed me with abundance. Please help me to choose
life and to choose Your way in the foods I eat.

Journal: Is there a connection between your favorite foods, instant gratification and the temptation to turn away from the living God?

—Roberta Wasserman

Sustaining the Weary

See to it, brothers, that none of you has a sinful, unbelieving heart that
turns away from the living God. But encourage one another daily, as long as it is
called Today, so that none of you may be hardened by sin's deceitfulness.
Hebrews 3:12-13

Shortly after joining First Place, I decided to take Hebrews 3:12-13 to heart and send each person in my First Place group a daily encouragement message. Writing is my joy and my passion, so I asked God to use me to strengthen others through a ministry of written encouragement. God answered that simple request in ways far beyond my ability to ask or even imagine. What began two years ago as a daily e-mail encouragement to seven women has increased over a hundredfold! Today "Winning Words for First Place Losers" goes out to more than 700 people every morning, and God is using this simple ministry to touch hearts in need of strength, encouragement and hope.

If that had been the only way God had answered my prayer to be an encourager, I would have been truly blessed. But God had more in store for me. What seemed so easy in the beginning turned out to be a double-edged sword! To encourage is quite literally to fuse courage into another, which meant that if I was going to encourage others daily, I was going to have to let God encourage me!

Today I understand that it is God's Word flowing through me that sustains the weary, not my clever way with words. How thankful I am that the God of heaven and Earth is willing to speak to me so that all of us who are weary and in need of His sustaining grace can be refreshed each morning.

PRAYER
Gracious and loving God, You are the giver of all good gifts.
Thank You for the life-giving gift of Your Word.

Journal: Take time today to write a note of encouragement to someone in your First Place group.

—Elizabeth Crews

Idolatry of Food

*See to it, brothers, that none of you has a sinful, unbelieving heart that
turns away from the living God. But encourage one another daily, as long as it is
called Today, so that none of you may be hardened by sin's deceitfulness.*
Hebrews 3:12-13

It was so subtle, so slow—just a little hardening here and a little hardening there. Before I knew it (or at least was willing to confess it), I was in the middle of full-blown deceit and my heart had hardened to God. The lies of Satan were much more real to me than the truth of God. "I'm just big boned." "I am healthy even if I'm 60 pounds overweight." "I can always diet next week and it will be fine." "God doesn't care what I weigh—He loves me just as I am."

It's true that God loves me just as I am, but He did not love the sin of gluttony and idolatry that was keeping me from turning my hardened heart toward Him. Actually, He loves me so much that He was not willing to allow me to remain in that bondage of sin. But it was not until I turned back to God through great conviction of the Holy Spirit and confessed my sin that freedom came.

This freedom is still a daily walk, but the accountability and the encouragement of my fellow First Place members keep my heart softened and turned to the reality of the living God.

PRAYER
*Lord, help me today to be one who turns my heart to You.
Please reveal to me any areas of deceit in my heart that
would keep this from happening.*

Journal: Is there any unconfessed sin that you need to turn away from? Confess your sin and turn your heart back to God in prayer.

—Becky Turner

When Everything Changes

*This righteousness from God comes through faith in Jesus Christ
to all who believe. There is no difference, for all have sinned and fall short
of the glory of God, and are justified freely by his grace through the
redemption that came by Christ Jesus.*

Romans 3:22-24

I didn't truly begin to grow in my Christian life until I became fully aware that the only righteousness I possess is Christ's righteousness in me. I wonder if any of us really learns this lesson without experiencing the devastating consequences of sin in our lives. This was certainly true for me. In December 1984, I had been a believer in Christ for many years, but He had never been given permission to be Lord of everything in my life. I was what people call a "carnal Christian," one who only cries out to God when in a real mess. The rest of the time I was in control of my life, or so I thought.

Through a series of devastating events, I finally came to the end of myself and cried out to God, "Change me, and please don't make it hurt too bad!" Christ's righteousness came into my life that day and began to change everything about me. He gave me a love for hurting women that I never had before and filled my life to overflowing with His love. Realizing that I have nothing worthy to give Christ has been the starting point of my daily walk with Him. I am only able to portray righteousness as Christ's righteousness works in and through my life.

PRAYER
*Dear Lord, thank You for the righteousness that comes through
faith for all who believe. Thank You that even though I sin, You have the
power to forgive and to use me in the lives of others.*

Journal: Write about something in your life that is standing between you and God's righteousness. Ask God to start changing you from the inside today.

—Carole Lewis

Power of the Holy Spirit

*This righteousness from God comes through faith in Jesus Christ
to all who believe. There is no difference, for all have sinned and fall short
of the glory of God, and are justified freely by his grace through the
redemption that came by Christ Jesus.*

ROMANS 3:22-24

Seven years after our first child was born, God gave us two more children. As you can imagine, our world was rocked. In the midst of all the excitement and blessings, there was incredible stress and chaos. At times I felt like I was just barely surviving. At the same time, I began to observe how all these changes were affecting our oldest child. Then it hit me. It seemed as though I was looking in a mirror when she acted out her stress. My heart broke that day when I realized how my moments of stress and anger had taught her how to behave. Although our sinful nature doesn't need any training, I still knew that my impatience and spouts of anger had spilled over into her life.

On my face before the Lord, I cried out, "Dear Lord, the damage is done!" The last thing I wanted to pass on to my children was one of my ugly and sinful attitudes. However, in my heartache and grief over how my sin had affected her, the Holy Spirit sweetly spoke to my spirit and said, "Just as I am in the process of sanctifying and transforming you, I will be faithful to do the same in her." I wept. The Comforter Himself had ministered to me. As we confess our sin, the blood of Jesus will cleanse and transform our hearts and mold us more and more into His likeness.

PRAYER
Thank You, Father, for Your Holy Spirit who convicts me of sin and comforts my heart. Thank You for cleansing me with Your blood. Thank You for changing me and sanctifying me.

Journal: Are there areas in your heart and life that you are feeling guilty about today? Confess the sins that the Holy Spirit is convicting you of, and allow Him to cleanse and comfort you.

—Denise Munton

Feed the Hungry

*This righteousness from God comes through faith in Jesus Christ
to all who believe. There is no difference, for all have sinned and fall short
of the glory of God, and are justified freely by his grace through the
redemption that came by Christ Jesus.*

Romans 3:22-24

Every Sunday afternoon, the church I belong to opens its doors to the homeless and poor living in downtown San Diego. An hour before Ladle Fellowship starts serving soup, the hungry begin lining up near the door to the dining area. As a result of this ministry, some of our Ladle guests have begun attending Sunday morning worship before they get in line to partake of the Ladle Fellowship meal. Those of us active in this ministry rejoice when we see the Word of God begin taking root in the heart of those who come seeking a bowl of soup for their hunger and find spiritual soup to fill their hungry souls as well.

But there are those in our congregation who do not share our joy. It's not that they feel that lost souls should be deprived of the gospel; they are all in favor of a message being preached before the meal. They just don't want to share a pew with them. I often wonder what they would do if Jesus, who was poor and homeless, sat down in the pew beside them!

Is it only when we realize that we also are destitute, foul-smelling, uneducated beggars before a holy God that we can begin to grasp the truth of Romans 3:22-24—that we have all sinned and fallen short of God's glory? We are all redeemed by the blood of Jesus Christ, the spotless Lamb of God, who came to seek and save the lost.

PRAYER

*Have mercy on me, O God, a sinner! You came to seek and save the lost. Help me join
You in that work as one poor beggar telling another where I have found the Bread of Life.*

Journal: Write about a time when you were able to minister to the least and the last, offering a cup of cold water in Jesus' name.

—Elizabeth Crews

Sin Is Sin

*This righteousness from God comes through faith in Jesus Christ
to all who believe. There is no difference, for all have sinned and fall short
of the glory of God, and are justified freely by his grace through the
redemption that came by Christ Jesus.*

Romans 3:22-24

We all think there is a difference between our sins and the sins of others. The murderer, his sin is far greater than mine. So I overeat a little bit and occasionally gossip. So what? I don't cheat on my taxes, and I have never been convicted of a felony. Surely there is a difference.

Yet there is no difference. We are all missing the mark of God's holiness. We have all fallen short of the standard of perfection displayed by Christ and established by the heavenly Father.

But praise the Lord for the other "all" in these verses. God is willing to give His righteousness to all who believe in Jesus Christ. There is no difference of sin and there is no discrimination of grace. God will give to everyone who believes.

Whether we need to lose 10 pounds or 250 pounds, only by His grace can we accomplish this task. There is no difference to those who believe.

PRAYER
*Lord, help me remember that it is a level field at the Cross.
Regardless of how "small" I sin, I am still missing the mark.
Help me receive Your grace today to walk in righteousness.*

Journal: How do you grade sin? How does your answer compare with Romans 3:22-24?

—Becky Turner

Washed Clean

*This righteousness from God comes through faith in Jesus Christ
to all who believe. There is no difference, for all have sinned and fall short
of the glory of God, and are justified freely by his grace through the
redemption that came by Christ Jesus.*

Romans 3:22-24

After a shopping trip the other day, I opened my van door only to have a gust of wind push the door open and graze the side of the neighboring vehicle. There was no dent, but definitely there was some marking. I had not intentionally done anything wrong. My doors even have a clear plastic strip to prevent dings. I rationalized that the marks were superficial, and I drove away.

I prayed for the owner of the vehicle, for his peace and forgiveness. I prayed that the marks washed off in the evening rain and that he never even knew they existed. I regretted that I had not sought out the owner and attempted to make amends.

It hurts to know that although I have a close relationship with God, I still sin. The marks may not have washed off the vehicle, but I am certain I have been washed clean through the sacrifice of Jesus.

All of us will continue to fall short, but God's promise of redemption endures. We confess our sins to God in order to keep a close relationship with Him. We learn from our mistakes because we love God and desire to please Him. But we do not earn our forgiveness. It is given freely. And because of His redemption, we live in grace.

PRAYER

*Lord, today I confess my sins to You. Surround me with Your love
and the knowledge that I am justified freely by Your grace through
the death and resurrection of Christ Jesus.*

Journal: In what areas do you need to accept His forgiveness and feel the peace that comes to you through His gift of grace?

—Becky Sims

Staying Close to Jesus

I am the vine; you are the branches. If a man remains
in me and I in him, he will bear much fruit; apart from
me you can do nothing.

John 15:5

A couple of years ago, I read *Secrets of the Vine* by Bruce Wilkinson. As I read chapter 15 of John's Gospel, I was intrigued by Jesus' words in verse 2. He says, "He cuts off every branch in me that bears no fruit, while every branch that does bear fruit he prunes so that it will be even more fruitful."

Shortly after I finished reading the book, we were in Ventura, California, for meetings at our publisher, Gospel Light. Since the California wine country is just about an hour's drive from Ventura, Johnny and I drove there and took a tour of a vineyard. I quickly saw what Jesus was talking about in this passage of Scripture. As the tour guide explained how the grapes are cultivated, she said, "You will notice that the limbs are tied to the pole, because they don't bear fruit when they hang down and drag on the ground." Instantly, I realized that the same is true of me. As long as I stay close to Jesus, I too will bear much fruit—for apart from Him I can do nothing.

PRAYER

Dear Lord, teach me what it means to stay close to You so that
my life will bear much fruit.

Journal: Think about areas of your life that need pruning so that you might be more fruitful. Ask God to do the work necessary to tie you closer to His side.

—Carole Lewis

Stuck in Unforgiveness

*I am the vine; you are the branches. If a man remains
in me and I in him, he will bear much fruit; apart from
me you can do nothing.*

John 15:5

When I think of the phrase "apart from me you can do nothing," I'm reminded of forgiveness. Apart from the Holy Spirit, forgiveness is impossible. From a human standpoint, however, forgiveness doesn't seem fair if we've been victimized or unjustly treated in some way. But from a spiritual standpoint, it holds the key to our freedom.

When we walk in unforgiveness, we miss out on the freedom that God has already purchased for us. But as long as we harbor unforgiveness, there will be personal consequences far beyond anything we can inflict on the person we don't want to forgive.

God's command for us to forgive is not because He doesn't understand what we feel; but rather, it is because He knows how this sin affects our hearts. He loves us so much that He sacrificed His beloved Son so that we can be free from the pain of unforgiveness and be healed. Don't believe the lie that your wound is too great to be healed and that the one who wounded you is unforgivable. When you do forgive, not only will you experience healing, but you will also reestablish your intimacy with the Lord.

PRAYER

*O God, help me! Heal my heart! I confess my unforgiveness toward
[name of person]. I need Your grace and power. Soften my heart.
Let me see them through Your eyes. Help me trust You daily and depend
on You for strength and wisdom. Thank You, Father.*

Journal: Is there someone you need to forgive? It is impossible to hate someone you are praying for. Who will you pray for today?

—Denise Munton

Bearing Fruit That Lasts

I am the vine; you are the branches. If a man remains
in me and I in him, he will bear much fruit; apart from
me you can do nothing.
John 15:5

I wasted a lot of years trying to lose weight apart from God. I bought every magazine in the checkout line that advertised a new diet on the front cover, thinking this would be the diet that worked. Little did I realize that I already had the book that held all the answers I needed. While many of the magazines made promises that failed, the Bible holds promises that never fail. I finally started to see results when I joined First Place and learned how to seek God first and remain in Him.

Without God, we are working in vain when trying to make lifestyle changes. Our attempts to get healthy and lose weight will be futile. Scripture says that with God we can do all things, which includes losing weight and living a balanced life (see Philippians 4:13).

When we remain in Him, we will also bear fruit. Just as an apple tree bears apples rather than some other fruit, true Christians will bear the fruit of the Spirit.

PRAYER
Father, help me remain in You. When I start to wander away,
remind me that apart from You, I can do nothing;
but with You, all things are possible. Amen.

Journal: Do a "fruit inspection." List the fruits of the Spirit that you see in your life. Then list the ones you need to work on.

—Joni Shaffer

Enslavement

I am the vine; you are the branches. If a man remains
in me and I in him, he will bear much fruit; apart from
me you can do nothing.

John 15:5

As a new First Place member, walking with my husband one afternoon, I shared with him how overwhelmed I felt trying to fit all my daily First Place responsibilities into *one* day. When my husband tried to encourage me, he paused to find the exact word, "Just do the best you can and don't worry about doing *all* those nine . . ."

"Enslavements!" I blurted out. The surprise and irony of that word popping out of my mouth made us laugh, though I felt a little sheepish about being so negative.

Moments later, the realization struck that this was God's word choice. He was revealing to me that my expectation of perfect obedience was enslaving me. I was not remaining in Jesus (relying on His power) but was trying to be a healthy branch and bear fruit on my own. God's convicting reminder came: "Apart from me you can do nothing." Yet I felt no condemnation, only the gentle chiding of a loving Father who wanted to get my nose off the grindstone and my eyes back on Jesus.

Just today, God helped me understand the continuing relief from the burden of perfectionism as I yield my efforts to Jesus, along with the incredible joy this freedom brings. Also, when I remain in the Vine, His life-giving Spirit can flow freely in me and produce the fruit of obedience. More joy!

PRAYER
Lord, thank You that You draw near to me when I draw near to You. Thank You that Your
Spirit will bring forth the fruit of a life pleasing to You. Be glorified, Jesus, in all of this.

Journal: What expectations for yourself are burdensome? How are these expectations causing you to focus on the process instead of on the person of Jesus? What helps you most to remain in Him?

—Molly Bascom

Parable of the Leaves

*I am the vine; you are the branches. If a man remains
in me and I in him, he will bear much fruit; apart from
me you can do nothing.*
J o h n 1 5 : 5

Several years ago, the Lord gave me a vivid illustration of this verse. I noticed that three large trees in my backyard had grown exponentially during the previous spring and now their branches were hanging dangerously close to my roof and my neighbor's roof.

I contacted a tree-cutting service that came out the following Saturday. Within hours, a huge pile of cut limbs, branches and leaves was stacked in my front yard and part of my driveway. The pile was at least six feet high and eight feet wide! Unfortunately, heavy-trash pickup day for my neighborhood was at least three weeks away. So, for the next 21 days, I drove in and out of my garage, maneuvering around this decaying pile of tree limbs and branches.

The first few days, the leaves of those cut-off branches were as green and healthy looking on the outside as those still attached to the tree. Over time, the deadness inside the branches began to show up on the outside. When heavy-trash pickup day finally arrived, the pile had shriveled to half its size, and the dead leaves lay like breadcrumbs across my driveway.

When we detach from the Vine, Jesus Christ, who is our source of life, we suffer spiritual decay. We become "like a branch that is thrown away and withers; such branches are picked up, thrown into the fire and burned" (John 15:6).

PRAYER
*Lord, help me remain in You today. Apart from You, I am nothing and
can do nothing. But with You, I can do all things!*

Journal: Recount a time when you experienced spiritual death from not remaining in the Vine. What happened? How did you feel?

—Eulalia King

Where Do You Run?

The name of the LORD is a strong tower; the righteous run to it and are safe.
Proverbs 18:10

This verse paints a beautiful word picture for me. I see myself standing on a barren plain, gazing at a huge castle. The castle has a moat all the way around it and water fills the moat. A drawbridge is in front of me, leading to the doors of the castle. When trouble comes, I have a choice. I can run across the drawbridge and into the doors of the castle, knowing that the drawbridge will come up after I cross over it. Or I can run to friends or family and try to deal with the circumstances in my own power and strength, making me vulnerable to the enemy.

Where we run in times of trouble is a real indicator of where we are spiritually, emotionally, mentally and physically. Do we run toward the arms of a loving Lord or away from them? Outside of His arms is nothing but barren plain—nothing to hide behind and nowhere to go that is safe.

The name of the Lord has great power. Call out His name when you want to eat something unhealthy. Call out His name when you are afraid. Call out His name when you need wisdom regarding finances, your children, your marriage.

PRAYER

*Dear Lord, Your name is a strong tower. Help me call out to You today
when I am tempted; help me run to You when trouble comes.*

Journal: What does the name of the Lord mean to you? How has His name kept you safe in times past?

—Carole Lewis

The Presence of God

The name of the LORD is a strong tower; the righteous run to it and are safe.
PROVERBS 18:10

The God of all grace was there and saw me in my darkest hour. When I found myself in circumstances beyond my control, He made His presence known. He literally engulfed me in His grace. Although my circumstances didn't change, the power and presence of the Holy Spirit in my life became manifest. Jesus was all I had, and Jesus was all I needed.

Three years after my first husband betrayed me and walked out of our marriage, Don, my current husband, proposed to me. I began to worry about what color wedding dress I should wear. I finally asked him what he thought. Without hesitation, he immediately said, "You'll wear a white dress, for the very same reason I can wear a white tux. I see you completely forgiven, cleansed as white as snow with the blood of Jesus. And you have forgiven your ex-husband. You've experienced the miracle of forgiveness."

I was stunned. Up to that point, I knew that I had been forgiven, but it was through Don's words that the Lord revealed to me how much He really loved me. The Lord loved me and ministered to me through my future husband. The Lord gave me a glimpse into His heart through Don's words. So as a symbol of Christ's cleansing blood and grace, Don wore a white tux in our wedding and I wore a white dress.

PRAYER

Father God, I thank You that Your name is a strong tower.
Help me know Your presence in my time of need. I don't understand
all that is happening—in fact, I don't know if I can
endure any longer, but God, I trust You.

Journal: When have you felt the presence of the Lord in your life most powerfully? What are you facing today? Do you trust Him to carry you through your circumstances?

—Denise Munton

Safe and Warm

The name of the LORD is a strong tower; the righteous run to it and are safe.
Proverbs 18:10

My 96-year-old mother almost died when she contracted the flu. After days of round-the-clock care, we were able to get away for the day with some friends to an outdoor festival. As the rain gently sprinkled the crowd of spectators, hundreds of opened umbrellas formed a colorful canopy over the crowd. My husband, Jim, and I sat under a red-and-white golf umbrella and listened to gospel music floating through the crowd from the musicians on stage. It was peaceful, and I felt safe. I could not help but thank the Lord for my husband who held the umbrella over me, keeping the rain off, and for this special quiet time. It was because of the rain that I was sitting next to my husband, not running off looking in different booths, talking to everyone but him. We were able to snuggle under the umbrella and feel safe, dry and warm.

This Scripture showed me that not only did the name of the Lord sustain me while I cared for my mother, but He also provided a safe place for her. How secure it feels to be in a safe place! And there is no safer place that in the strength of the Lord.

PRAYER
*Thank You, Lord, for being my strong tower that keeps me safe
no matter where I am or what situation I am facing.*

Journal: What makes you feel secure?

—Bev Schwind

A Familiar Face

The name of the LORD is a strong tower; the righteous run to it and are safe.
PROVERBS 18:10

Cracks of thunder and flashes of lightning brought our three little children jumping into our bed. They had found a safe place. The thunder could continue and the lightning flash in the same way, but now there was no fear as our darling children felt safe with us.

It reminds me of when one of our children, who was lost for just a few minutes in a crowded store, thought he was with me, but he looked up only to realize he was walking with a woman wearing the same color coat as mine. When he realized it was not me, he panicked. Soon after, he ran toward me and came crashing into my body. I could sense his body relax as he felt my familiar arms. Although I had him in view all the time, he had not seen me. In the same way, God has us in view all the time, but we need to run to Him to feel the safety He provides.

PRAYER
*Lord, I know that all I need to do is call out Your name and
You are there for me in every type of situation, to share in
my trials as well as my joys.*

Journal: Describe a time when you felt alone and afraid and then a sudden relief flooded over you as you saw a familiar face or heard a familiar voice—or remembered God's faithfulness.

—Bev Schwind

What's in a Name?

The name of the LORD is a strong tower; the righteous run to it and are safe.
Proverbs 18:10

I often wondered why the word "name" is used so often in Scripture. What could it be about a name that to us may not seem so important but to God means everything? Through studying this Scripture regarding God's name as "Lord," He began to show me His character revealed in His name, in what He does and is doing within me! As He becomes my fortress and safety, His lordship is established in my life.

When I begin to feel my old weakness for bad choices and unbalanced living sneak in, I don't wait around; I run to Him! As I thank Him for His names, they become evident in my life: my safety, my salvation from sin and from myself. My old evil desires no longer have their way in my life; they cannot reach me in my Strong Tower. I don't find any security in food; my strength isn't found in what is in my hands (food) but what is in my heart (His Word), and therefore His praises fill my mouth and satisfy my soul. I actually can picture in my mind an old, strong tower, high upon a hill. It is a mighty fortress that cannot be shaken!

PRAYER
Heavenly Father, may I truly come to know Your Name as my Lord,
that I may trust, seek and run to You. Be my strong tower of safety as
I remain in Your Word and experience Your presence in prayer.

Journal: Allow God to reveal to you any area of your life in which you do not trust or know Him. What does His name mean to you?

—Tammy M. Price

Live in Him

So then, just as you received Christ Jesus as Lord, continue to live in him,
rooted and built up in him, strengthened in the faith as you were taught,
and overflowing with thankfulness.

Colossians 2:6-7

When my husband, Johnny, was diagnosed with stage-four prostate cancer in October 1997 and given one-and-a-half to two years to live, we were both in shock. But in a few days, we were able to settle into the reality of living with a disease such as cancer.

A few weeks after the diagnosis, Johnny was driving down the freeway, and he asked God if he could know how long he had to live. Johnny said it was as if a piece of newsprint appeared in front of his eyes with only two words on it, "Nobody does."

Johnny shared the experience with me, and we both realized how profound those two words were. Only God knows when we will take our last breath. Because of this, God's desire for us is to continue to live in Him as long as we have breath in our bodies.

As I write these words, it has been more than eight years since Johnny's diagnosis. He and I are overflowing with thankfulness today for eight more years together. God has taught us both what it means to live in Him, rooted and built up in Him, strengthened in our faith.

PRAYER
Thank You, Father, for Jesus and the power You give us to
live each day to the fullest. Thank You also for being the only
One who knows how many days we have left.

Journal: Write about something you are concerned about today, thanking God that He has the answer.

—Carole Lewis

Redeeming the Past

So then, just as you received Christ Jesus as Lord, continue to live in him,
rooted and built up in him, strengthened in the faith as you were taught,
and overflowing with thankfulness.

COLOSSIANS 2:6-7

If you have succumbed to the belief that God can't use you because of the sins you've committed, consider the life of Peter. He passionately loved the Lord and believed in his heart that he was ready to die for Him. Yet even though he had absolutely no intentions of denying Christ, in a matter of seconds, he denied knowing the Lord he dearly loved not once, but three times.

As Peter yielded to his flesh in a moment of pride and fear, Satan thought he had him right where he wanted. Satan knew that if he could keep Peter in the depths of despair and guilt over his failure, Peter would never fulfill the destiny of his calling. Satan's plan was to enslave Peter and cause him to live a defeated and powerless life.

Instead of wavering in unbelief, Peter experienced true godly sorrow and repented of his sin. God's plan for Peter's life was never thwarted. The key to Peter's complete restoration and reconciliation to Jesus was his brokenness over his sin. He truly repented and followed Christ from that time on.

The same is true for us. Our past does not thwart God's plan for our lives when we let Him redeem our past actions and we continue to abide in Him.

PRAYER

Praise to You, Father God! Your great mercy has given me
new birth into a living hope through Your Son, Jesus. Restore and
reconcile my heart back to You. Reveal Your heart to me.

Journal: What is the impact of Peter's failure and complete restoration on your life? What do you believe God is calling you to do?

—Denise Munton

Living by Faith

So then, just as you received Christ Jesus as Lord, continue to live in him,
rooted and built up in him, strengthened in the faith as you were taught,
and overflowing with thankfulness.

Colossians 2:6-7

Faith is risky, but it overcomes the world and strengthens us daily. Faith is a vital component in our relationship with God and our ability to be content. Christ is the trustworthy object of our faith. He doesn't demand that we have blind faith. But He does want us to have abandoned faith that trusts Him fully and is rooted in His character and based on His Word, not on our feelings or circumstances.

Noah lived by abandoned faith. Suffering ridicule and loneliness, he worked 110 years in the desert without knowledge of rain or boats. Yet Noah practiced his faith daily with every wooden peg he pounded. Walking by faith is difficult because we're asked to believe what we can't see. Although I like lighted paths, if I can see what God is doing every step of the way, I don't need faith. When the Israelites were caught between the advancing Egyptian army and the Red Sea, Exodus 14:21 tells us, "All that night the LORD drove the sea back"—He was at work in their night creating the miracle they couldn't see at the moment.

The more we trust God, the more faith we have; the more faith we have, the more we trust Him. We trust our faith and know that everything happening to us has been thought out by our infinitely wise God. And all that happens will ultimately be for our good and His glory. What more strength do we need?

PRAYER

Lord, I am so thankful that because You have overcome the world,
I, too, can overcome the world by having abandoned faith in You.
Thank You for working in my nights when I can't see.

Journal: Is there an area in which you need to practice abandoned faith in God and His work on your behalf?

—Judy Marshall

Celebrate Your Life

So then, just as you received Christ Jesus as Lord, continue to live in him,
rooted and built up in him, strengthened in the faith as you were taught,
and overflowing with thankfulness.

Colossians 2:6-7

If you woke up today without a white chalk mark around your body, it is cause for celebration. It means that you are alive. God has given you another day, a new chance to fulfill your God-given purpose on Earth. In order for that to happen, you need to get out of bed, get dressed, eat something and spend some time with God to find out what *His* purpose for the day will bring. How do you know what God's plans are if you never take time to be alone with Him?

You have been chosen by God to live your life with His strength guiding you. He chose you to make a difference in your world today. Be overflowing with thankfulness that God has given you another day to live for Him. He has chosen no one else to do your part. He only wants you to fulfill your plan.

Every day is a precious gift, so don't waste a minute of it!

PRAYER

Lord, I choose to live centered on You and Your plans for me.
Thank You for reminding me that I can celebrate Your work in and through me.
Thank You for choosing me to be part of Your wonderful plan.
In Jesus' name, amen.

Journal: Make a choice today to live the life God is calling you to live, and do it with passion, excellence and celebration. To begin, how can you be a blessing to others today?

—Barbara Lukies

Have a Great Day!

And whatever you do, whether in word or deed, do it all in the name
of the Lord Jesus, giving thanks to God the Father through him.
Colossians 3:17

I learned the power in this verse when I was writing the devotionals for *Today Is the First Day*. It had been only six weeks since the death of our daughter Shari at the age of 39. I had no power inside myself to write 80 devotionals, but every morning for eight days my "whatever you do" was to write devotionals. I set my alarm for 4 A.M., went to my favorite chair and began to pray. I told God that unless He wrote those devotionals, they wouldn't get written. I thanked Him that because of Jesus, I would be able to accomplish the task. Sure enough, after eight days, all the devotionals were written and my part of the book was finished.

How different the writing for this book has been. I am not in crisis mode, so I forget that I still have no power to do anything myself. The Lord Jesus must be the One who does the writing, and He wants to use my hands, heart and mind to do it.

Your life isn't much different from mine. We wake up every morning, get dressed for the day, eat, work, run errands, pay bills. The biggest difference today can be whether or not we do everything in the name of the Lord Jesus. If we do, today will be a great one.

PRAYER
Dear Lord, whatever I do today, I want You to do through me.
Use me today to do Your will.

Journal: Write down all the things you will do today. Thank God for your "whatevers" and ask Him to do them all through you, in the name of Jesus.

—Carole Lewis

Giving Our Best

*And whatever you do, whether in word or deed, do it all in the name
of the Lord Jesus, giving thanks to God the Father through him.*
Colossians 3:17

Recently, our family had the opportunity to serve a friend and sister in Christ in a very special way. Ralpha, a 77-year-old woman, had just been diagnosed with breast cancer and needed to travel to Houston, 12 hours from her home. When we found out that she was coming here for treatment, we tried to find a host home for her. (We are a family of five with only three bedrooms, and I never considered that anybody might want to stay in our home with all the kids.) However, when there were no other openings, we apologetically offered her our master bedroom.

Don and I camped out in our daughter Abby's room, and Abby camped out in her brothers' room. Ralpha was here for two weeks. She later told us that it had been her desire all along to stay in our home. She joined in just like one of the family. She helped Abby with her homework, read to the boys and insisted on helping around the house.

We weren't quite sure how all the details would work out before Ralpha came, but the Lord had it all divinely planned beforehand. And although Ralpha and her husband back home felt like they could not thank us enough, it was the five of us who were blessed the most.

PRAYER
*Father, thank You for the opportunities You've given me to serve You with my
whole heart. Show me ways to join You in meeting others' needs. And thank You for
all the ways You have so faithfully met my needs through others.*

Journal: What are some ways that you have allowed God to meet the needs of others through you? What impact did that have on your life?

—Denise Munton

Modeling Christ

And whatever you do, whether in word or deed, do it all in the name
of the Lord Jesus, giving thanks to God the Father through him.

Colossians 3:17

Have you ever asked yourself, "How can God use me?" You may feel like you do not have any talent or special gifts that God can use. If you feel this way, you only have to search the Scriptures to discover that if you are a child of God, He has already given you all the gifts you need to follow Him and be used in His service.

I have three very special Christian friends who love the Lord and serve Him with such passion. They are excellent role models. They each have different gifts, and they use their special spiritual gifts in His service by modeling Christ in their lives. They model His grace and freely extend grace to others. I thank God for giving me these very special friends.

When I think of how many times God has extended grace to me, and how He is always so willing to forgive, forget and give me yet another chance to begin again, I know it pleases Him when I, in some small way, model this message to those around me.

PRAYER
Lord, thank You for giving me friends who have taught me so much about
Your love and Your grace through their own lives. Thank You for giving me so
many chances to begin again and learn to live in Your grace.

Journal: Ask God to reveal to you the gifts He has given you and how He wants to use you.

—Janet Kirkhart

My Name in Heaven

And whatever you do, whether in word or deed, do it all in the name
of the Lord Jesus, giving thanks to God the Father through him.
Colossians 3:17

"PJ" doesn't rhyme with "fatty," "fat" or "two-by-four," so it has become the name I use as an adult, both privately and professionally. My birth name is Patrice; but while growing up, I was nicknamed Patty. For as long as I can remember, I was dubbed Fatty Patty by both kids at school and family members. A breakthrough came when I was 10 years old. My oldest brother was in Vietnam and addressed me in one of his letters as Patti. I decided to start using that spelling because it looked "thinner" without the *Y* on the end.

My husband, when we were dating, began calling me PJ because my maiden name started with a *J*. I loved it! Not only was PJ very thin-looking, it also did not rhyme with any words that were associated with fat. I changed my notary seal, driver's license and everything else I could think of to reflect this new name.

It wasn't until I joined First Place and began to memorize Scripture that I really saw Colossians 3:17 in a new light and could apply it to my life. God showed me that it doesn't matter whether or not my name rhymes with words that sound like fat, because if I am a child of God, I do all things in the name of the Lord Jesus. My name is insignificant if I am doing *all* things in *His* name!

PRAYER
Thank You, Lord Jesus, that You love me no matter what my weight is.
Thank You that I can look to heaven and can know that when I am in heaven
with You, I will never be called names that are hurtful or painful.

Journal: What names are you recalling from your childhood that you can nail to the cross with Christ? Thank Him today that everything you do or say is in His name and that your name is written in heaven.

—PJ Bahr

God's Agenda

Therefore go and make disciples of all nations, . . . teaching them to obey everything I have commanded you. And surely I am with you always, to the very end of the age.
Matthew 28:19-20

Sometimes I forget that every day is a new opportunity to live this verse. In my daily encounters with people, I have no way of knowing whether they know Jesus or not. It is more than a little sobering to realize that my life, and how I live it, is the greatest teacher of all. I make disciples by being a disciple myself. I teach others to obey the commands of God by obeying them myself.

Last week, it was late and I was trying to get out of the office for my 45-minute drive home. The phone rang, and out of habit, I answered it. The lady on the other end of the phone was selling copy machines, and her call was to inquire whether or not I was in the market for a new copier. After I told her that she had reached the wrong department, she just kept talking. She asked who the contact person was, what her telephone number was and where her office was located. By the time the call was over, she knew by my tone of voice that I was irritated.

I completely failed a test that day, and I asked God to forgive me. That call might have been a divine appointment, but I didn't find out because my agenda came before God's. God is with me and wants to speak through me and use me, even when someone calls my number by mistake.

PRAYER
Dear Lord, I want my agenda today to be Your agenda.
Help me remember that everything I do and every word I say has the power
to teach others about You and Your love for them.

Journal: Is there something you did or said recently that you regret as a missed opportunity to let Christ be seen in you? Tell Him about it. Today is a new beginning for you and for me.

—Carole Lewis

Walking in His Desires

Therefore go and make disciples of all nations, . . . teaching them to obey everything I have commanded you. And surely I am with you always, to the very end of the age.

Matthew 28:19-20

After a bout of depression, I began to ask the Lord, "Why was I born? Why did You make me?" As I asked, two things kept coming to my mind: I was born to know God and I was born to proclaim His name. That was it! And that was all I needed. The Holy Spirit once again revealed Himself to me.

I love to study God's Word, but when it came to proclaiming Him, I felt ill equipped. I loved mentoring and encouraging younger women in the faith, but actually sharing Christ and teaching His Word was another thing altogether.

But eight years ago, I began to study God's Word. From that point on, I have had a desire to teach God's Word, but fear began to cover up the desire and push it aside. When I began to ask the Lord how I could possibly proclaim His name, He revealed to me that He was calling me to teach His Word. He was the One who put that desire in my heart. Every time I pushed that desire aside, I was pushing God's desire for me aside. When I began to live out His desire for me by faith, His desires became my desires. As I obediently walk by faith, fear has now been pushed aside. Living a passionate life for Him and walking in His desires has become the most exciting adventure of my life.

PRAYER
O Father, I know that I was made to know You and proclaim Your name. Show me how I can do that.

Journal: Ask the Lord to reveal His desires for your life. Begin to make a list of your desires and passions and see how they line up with His voice.

—Denise Munton

Who, Lord? *Me?*

Therefore go and make disciples of all nations, . . . teaching them to obey everything I have commanded you. And surely I am with you always, to the very end of the age.
Matthew 28:19-20

When I joined First Place, I never dreamed that I would become a leader. But in my second class, when my leader had to quit in the middle of our session, she approached me about taking over the class. God spoke to my heart and I knew I had to say yes. Later I thought, *Lord, why me?* Surely, there was someone better prepared.

What a blessing I would have missed if I had not stepped out in faith! It's amazing to watch my class members have success in their spiritual and emotional growth, as well as see them lose weight and improve their health. I know that it is not due to anything I have done. The glory goes to Jesus, for He is the One who is with us and makes the changes within us. But when we step out, He comes to meet us.

If God speaks to your heart about leading a class in your church, step out in faith and God will be with you. You will be a part of His work. Don't feel like you have to arrive to where you want to be in First Place before you stand before a class. Just be transparent, letting them know that you will grow with them. This type of teaching commitment is sweeter than any dessert you could ever taste. And guess what? No calories!

PRAYER
Heavenly Father, we do not deserve all that You have done and continue to do for us, but You do it anyway. What an awesome God You are! Thank You, Father, for never giving up on us. In Jesus' most precious name, amen.

Journal: If you feel that God is calling you to a ministry, write down all the reasons why you think you should not do it. Then ask yourself, *Is my God big enough to overcome everything on my list?* Don't miss out on the blessings He has for you.

—Mary Etta Jackson

Be an Action Figure!

Therefore go and make disciples of all nations, . . . teaching them to obey everything I have commanded you. And surely I am with you always, to the very end of the age.
Matthew 28:19-20

I remember as a child learning to read from the Ted and Sally reading series. Ted and Sally would be running, and under them in large letters would be the word "Go!" The picture made it obvious from Ted's and Sally's body language that they were going somewhere.

I remember that when I weighed in at 310 pounds, I desired to do something for the Lord. He loved me just the way I was, but I didn't feel like doing much or going anywhere for Him. I remember that to others, my body image conveyed the idea that I was a lover of eating food and sitting around. Once I put the word "go" to work in my life, my body image for the Lord changed. I became an action figure for the Lord!

This past year, I was injured. People e-mailed me to tell me they were praying for me because they knew how hard it is for me to sit still—to take time out to heal. When people tell me that, I say, "Thank You, Lord," because I know my body image has changed from that of a sedentary eater to an action figure working for the Kingdom. I can truly go into the world and preach the gospel—and feel like I have the energy to do it!

PRAYER
Father in heaven, only You can change a heart. I thank You for changing my heart to one that loves to move and go!

Journal: When it comes to exercise, what are your challenges? Write a prayer to the Lord, asking Him to change your heart concerning exercise.

—Beverly Henson

A New Creation

Introduction

I am awed by creative people. My mom was creative, and my middle daughter, Shari, inherited the creative gene. They both sewed and created beautiful objects for their homes. But more than the awe I experience when I look at the creative abilities of people around me is the awe I experience every day when I look at the evidence of our creative God.

Our God created a world of beautiful sights. He spoke into existence gorgeous sunrises and sunsets and beautiful beaches. Greater still was the beauty of God's supreme creation: man and woman. Yet because of Adam and Eve's sin in the Garden, God's greatest creation was in need of divine help. Jesus' death on the cross at Calvary and His resurrection from the grave provided the way for anyone who asks to be created all over again—to be made a new creation in Christ.

This section and the verses contained in it all speak about what a person looks like when he or she has experienced the new birth and is now a new creation in Christ. Susan Sowell, a Christian psychologist and former First Place leader, wrote this First Place Bible Study, *A New Creation*, and she chose the 10 Scripture memory verses used in this section. You will find Susan's devotions immediately following mine.

The Power and the . . . Obedience

We were therefore buried with him through baptism into death,
in order that, just as Christ was raised from the dead through the
glory of the Father, we too may live a new life.

Romans 6:4

My life will never become new until I realize that this verse is about so much more than my actual baptism. Yes, my baptism was a special time of telling the world that I was dying to my old life to live a new life in Christ. But every day I must continue to die to myself in order to experience what new life really means.

The power that raised Christ from the dead is living inside of me. What a thought! That same power is great enough to help me eat healthy foods, think healthy thoughts and do healthy things. Today, when I am tempted, all I have to do is ask God for help, and when the help comes, I must obey. This is the first step toward a new life.

Step two is just more of the same: I am tempted; I ask for help; I obey. As I learn to do this, my life truly becomes new. Others will begin to see the power of God living inside of me as I lose those extra pounds. I'll look different on the outside, but I'll be different on the inside as well.

PRAYER
Dear Lord, may I die to myself today so that I may live a new life, in You.

Journal: Write about an area of your life that needs to die in order for you to truly begin living. Ask God to come in with His power to help you change.

—Carole Lewis

Gift of New Life

We were therefore buried with him through baptism into death,
in order that, just as Christ was raised from the dead through the
glory of the Father, we too may live a new life.

Romans 6:4

There is an undeniably powerful truth in the above verse. Our gracious heavenly Father chose to give us a new life using the same method He used to raise His beloved Son from the dead. God chose to resurrect Christ through His glory. God chose to give us new life through His glory.

What is so profound about this truth? When we came to Christ as sinners in need of a Savior, we had to experience a death in order to receive our new life. Our old self died when we accepted Christ as our Lord and Savior, and we were given new life through the gift and power of God's glory as we trusted in His Son. We did not suffer the agonizing death on the cross, yet we died and were raised again to new life. We now drink from the same stream of glory that flows from our Father's hand—the same glory that resurrected Christ.

I am so thankful that God chose to give me new life. I came to Him in filthy rags. I drank from His life-giving stream and was given a robe of righteousness and eternal life. Isn't that grace too marvelous for words?

PRAYER

Father, thank You for giving me a new life. Thank You for that fountain
of life that You allow us to freely drink from. God,
help me to consider the cost of my new life and to honor You.

Journal: Do you see yourself still wearing filthy rags, or do you see yourself wrapped in the robe of Christ's righteousness?

—Susan Sowell

Robes of Righteousness

We were therefore buried with him through baptism into death,
in order that, just as Christ was raised from the dead through the
glory of the Father, we too may live a new life.
Romans 6:4

I laughed out loud when I saw the book *You Can Wear It Again: A Celebration of Bridesmaid's Dresses.* In this little tome, Meg Mateo Ilasso humorously illustrates the fallacy that those fluffy, frilly, frivolous dresses worn in someone else's wedding can never serve a useful purpose! As I thumbed through the pages, I recalled the dresses my daughters had worn in their friends' weddings: The colors weren't flattering, the styles weren't flattering, and the prices certainly weren't flattering to my budget. To paraphrase the words of C. S. Lewis, just as there is no way to make a bad egg into a good omelet, there is no way to make a bridesmaid's dress into something that can be worn again!

Today I celebrate because when I was clothed in the world's fluffy, frilly, frivolous clothing, God didn't dispose of me or even try to remake me into something useful. He made me into a new creation. He gave me a new heart of flesh to replace the stony, cold heart that kept me from being His bride. Today I rejoice that I am a new creation in Christ Jesus. His grace, and His grace alone, has allowed me to live a new life. Praise God!

PRAYER
Lord Jesus Christ, today I celebrate the new life I have in You.
I can serve a useful purpose in Your kingdom because the old has
passed away and I have been given new life in You.

Journal: Think about a time when you wore the world's finery. Then describe how God, in His grace, has now clothed you with Christ's robes of righteousness.

—Elizabeth Crews

New Life, New Power

We were therefore buried with him through baptism into death,
in order that, just as Christ was raised from the dead through the
glory of the Father, we too may live a new life.

Romans 6:4

I just love new things: the smell of a new car, the excitement of pulling the tag off a new dress, the joy of holding a newborn baby! When I consider the word "new," here are some things that come to mind: freshness, a new coat of paint, a first-time experience, a new approach, something novel or unfamiliar, something changed for the better, having new energy.

Praise God that our new life as a believer in Jesus Christ is always fresh. Many times there are new experiences and encounters that are novel and unfamiliar. I have been established in a new place beside the King of Glory. I have been changed for the better and rejuvenated. I am no longer like my old self—I am different. I live a completely new life!

As I struggle with breaking destructive, unhealthy habits, the enemy wants me to think that I am still my old self—that the Holy Spirit living inside of me makes no difference. Like all of the evil one's false illusions, this too is a lie! Today I choose to walk in the truth: God's Word assures me that I have a new life and the power to make healthy choices.

PRAYER

Lord, thank You for my new life in You. May I be willing to
use the power of the Holy Spirit, who dwells
in me, to make wise choices.

Journal: Write about a facet of the word "new" that has special meaning for you and explain why that meaning has importance in your new life in Christ Jesus.

—Becky Turner

Running on God Power

Delight yourself in the LORD and he will give you the desires of your heart.
PSALM 37:4

I have not experienced a year like 2006 in more than 20 years of full-time ministry! In January, my long-time friend and associate Kay Smith resigned because of changes in our church policy, which prohibited her from working at home. In March, Nancy Taylor, my dear friend and First Place Leadership Training Director, resigned to go home and spend more time with her family. Nancy's passion is Scripture memory, and she knows God is calling her to speak and write on this subject.

These staff changes took us back to where we were 20 years ago staff-wise, but the workload has exploded since then! Pat, Lisa and I have witnessed firsthand what God's power looks like as we pray for His help and then watch Him work. In many ways, it has been a time of delighting in God as we expectantly wait to see how He is going to work everything out.

Just two examples of His work: Vicki Heath, a long-time First Place leader who lives in Charleston, South Carolina, agreed to work with our First Place Networking leaders. First Place leaders from our church and other Houston churches have also stepped forward to volunteer their time in our office as we continue to pray about who God will send to us.

PRAYER
Dear Lord, help me today to delight myself in You.

Journal: Write some of the ways you might delight yourself in the Lord today.

—Carole Lewis

Guard Your Heart

Delight yourself in the LORD and he will give you the desires of your heart.
Psalm 37:4

The word "delight" in this verse comes from a Hebrew word meaning "to be delicate." What does it mean to make ourselves delicate in the Lord? When I think of the word "delicate," I think of something that requires special care and protection.

I am not a woman who collects china or fine crystal. In fact, most of the items in our home are not very delicate—if they were, they simply would not survive. However, when I think of delicate items in my life that require special care and protection, I think of my children's hearts. Their precious hearts need my special care and protection.

We are responsible for giving our relationship with God special care and protection by not allowing things to come between us and our love for God. We protect our hearts and minds from the ungodly trappings of the world that come into our homes through television, books, music, the Internet, sinful conversations and unconfessed sin. We place high priority on the reading of God's Word and on prayer.

What are we promised when we give such loving care to our relationship with our God? The Lord begins to put His desires in our heart. What is important to God becomes important to us. What is closest and most tender to His heart becomes what is closest and most tender to us.

PRAYER
Lord, teach me to take special care and protect my relationship with You.

Journal: How can you begin today to give more special care to your relationship with God?

—Susan Sowell

Providing for Needs *and* Desires

Delight yourself in the LORD and he will give you the desires of your heart.
Psalm 37:4

Kelly, one of our First Place leaders, wanted to buy mums to decorate her yard, but her family was on a strict budget. Every time she shopped she longingly looked at the mums, but then reminded herself to walk in obedience.

Her husband, knowing her desires for the mums, met a man who owned a nursery in the next town. He arranged for Kelly to pick up 22 huge mums that she would then sell out along the street near a deserted gas station. The response was overwhelming—she sold them all. She went back to the nursery many times for mums and took them in offices, banks and anywhere else she could think of.

When Kelly told the Lord that she really wanted some mums, she suddenly found herself with a yard full of them ready to be loaded up and sold. Over a period of several weeks, Kelly sold 125-plus mums and earned over $1,000. She was able to testify that two years before this time, she was not physically, mentally or spiritually prepared for this blessing. God had given her the desires of her heart and a unique way to witness to others.

PRAYER
Lord, You are Lord of more than enough. Thank You for Your Word and the way You provide for our needs and the desires of our hearts.

Journal: How has God worked in a different way to help you obtain the desires of your heart?

—Bev Schwind

God's Generosity

Delight yourself in the LORD *and he will give you the desires of your heart.*

Psalm 37:4

One morning as I was studying the Bible, I became captivated by the story of the bent-over woman in Luke 13. I began to ponder what she must have gone through. I am a nurse, so I could not quit thinking about her physical challenge.

It had been my desire to write a book some day. As I began jotting down some meditations in my journal, the words began to flow. I did a great deal of research regarding this particular biblical figure and was thrilled when I read that she had met Jesus. I asked God to help me feel her heart.

Soon, Jesus sent people into my life who encouraged and assisted me in many areas. I became aware of the people in my church and community who were in need of mental or physical healings, who were addicted to food and drugs, or who had been mentally abused.

I began a jail ministry and gave a weekly Bible study to the "bent-over" women in the jail. I started a First Place program in my church for myself and the other bent-over women there. I finished writing the book, which was the desire of my heart. But as usual, God gave me abundantly more than I could ever have imagined.

PRAYER
Lord, help me be more and more aware of the physically challenged
people whom I can reach with Your salvation message.

Journal: What has you bent over in life? Is it an attitude? Does a spirit of discontentment, unforgiveness, pride or prejudice have a stronghold?

—Bev Schwind

Put Down the Mirror!

Delight yourself in the LORD and he will give you the desires of your heart.
PSALM 37:4

As I jumped (well, almost) out of bed this morning and stumbled into the bathroom, what I beheld wasn't too pleasant: messy hair, puffy eyes, new wrinkles and a double chin. Thank goodness for makeup and curling irons! Within about 30 minutes, my reflection in the mirror went from horrible to passable.

It was then that God spoke to my heart and said, *What is more important to you, your physical or spiritual appearance?* God wanted me to be concerned about all the areas of my life, not just the way I looked. He was more concerned about the state of my heart than the state of my hair or the way I looked that particular morning.

As I bowed my head, I prayed for God to create in me a clean heart. I asked Him to search my heart and test my thoughts to see if there were any offensive ways in me. I asked Him to lead me in the way everlasting (see Psalm 139:23-24).

God doesn't need a mirror. He created us in His image! If we are His children, we are beautiful to Him all the time. He just wants us to delight ourselves in Him.

PRAYER
Lord Jesus, help me daily to delight myself in You and experience great pleasure just being with You as I read, study and memorize Your Word.

Journal: How much time do you spend each day looking into a mirror, "repairing" your physical appearance? What about your spiritual repair time? Are there physical benefits to spiritual beauty?

—Barbara Brown

Don't Let Your Emotions Drive

Since, then, you have been raised with Christ, set your hearts on
things above, where Christ is seated at the right hand of God. Set your
minds on things above, not on earthly things.

Colossians 3:1-2

Why did the apostle Paul phrase these verses in this particular way? Why did he direct us to set our hearts on things before instructing us to set our minds on things above? It seems backward. We all know that our thoughts come first, and then our heart acts on our thoughts.

I believe that the Holy Spirit inspired Paul to write these verses in this way because most of us act on our *feelings* without ever taking the time to think about what we are doing. We eat that candy bar because we're feeling anxious or blue. We order the hamburger with fries because we've had a bad day. We don't exercise because we didn't sleep well last night.

When our emotions (heart) do the driving, we can get into a lot of trouble. Most of us know the right thing to do in any given situation, but many of us don't take the time to think before we act. Setting our heart (emotions) on things above means that because Christ is in us, we don't have to act on every impulse. Setting our mind on things above means that we think about what Jesus wants us to do before we act.

PRAYER
Dear Lord, help me today to think before I act.

Journal: Write about the area of your life that is ruled by your emotions. Ask God to help you become aware when your emotions are causing you to get off track.

—Carole Lewis

Yielding to the Divine Gardener

Since, then, you have been raised with Christ, set your hearts on
things above, where Christ is seated at the right hand of God. Set your
minds on things above, not on earthly things.
Colossians 3:1-2

As a professional counselor, I have visited the hearts and minds of countless individuals. It's important for me to know how a person feels and thinks before I can identify, with help from God, the root or source of the person's wounds and then help him or her heal.

In the same way, the Lord desires to uproot the areas of our hearts and minds that bear rotten or painful fruit—or perhaps no fruit at all. Our God is passionate for us to have a thriving garden in our hearts and minds. If our minds are focused on our problems, our failures, our weaknesses or our inabilities, we will produce the fruit of doubt and fear. If our hearts are focused on our past hurts or failures, or we hold on to unforgiveness, our hearts will produce the fruit of bitterness.

I don't know anyone who needed more uprooting in her heart and mind than I did. For years I struggled with self-defeating thoughts and feelings. My mind felt like a prison with no way out, and my heart felt enchained.

As a counselor and as a woman who has been healed and set free, I plead with you to set your heart and mind on Christ. Read God's Word and do not let your mind wander from His truth so that your life can become like a well-watered garden that bears much fruit.

PRAYER
Lord, I choose this day to set my mind on what is true and to believe Your Word. Thank
You that as I set my heart and mind on You, You will produce good fruit in my life.

Journal: Write down any thoughts that are causing bad fruit to grow in your life. Ask God to heal you of the wounds that He reveals are in your heart.

—Susan Sowell

Clueless and Busy in Illinois

Since, then, you have been raised with Christ, set your hearts on
things above, where Christ is seated at the right hand of God. Set your
minds on things above, not on earthly things.

Colossians 3:1-2

I became aware of the hectic nature of my life one time when I found myself dyeing my hair at midnight! During the 20 minutes I had forced myself to stay awake so that I could cover the gray, I had just enough reflection time to say, "My life has been w-a-y too busy for the last week."

I should have had a clue on Sunday when I left for church at 8 A.M. and didn't look at the time again until I unglued myself from my computer at 9 P.M. That was my day of rest, the Lord's Day. I should have had a clue, but I didn't because that is what busyness does— it keeps us clueless in a life void of reflection, quiet and undisturbed time with God.

But, hey, after all, it was only for a week, and I was doing really important stuff! I was able to keep up with my e-mail and phone messages, go to my appointments, finish my projects and run errands for my kids. So what got shorted?

Well, I fell asleep during prayer, "glanced" at my husband, ignored my Bible study, gobbled junk food suppers, and reduced my sleep to deprivation levels. I didn't hurt anything other than my spiritual, emotional, relational and physical wellbeing!

PRAYER

Lord, help me to see my life from Your perspective. Slow me down
when busyness threatens to sabotage Your plan for me.

Journal: Write down two things that you can let go of today in order to have more quiet time with God.

—Barb Lee

Winning the Battle

*Since, then, you have been raised with Christ, set your hearts on
things above, where Christ is seated at the right hand of God. Set your
minds on things above, not on earthly things.*

Colossians 3:1-2

The heart is the dwelling place of the Holy Spirit. We choose each day whether we will yield our heart to God and choose to obey Him. Our heart represents our innermost being—the place where the battle between our old sinful nature and our new nature begins. When we set our hearts on heavenly things, we allow God to help us grow as new creations.

Temptation begins in the mind. We first think about having that one dip of ice cream. If we allow our mind to continue thinking about it, we can imagine how good it will taste and how much we really want it. Before long, we are looking for the ice cream shop. When we get there and see the large selection of enticing flavors, we end up eating several dips. I know this from personal experience.

For me, making sure that I have my quiet time each morning with the Lord is the most important step I take for the day. This is where the battle is won or lost. I praise and worship Him. I tell Him how much I love Him. When I begin the day by focusing my eyes, my heart and my mind on Christ, the victory is already half won!

PRAYER
*Lord, help me to keep my eyes focused on You alone.
I choose to set my heart and my mind on You today.*

Journal: Spend some time praising and worshiping God. Write a letter to Him, telling Him how you feel about Him.

—Janet Kirkhart

Baby Steps

For I am the LORD, your God, who takes hold of your right
hand and says to you, Do not fear; I will help you.

Isaiah 41:13

When our daughter Lisa started to walk, we were overjoyed. Every time she fell down, we took hold of her right hand, helped her stand and held her hand as she took a few more steps. She was without fear, because she knew that every time she fell we were there to help her up again.

As new creations in Christ, we are like babies learning to walk. We fall more than we walk, and we need help to stand up each time. As we grow in Christ, we find that we are able to walk longer and farther before falling. Our fears lessen as we learn about the true character of our heavenly Father. He is the perfect parent. He never sleeps, never forgets, always cares, and is always there for us when we fall.

Where are you in your Christian walk? Are you like a one-year-old baby, just beginning to walk, always thinking you will fall? Or are you like a rebellious two-year-old, running headlong into trouble but never knowing you need help? When we are mature Christians, we desire to hold God's hand not because we are afraid of falling or because we need to be kept from rebelling, but just because we love Him.

PRAYER
Dear Lord, hold my hand today and walk with me.
I won't be afraid, because You are with me.

Journal: As you write in your journal today, ask God to reveal your spiritual age to you. Ask Him to continue to help you grow up in Him.

—Carole Lewis

Letting Go of Fear

*For I am the LORD, your God, who takes hold of your right
hand and says to you, Do not fear; I will help you.*

Isaiah 41:13

To leave something that is known and enter a place that is unknown might seem adventurous to some, but most folks who encounter change experience some level of fear. I began pursuing a different life for myself when I turned 22. After spending years walking a path paved by self-destruction, I made a decision to flee from the only life I had known to pursue the unknown. I knew very little about God, but I was certain that I wanted a different life.

Nearly 20 years have gone by since I took my first few steps into that new life of freedom. I know that I could not have taken one step without my Daddy's hand holding me up and giving me the strength and courage to face my fears. My Daddy is still holding on to my right hand and helping me overcome my fears.

We don't know what trials, tribulations, gains or losses will enter into our lives tomorrow, next week or next year. The unknowns in life pop up without warning. How can we live our lives free of fear? How can we leave what is comfortable and embrace a path of healing and freedom? Only by reaching out a hand for our Daddy to hold. God will give us the strength, the courage, the grace and the power to take each step.

PRAYER

*Lord, I choose to trust You today. I will not embrace fear but instead
will embrace Your faithfulness. In Jesus' name, amen.*

Journal: Write down some of the fears that you are currently facing. Choose to lay each fear at the feet of Jesus, and then make a decision to trust Him.

—Susan Sowell

Healthy Pregnancy, Happy Heart

*For I am the LORD, your God, who takes hold of your right
hand and says to you, Do not fear; I will help you.*

Isaiah 41:13

It was a joyous day. After a long wait, I was expecting my second child. My husband and I eagerly anticipated holding our precious one in our arms. Yet at the same time, my heart was filled with the common fears of an expectant mother: *Will the baby be healthy? Remember those awful labor pains? How much weight will I gain?*

The last thought might seem superficial, but it was a very real concern. During my first pregnancy, I gained about 90 pounds. Fortunately, with the help of my First Place group, I was able to get back on track. But the fears still plagued me. Had I learned the lessons of the past? Or would I again use the pregnancy as an excuse to disregard eating in moderation?

The months passed, but with the Lord's help I was able to faithfully record my daily food intake, stay on the Live-It plan (at a doctor-approved calorie level), exercise and keep the First Place spiritual commitments. As my baby and the numbers on the scale grew, I could feel the Lord comforting me. It was as if He were whispering, "Do not fear; I will help you."

As promised, the Lord never relinquished His hand. The added pounds were reasonable, and the pregnancy was much healthier this time around. The baby's delivery was glorious, and the spiritual blessings I've received are eternal.

PRAYER
*Lord, many challenges in life seem insurmountable, but You promise that You are here to
hold our hand and help us prevail. Give us the grace today to surrender our lives to You.*

Journal: Write down some of the things that seem too difficult to manage right now. Reflect back on these periodically and think about how the Lord has held your hand through these times.

—Laura Hartness

Gym Phobia

For I am the LORD, your God, who takes hold of your right hand and says to you, Do not fear; I will help you.
Isaiah 41:13

I always feared going to a gym. I thought it was only for skinny people! I didn't want to be the only fat person there. So I told God that if He wanted me to go, He had to get me an exercise partner.

During my quiet time, I kept hearing the words, "Look for a gym." So I searched the Internet and found a free guest pass to try out a gym for two weeks. At 5:00 P.M., one of my First Place members called and said, "I have just joined a gym, and I was wondering if you would come with me. I'll even hold your hand." When she told me the name of the gym, I laughed and said, "I was looking online today at the same gym, and I was thinking about joining. It must be a God thing."

Shortly thereafter, when I took my first step inside a gym, I could hear God whisper, "Do not fear. I will help you." I ended up signing up for a full-year membership! As part of the membership package, I even received three free sessions with a personal trainer. The lady who signed me up offered these parting words: "You have support now. Your choice to join the gym is for a total lifestyle change!"

PRAYER
Lord, we thank You that You care enough to show us You want what is best for us.

Journal: What is holding you captive or preventing you from making choices that will lead to a healthy lifestyle?

—Barbara Lukies

In God's View

For I am the LORD, your God, who takes hold of your right
hand and says to you, Do not fear; I will help you.
Isaiah 41:13

My daughter brought a baby bird over to our yard to set it free. Her children had saved it from the jaws of their cat and had placed it in a cage, lovingly feeding and nourishing it for several weeks. They had reached in to feed the bird with their tiny hands, and now it was not afraid to take food from them or perch on their fingers.

My daughter tried to place the bird on a low-lying limb, but the bird refused to get off her finger. When she pushed it, it just scurried on the ground, unaware that it could fly. "It's not ready," she said. So they took the bird back to their house.

The next week, the children came back with the bird. My daughter removed it from the cage and placed it on her right hand. She lifted it up to a higher branch. The bird responded to the chatter of other birds and soon began to realize that it too could fly. It flapped its wings and began to fly. Soon it was out of our view.

God reaches into our lives and helps us in much the same way. He holds us close until we can take the next step. He watches over us, looking into our eyes and hearts until we are ready to fly. God has us in His view today—and He always will.

PRAYER

Lord, thank You that I am always in Your view. Thank You for holding my hand when I
feel weak. Thank You that You are there for me.

Journal: Has there been a time when you have not been ready to let go of something? What did you do to get strong enough to be able to let go?

—Bev Schwind

Leave the Fighting to God

For the LORD your God is the one who goes with you to fight for you
against your enemies to give you victory.

DEUTERONOMY 20:4

My husband, Johnny, loves world history. Yesterday, he asked me if I knew why the first movies during World War II always depicted the Japanese as our enemies, even though we were at war against both Germany and Japan. When I didn't know the answer (as I usually don't), he said, "Because the Japanese looked different. If the movies showed us fighting the Germans, we would have looked too much alike."

As I looked at this verse in Deuteronomy, I was reminded of this history lesson and what I could learn from it. Today, most of my enemies probably look a lot like me. In fact, most of the time, my greatest enemy *is* me. That's the problem with trying to fight our enemies instead of allowing God to do the fighting—most of the time, we don't have a clue about who our enemies actually are. Someone who pretends to be our friend might really be our enemy, and someone who seems like an enemy might actually be a future best friend.

God is the only one who truly knows who the enemy is. He also knows how to fight and how to win the battle. This life and its battles are all about future victory for believers in Jesus Christ. That's why it is so important to let God do the fighting.

PRAYER
Dear Lord, help me to let You do the fighting against
my enemies for a sure victory.

Journal: Is there a battle you have been fighting that you need to give to God? Write about it, asking God to take over the fight.

—Carole Lewis

Spiritual Warfare

*For the LORD your God is the one who goes with you to fight for you
against your enemies to give you victory.*

Deuteronomy 20:4

God's Word makes it clear that Satan is real and that he has an army out to get us. Just as God has a plan for our lives, so does Satan. He wants us to live in bondage to addictions, fears, bitterness, unforgiveness, loneliness, depression, materialism, debt, insecurity, people pleasing and guilt. He wants to destroy our kids, our marriage and our lives.

God made the provision—through Jesus Christ—for us to live a life of freedom. Christ came to Earth so that we could have eternal life and be set free to experience the abundant life that brings Him glory. Children of God in bondage do not bring God glory!

Satan wants to rob us of our inheritance—our abundant life. Ignorance or fear of the enemy is a tool he uses to keep us from being successful in battle. But our enemy has already been defeated! Christ defeated him on the cross and has given us the resources to defeat him in our lives as well.

Our victory against our enemy does not depend on how well we fight or how hard we fight. Our victory depends on whether we fight using our own weapons or the weapons that God has given us. Prayer and God's Word will defeat the enemy every time.

PRAYER

*God, I praise You that You have defeated my enemies and that
You fight my battles for me. Teach me to rely on prayer, knowing
that victory is guaranteed. In Jesus' name, amen.*

Journal: What do you rely on to gain victory in the areas of your life in which you struggle?

—Susan Sowell

V.I.C.T.O.R.Y.

For the LORD your God is the one who goes with you to fight for you
against your enemies to give you victory.
Deuteronomy 20:4

As a daughter of the King, I recognize that I am a new creation by God's divine grace. But after gorging down a super-sized dish of sugar-filled ice cream, I didn't feel like a new creation. In fact, I felt like a defeated woman—old, not new.

Carol, my best friend, encouraged me over the phone. "You don't have to fight these temptations alone," she said. "Remember the amazing acronym you shared with me for 'victory'?" After hanging up the phone, I pulled out my journal and reviewed this acronym.

Voice it to God. Go ahead, tell Him all about it. He knows anyway. He is ready to defend His children.

Include others. Reach out! Don't keep your failures to yourself. Allow others to encourage you to keep fighting.

Confess your sins. If you have fallen short of God's glory, confess, repent and allow Him to cover you with His grace.

Trust God's truths. Dive into His Word. Don't allow the enemy to creep in and start his accusatory chatter.

Obey. Start over. Listen to God's voice. Obey the truth and move forward one step and one prayer at a time.

Recognize the enemy. Be aware of his agenda. He wants to steal from you and kill and destroy you.

Yield to God's will. Remember that when you seek God, He will be found.

PRAYER

Dear heavenly Father, sometimes I mess up and don't behave as
a child of God. As I continue my day, help me to remember that VICTORY
is found in You alone. In Jesus' awesome name, I pray. Amen.

Journal: Is it difficult to fully accept the fact that you are a new creation in Christ? What would a day of victory look like to you?

—Carol Van Atta

Quiet Time:
The Ultimate Weapon

For the LORD your God is the one who goes with you to fight for you
against your enemies to give you victory.
Deuteronomy 20:4

It was time for our yearly trip to get our two cats their shots at the Mobile Pet Unit. My job was to stay in the car with the cats while my husband stood in line to pay for the shots. As I watched the people bringing their animals, one man in particular caught my attention. He had his dog on a leash securely held in hand. As I watched, the dog went behind the man and wet on his right pant leg and then proceeded to move over and wet on his left pant leg. The man never knew what happened!

Aren't we all like this man? We think we have our life under control, when in reality Satan is slipping up behind us and "soiling" us. We don't even realize it until it's too late—until we've been robbed.

We need to recognize that God is all-powerful and that He will fight for us and give us victory over any attempts by Satan to cause us to stumble and not keep our commitments. Our responsibility is to spend time with Him. I have found that if I have my quiet time—which includes reading the Bible, praying and listening to God—the first thing in the morning, I can be on guard against Satan's attempts to make me stray from my commitments.

PRAYER
Holy Father, help me to remember that You go with me, will fight
for me and will give me victory against my enemy.

Journal: What are your plans to keep the enemy from soiling you? Remember, you either plan to succeed or you don't plan at all—and will fail.

—Barbara Brown

View from the Top

For the LORD your God is the one who goes with you to fight for you
against your enemies to give you victory.

DEUTERONOMY 20:4

Last summer, my husband and I spent a week at the Philmont Scout Ranch in Cimmaron, New Mexico. My husband is the hiker in the family, but I exercise four to five times a week, so I thought the four-mile mountain trail would be a breeze.

The trail looked easy, but five minutes into the hike, I was huffing and puffing. I'd walk a few yards, rest, walk a few yards, then rest again . . . at that rate, it was turning into an all-day event! Maybe it was just the determination to make it, but before I knew it, we were at the top. What an awesome view! It was certainly worth all the huffing and puffing necessary to get there.

There are going to be days when we feel we just can't make it. Everywhere we turn, there will be another temptation. Occasionally we might even give in, but that's no reason to give up. Part of being human means that we won't succeed every time we try something. When we find ourselves tempted to give in, we need to call on God and ask Him for the strength and determination to overcome. God will send forth His mercy and truth, and we will be able to pick up where we left off and do even better the next time!

PRAYER

Heavenly Father, give me the strength and courage to achieve my
healthy-lifestyle goals—even when I am tempted to give up.

Journal: What is keeping you from achieving your goals? Are you missing the view from the top because you give up too easily?

—Judy Dorn

Approach the Throne with Confidence

Let us then approach the throne of grace with confidence, so that we may
receive mercy and find grace to help us in our time of need.
Hebrews 4:16

I have a long history with God regarding His mercy and grace. Every single time I have cried out to God since the day, as a 12-year-old, I asked Jesus to come live in my heart, He has been there flooding me with His mercy and grace—even during times of rebellion and unbelief. He has been there even when I refused to turn from a particular sin.

He has shown mercy and grace in the middle of financial difficulties. He has shown mercy and grace during times of grief and loss. He has shown mercy and grace when I couldn't figure out the answers to the problems I was facing. Whatever the problem, God's mercy and grace have been the answer.

My long history with God makes it easy for me to approach His throne of grace. Am I able to do this because I deserve His mercy and grace? Quite the contrary! I can confidently approach God's throne because of Jesus Christ, who covers me with His righteousness before the Father.

PRAYER
Dear Lord, help me to show the same mercy and
grace today that You have shown to me.

Journal: Is there someone to whom you have trouble showing mercy and grace? Ask God to show mercy and grace to that person through you.

—Carole Lewis

Awesome Invitation

*Let us then approach the throne of grace with confidence, so that we may
receive mercy and find grace to help us in our time of need.*
Hebrews 4:16

Our God is the one and only true God. There is no other like Him. He is the Alpha and Omega, the King of kings and the Lord of lords. Our God reigns for all eternity, yet we are invited into His presence. We are welcomed into His holy sanctuary, and when we enter in, we are met with an indescribable love and acceptance that melts all our fear away.

How can it be that we feel as if we are at home when we are surrounded by such glory? Grace. The King of kings determines that His throne will be a place where grace has authority over anything that our hearts bring into His sanctuary. How else could we come into His holy presence with confidence?

How do you enter into the presence of God? Are you afraid to enter in? Are you counting on some good works to make yourself feel more worthy before you come before Him? Are you approaching His throne of grace without first acknowledging the glory that fills that place?

We need to enter into God's presence with an awareness of His power, glory and majesty. We need to come to the feet of our King with a thirst and hunger to feast on the blessings that fill the table in His sanctuary. We will never feel more at home than we do when we are in the presence of the King of glory.

PRAYER
*God, create in our hearts a holy passion to be in Your presence. Thank You for the
grace that allows us to come before You with confidence.*

Journal: Are you ever afraid to enter the presence of God? Do you feel that you need to make yourself worthy to come before His throne of grace?

—Susan Sowell

Enter In!

Let us then approach the throne of grace with confidence, so that we may
receive mercy and find grace to help us in our time of need.

HEBREWS 4:16

I knew that I was failing miserably in my commitment to exercise self-control in the area of my mouth. This mouth of mine was causing considerable grief in two ways. First, I was lashing out at my family with critical comments. Second, I was eagerly shoving food into my mouth.

I realized that I was failing in my commitments and that it was time for me to take care of business before God on my knees. Yet instead of confidently approaching God, I entered His presence with my head hung in shame, expecting the worst. Once again, I'd bought into the lie that I had to somehow be good enough for God. Thankfully, I recognized the mistake and adjusted my attitude according to the truth of His Word.

Because of what Jesus did for us, we don't have to cower in terror at the thought of reaching for God. His Word instructs us to enter His presence boldly and with confidence. Not only are we able to enter the Holy of Holies, but we can also expect to find mercy and grace there to help us in our times of need. It's only through His incredible love that we can actually become the new creations we were called to be. So go ahead and enter in. The heavenly Father is waiting with mercy and grace.

PRAYER

Dear heavenly Father, help us to remember that we don't have
to hide from Your presence. Help us to enter Your loving arms with
any need we might have. In Jesus' name, amen.

Journal: Do you dread your personal time with God? After reading Hebrews 4:16, do you feel differently? Why, or why not?

—Carol Van Atta

With Humble Boldness

*Let us then approach the throne of grace with confidence, so that we may
receive mercy and find grace to help us in our time of need.*
Hebrews 4:16

I came from one of those families in which asking for help—even in times of obvious need—left me open to ridicule, humiliation and shame. Self-sufficiency became my credo, my obsession and the idol that separated me from a sovereign, supreme and all-sufficient God.

Hebrews 4:15 tells us that we have a high priest who is able to sympathize with our weaknesses. When we come to Him for help, we can be confident that He will never chide, shame or ridicule us because of our weakness. Jesus put aside His divinity and took on human flesh so that He could fully understand what it means to be dependent on God the Father for every good thing.

In my former way of thinking, being confident and asking for help were opposites. To me, confidence meant never having to ask for help. How thankful I am that God patiently taught me the true meaning of humble boldness. This boldness is only possible because Jesus came to Earth to show us that the only way to approach our Father is by admitting that we are utterly dependent on His mercy and grace. Humble boldness is about being sufficient in Christ's sufficiency, not our own "just do it" prideful sufficiency.

PRAYER
*My Lord and Savior, I am thankful that You are the High Priest who can
sympathize with my weakness. You came to Earth in human form to show
me how to approach the throne of grace with humble boldness.*

Journal: Write about the pride that keeps you from being totally dependent on the sovereign, supreme and all-sufficient One. Resolve today to no longer trust in your own ability.

—Elizabeth Crews

Amazing Calling

For we are God's workmanship, created in Christ Jesus to do good works,
which God prepared in advance for us to do.

Ephesians 2:10

My mom was a fabulous seamstress. She made everyday dresses for me to wear to school and beautiful dresses for parties and proms. The everyday dresses were easy for her to make, but the prom dresses were another matter entirely.

Weeks before the date of the prom, we would visit the most expensive stores in town. We would spend hours finding the perfect dress, and after we found it, Mom would meticulously write down every detail so that she could go home and duplicate the dress perfectly. Sometimes she took part of the pattern from one dress and part of the pattern from another to make my dress turn out exactly like the one in the store.

This verse in Ephesians tells me that, much like my mom, God is great at creating "hits." Of course, He is even more so than she could have ever been, for He is in the business of creating lives that will resemble His Son, Jesus. God knew me when I was still in my mother's womb. He made me, and I am His workmanship. The day I accepted Jesus into my heart was the beginning of a brand-new life—one created to do good works.

It is quite humbling to realize that God already knew, before I even took my first breath, all the good works that I would do in my life.

PRAYER

Dear Lord, I want to do good works for You.
Please do whatever it takes to make that happen.

Journal: Is there something in your life you need to let go of so that God can remake it into something beautiful?

—Carole Lewis

God Doesn't Waste a Thing!

For we are God's workmanship, created in Christ Jesus to do good works,
which God prepared in advance for us to do.

EPHESIANS 2:10

Growing up in a dysfunctional family, I learned to grab hold of every self-defeating tool around me. By the time I was 21, I had a toolbox filled with destructive behaviors, thoughts and beliefs about my life. If you had told me that I would one day be serving God in full-time ministry through counseling, writing and speaking, I would have said that you had lost your mind!

It took a long time for me to realize that God uses mixed-up and messed-up people like myself to showcase His glory. He uses our pain, our failures and our sins to reveal to the world that He is true to His Word. Christ came to heal the brokenhearted and set the prisoners free, and He has given us the authority to have victory in our lives. God's love for us is unconditional. His grace is real.

God prepared in advance how our lives would be used to do His work. In my life, His plan all along was to use my past to reveal His heart for me so that I could help others know His heart for them. In the same way, His plan all along for you has been to use the trials and tribulations in your life to reveal His heart for you. When you allow Him to use your past to His glory, He too will enable you to help people know His heart.

PRAYER
Lord, thank You for healing our broken hearts and setting us free.
Thank You that You use our healing and our freedom to
display Your glory. In the name of Jesus, amen.

Journal: What work has God prepared you to do for His kingdom? Have you allowed your feelings to hold you back from doing God's work?

—Susan Sowell

Living Beyond Our Weaknesses

For we are God's workmanship, created in Christ Jesus to do good works,
which God prepared in advance for us to do.
Ephesians 2:10

My sister, Ann, died several years ago after struggling for 34 years with multiple sclerosis. Ann took part in several First Place classes in her church. The commitments she made during these First Place classes were always magnified a hundredfold for her.

Because Ann was confined to a wheelchair, drinking the necessary amount of water was a problem. She was alone during the day, so bathroom trips were a struggle, a risk and a drain on her energy. Her limited exercise, when she had the strength, was on her stationary bike. Cooking was also a problem for her because of the loss of the dexterity in her hands.

Yet through all of these challenges, Ann never complained. Whether cooking for someone who was sick in her community or church, sending encouraging notes, or praying for someone's need, Ann never let her illness keep her from doing what God had created her to do: His good works.

No matter what our situation might be, we are God's workmanship and are created to do His good works. As long as God leaves us here on Earth, His plan and purpose is for us to enter into what He planned for our lives. Think about how important we are to Him! The fact that He created a detailed plan for each of us should inspire us to see and live beyond our limitations and weaknesses.

PRAYER
Lord, thank You for making specific plans for each of us. Thank You that You make it
possible for us to achieve good works, even in our weaknesses and limitations.

Journal: Are you looking and living beyond your limitations? Are you turning your weakness into a testimony to God?

—Susan Jones

Forget the *Mona Lisa*

For we are God's workmanship, created in Christ Jesus to do good works,
which God prepared in advance for us to do.
Ephesians 2:10

In the newly built Salle des Etats room at the Louvre Museum in Paris, the world's most famous portrait, the *Mona Lisa*, is encased behind triplex, nonreflective, unbreakable glass. The 500-year-old painting by Leonardo da Vinci attracts over 1,500 visitors a day. Artists around the world agree that this portrait is a masterpiece.

Ephesians 2:10 says that we are God's work of art, the tour de force of His creation. Through Jesus, God purchased us and redeemed us from all wickedness in order to purify a people of His own (see Titus 2:14). Having been re-created in righteousness and true holiness, we are set apart for His purposes. This new birth in Christ is the supernatural work of the magnificent Creator.

God filled us with His Holy Spirit, inspiring and empowering us to carry out the plans and purposes He has for our lives. Now, compelled by His love, we go into the highways and byways of life, letting our light shine so brightly before others that they see our good deeds and praise our Father in heaven (see Matthew 5:16). Through these good works, although they were never meant to save us, we point others to the One who has saved us and become His living masterpieces.

So today, go forward and display His glory and power in your body and your life. Mona Lisa has nothing on you!

PRAYER
Thank You, Lord, for You rejoice over me with singing and take
great delight in me (see Zephaniah 3:17). Help me to complete the good
works You have prepared for me so that You may be glorified in me.

Journal: Do you esteem yourself as highly as God esteems you? If not, explain your reasons why.

—Eulalia King

Make Him Proud

For we are God's workmanship, created in Christ Jesus to do good works,
which God prepared in advance for us to do.
EPHESIANS 2:10

I love to go to craft fairs and talk with people as they display their creations and eagerly tell others about their workmanship. They are proud of their work and often spend hours creating the objects they have on display. They are completely familiar with their works and understand both the strengths and imperfections of creation. They also know that no two of their handmade creations are exactly alike.

God prepared us in advance for what we would do and provided us with the talents we would need to do His good works. Like the works of the craftspeople, He knows our strengths and weaknesses. He has created each of us with our own individual talents and abilities.

I can just imagine God creating me in my mother's womb before I was born, knowing ahead of time what gifts He had given me and which ones I would use or not use. In my life, I know that I can best serve Him by keeping my body in balance, by memorizing His Word, and by doing the good works He has created me to do. I want God to be proud of His creation, and I want to serve Him not because He saves me but because He has created me to be of service in Christ Jesus. It is fulfilling to be of use to the Lord.

PRAYER

Lord, what other things have You created me to do of which
I am unaware? Help me to always look for ways to serve You.
Thank You that I am handmade and unique.

Journal: Has God nudged you to take on a project that you have ignored because You deem it unworthy of your time? Do you choose to do only things you enjoy?

—Bev Schwind

Love Songs

The LORD your God is with you, he is mighty to save.
He will take great delight in you, he will quiet you with his love,
he will rejoice over you with singing.
Zephaniah 3:17

Recently, I took an extensive battery of tests including ones that rated my personality, abilities and learning style. I was shocked when my friend Elizabeth Crews, who has been trained to score and teach this particular model, informed me that the tests revealed I am musical.

The shock was partly because, even though I took seven years of piano lessons, I still cannot even play the first page of "The Spinning Song" today. I was in choir from the age of nine until I graduated from high school, but today I would have trouble reading the alto line of a song.

Elizabeth said that she should have known I was musical, because when she stayed in my home, instead of talking to the bird, the cats and the dog, I sang to them! I realized that this is true. I have little songs for each of our pets, and each of them knows his or her song. I delight in singing over our pets, just as God delights in quieting me with His love and singing over me.

My pets belong to me, and I keep them safe from harm. How much more does God love me than I love those pets?

PRAYER
Dear Lord, thank You for being with me and keeping me safe.
Thank You for delighting in me and singing over me.

Journal: Do you have trouble believing that God delights in you? If so, tell Him how you feel and ask Him to show you the truth about His love.

—Carole Lewis

You Are Loved!

The LORD your God is with you, he is mighty to save.
He will take great delight in you, he will quiet you with his love,
he will rejoice over you with singing.

Z e p h a n i a h   3 : 1 7

John Crawford served as the associate pastor at Kingsland Baptist Church in Katy, Texas, before the Lord took him home in 2001. People from all over Katy who knew this man described him as "Jesus with skin on." Pastor John made every person he met feel as though he or she were personally significant to him.

Pastor John's love for people was extremely powerful, yet his nature was as gentle as a soft breeze. He spent his life ministering to the hurting. He wanted to be next to the mom and dad who had just buried their child. He wanted to travel down the path of healing with a woman or man who had been abused, rejected or abandoned. He wanted to celebrate the joy of a child's decision to trust Christ. He wanted to help an old heart experience a childlike faith.

One of Pastor John's favorite verses in the Bible was Zephaniah 3:17. He passed this verse on to many hearts that needed to hear that their heavenly Father loved them. Pastor John knew that we all need God's love, and he lived out this important truth as he allowed his life to be a vessel for God.

We need to feel significant. We need our heavenly Father to think we are delightful. We need our heavenly Father's love song sung over our hearts. We need to feel special and cared for by our heavenly Father.

PRAYER

Father, my heart desperately needs to be filled with Your love. Remove from my heart and mind anything that may be preventing me from receiving Your love for me this day.

Journal: Do you find it difficult to receive God's love? Ask God to help you receive His love and strengthen your faith in His love for you.

—Susan Sowell

The Blessing

The LORD your God is with you, he is mighty to save.
He will take great delight in you, he will quiet you with his love,
he will rejoice over you with singing.
Z e p h a n i a h   3 : 1 7

I flopped open my Bible on my lap in order to create a stable writing surface while I took sermon notes. Letting my eyes briefly glance to the left of the page, I noticed Zephaniah 3:17. I was immediately distracted and transfixed by the words. I don't think I had ever read that passage before.

The next day while doing my Bible study lesson, I again heard those words. My radio, softly playing in the background, was set to the local Christian station. As I again sat in amazement, I heard those same exact words from Zephaniah being spoken!

Later that same morning, my sister asked me to pray for her daughter who was undergoing a minor surgical procedure that day in New York. I sent her the words from Zephaniah 3:17. In the afternoon, a coworker shared a frustration she was having with her job. I wrote down the promise from this verse for her. Immediately after that, another coworker shared that just the day before, he had to put down the family dog. Again, the words from Zephaniah encouraged a hurting heart.

Within a day and a half, the words from just one portion of Scripture had blessed the lives of me and several people around me. How grateful I am for God's Word and the freedom we have to share His Word in our country.

PRAYER
Dear God, thank You for Your Word. Thank You that we can freely open our
Bibles and find encouragement, comfort, motivation and hope within.

Journal: Think of a verse of Scripture that has particularly blessed you during the past year. Thank God for that blessing.

—PJ Bahr

It's All About You!

The LORD your God is with you, he is mighty to save.
He will take great delight in you, he will quiet you with his love,
he will rejoice over you with singing.
Zephaniah 3:17

I had just been sharing with other ladies in church how difficult it had been for me to receive this verse in Zephaniah. Because I wasn't able to receive it, I also couldn't remember it. The words got twisted in my head.

However, as I continued to press on and seek God as to why I had so much trouble with this one verse, He revealed that I had not taken this verse as His Word, but just as mere words. This passage could not change me until I considered it to be something that God was actually speaking to me. I had tried to dissect the verse to discern its meaning, but my attempts had yielded nothing. Now, when I looked at it with this new perspective, I was finally able to see.

How the Lord does love me! What comfort it brings me to know that God loves me, saves me and quiets me so that I can hear His voice. He delights over me and rejoices over me with singing. He is ever faithful and strong. He is truly my rock and my fortress. Although He sees all my faults and shortcomings, He loves me unconditionally. Because of this fact, I can persevere during any and all challenges that life sends my way.

PRAYER

Lord God, I praise Your holy name, for You are our worthy
and almighty God. I thank You that You quiet me with Your love.
Hallelujah, in Your mighty name, Jesus!

Journal: Have you taken the time today to praise God for who He is? Have you thanked God for your salvation? Go for it. You will truly be blessed.

—Millie Aviles

Put a Song in God's Heart

The LORD your God is with you, he is mighty to save.
He will take great delight in you, he will quiet you with his love,
he will rejoice over you with singing.
Zephaniah 3:17

I love this verse in Zephaniah because it has given real purpose to my life. I was so amazed when, as a teenager, I realized how much God loves me—so much so that He gave His Son to die on the cross for me. Now, I knew that I could be certain of spending eternity with Him and live as His child on this earth. Imagine, to be a child of the living and majestic God!

He is indeed mighty to save. I am so grateful that I have three wonderful children who have brought me much joy. They have done many totally unexpected things that have brought great delight to my life. In the quiet of the night, thinking of them has brought a smile to my face and warmed my heart.

That is what I want to do for my Lord. Yes, I want to be obedient to Him and do all that He tells me to do in His Word; but for me, that is not enough. I want Him to take great *delight* in me. I want to surprise Him in ways that are totally unexpected. I want Him to quiet me with His love. More than anything, I want God, the Creator of heaven and Earth and the One who has redeemed me, to rejoice over me with singing.

PRAYER
Father, I am so grateful that I am Your child. Quiet me with Your amazing love and let me live in a such a way that You will rejoice over me with singing.

Journal: Look at the journal entry you wrote yesterday and list the ways God brought delight to your life. Ask God to show how you can delight Him today.

—Dee Matthews

To Love God More

We demolish arguments and every pretension that sets itself up
against the knowledge of God, and we take captive every
thought to make it obedient to Christ.
2 Corinthians 10:5

My nine-year-old granddaughter, Harper, loves every kind of creature. If it moves or breathes, she wants it for her own. When she is at the bay, she spends most of her time on the rocks capturing minnows, jellyfish and whatever else is moving around. At night, she gets a jar to catch fireflies. She loves books about any living thing.

Ever since Harper was a baby, we have known that she was a thinker. She thinks and feels more deeply than most children, and so her thoughts have led her to make a momentous decision regarding food: She loves God's creatures so much that she has decided she won't eat them anymore! Because her favorite food is steak, this was not an easy decision for her to make. But after months of thinking about it, Harper decided to become a vegetarian.

What if we loved God so much that we couldn't stand the thought of doing or thinking something that would hurt our Lord? What would happen if we started taking every thought captive and made those thoughts obedient to Christ? If we all did this, we would surely be able to demolish every argument and pretension that sets itself up against the knowledge of God.

PRAYER
Dear Lord, help me learn how to take captive every thought
I have today and make it obedient to You.

Journal: Is your thought life helping you become a better person, or is it holding you captive?

—Carole Lewis

Escaping Bondage

We demolish arguments and every pretension that sets itself up
against the knowledge of God, and we take captive every
thought to make it obedient to Christ.

2 Corinthians 10:5

As a Christian counselor, I see the bondage that many people are living in today. I am convinced that the main reason God called me into the ministry of counseling is because I personally experienced severe bondage through pain, sin and an ungodly belief system. Like many of those whom I counsel, my mind was a battlefield and my thoughts were arrows that pierced my heart.

When we allow thoughts that go against God's Word to enter into the battlefield of our minds and camp out, we give Satan permission to build a belief system in our lives. This stronghold that Satan builds using the tools of deception will leave us in bondage.

We can't use the worldly teaching of positive thinking to free ourselves from bondage. Others can't love us out of bondage; we can't work ourselves out of our strongholds; and denial certainly won't set our hearts free. Only Christ can set us free.

Although Christ set me free from the strongholds in my life, I know that I must stand firm daily against thoughts that make me feel defeated in my walk with Christ. We all must recognize these thoughts that are inconsistent with God's Word and not allow them to camp out in our minds. It is God's desire that our thoughts and beliefs are based on His Word so that we can live a life of freedom.

PRAYER

Jesus, I will never know the cost You paid for my freedom. Help me to recognize thoughts
and beliefs that are untrue. I want to walk in Your truth. Amen.

Journal: Write out a verse to use when an arrow of deception comes your way. Ask God to reveal any thoughts or beliefs that you have about yourself that are untrue.

—Susan Sowell

To Arms!

We demolish arguments and every pretension that sets itself up
against the knowledge of God, and we take captive every
thought to make it obedient to Christ.
2 Corinthians 10:5

In 2 Corinthians 10:4, Paul says, "The weapons we fight with are not the weapons of the world. On the contrary, they have divine power to demolish strongholds." Whether we realize it or not, we are at war! We are in a daily battle against Satan and his evil forces of this world.

Paul uses military terminology to describe the spiritual warfare that goes on continually in our lives as Christians. We must choose to allow God to be Commander in Chief of every thought we have and make it obedient to Him. He must be in total control in order for us to win the war for our hearts and minds. As we use the weapons of prayer and God's Word, we can know the truth and not be deceived by Satan's lies.

Our daily quiet time is the place in which we receive God's marching orders for the day. Scripture memory is another weapon that can help us to take captive every thought to make it obedient to Christ. For when Christ is in control of our thoughts, Satan is defeated.

I cannot count the times during the day when a Scripture verse comes to mind that helps me through a challenging situation. I do not always have a chance to run for my Bible, but as I hide God's Word in my mind and heart, His mighty weapon is readily available.

PRAYER
Dear Lord, thank You for reminding me that You have already given me everything I need
to fight and win the daily battles against sin and Satan's strongholds in my life.

Journal: Make a list of any strongholds that Satan has created in your life to try to defeat your efforts to serve the Lord.

—Janet Kirkhart

Pulling the Weeds

We demolish arguments and every pretension that sets itself up
against the knowledge of God, and we take captive every
thought to make it obedient to Christ.

2 Corinthians 10:5

Long before the days of weed whackers and chemical sprays, there was only one way to get rid of the pesky weeds that threatened the survival of the fruit-bearing plants: with a hoe and lots of hard work. During the summers I spent at my grandparents' farm in Arkansas, my grandmother, who was very protective of her vegetable garden, made sure daily weed pulling was a priority.

Just cutting the tops off at the ground wasn't enough to please Grandma. She insisted that we pulled the obnoxious plants out by the roots, which meant backbreaking work! Grandma knew that cultivation was more than sticking seeds in the ground and hoping they would thrive. Feeding what was good and destroying what was not was the only way to ensure an abundant crop!

As unpleasant as the task was at the time, today I can see this was part of the preparation process that God was using to teach me how to live a life pleasing to Him. Much like the unwanted plants in Grandma's garden, the negative thoughts in my mind threaten my ability to produce a crop pleasing to the Master Gardener, who calls me to bear fruit—fruit that will last. Yes, it is often a hard row to hoe, but half-measures will not work. God calls me to demolish those pesky weeds that keep me from being about my Master's work.

PRAYER
Gracious Lord, thank You for lessons that prepared me to
live a life pleasing to You and for a grandmother who taught me that
hard work is part of producing an abundant crop.

Journal: Write about a childhood experience that God used to prepare you for the work He has called you to do in His kingdom.

—Elizabeth Crews

Radiant

And we, who with unveiled faces all reflect the Lord's glory,
are being transformed into his likeness with ever-increasing glory,
which comes from the Lord, who is the Spirit.

2 Corinthians 3:18

Have you ever thought about what Moses must have looked like after he experienced the glory of the Lord? Exodus 34:29-31 states that when Moses came down from the mountain:

He was not aware that his face was radiant because he had spoken with the Lord. When Aaron and all the Israelites saw Moses, his face was radiant, and they were afraid to come near him. But Moses called to them; so Aaron and all the leaders of the community came back to him, and he spoke to them.

You and I are capable of having that same radiance on our face every day. As we seek after God and begin desiring to live holy lives dedicated completely to Him, we will take on the likeness of Christ. Our part is to turn from any known sin that the Holy Spirit brings to our attention.

As we ask God to change us, He will do just that. God's part is to make us look more like Jesus every day as we are obedient to Him. This is all possible because the Holy Spirit lives inside each of us.

PRAYER
Dear Lord, I want to reflect Your glory today. Make me look like Jesus.

Journal: Is there something you refuse to give up that is keeping your face from reflecting the Lord's glory? Write a letter to God asking Him to remove that barrier.

—Carole Lewis

Seek His Presence

And we, who with unveiled faces all reflect the Lord's glory,
are being transformed into his likeness with ever-increasing glory,
which comes from the Lord, who is the Spirit.

2 Corinthians 3:18

God has a calling on our lives. We are called to resemble Christ to those who love us and to those who hate us. We are to reveal the heart of our God to the little children down the street and to the checker at the grocery store. We are called to be Christlike in the most challenging place in our lives: our own homes.

There is nothing simple about being Christlike in the world that we live in today. There is nothing easy about being Christlike to people who have hurt us and disappointed us. Living our lives full of God's love and peace and having a passion for His kingdom is not something we naturally possess. Being Christlike and living our lives for God come from a life spent in the presence of our Lord.

We become more like Christ through our encounters with God as we seek Him in prayer and in His Word. This process will not be complete until we meet our Lord face to face. As we spend time in His presence and yield our lives to Him, the glory that God reveals through our lives will increase.

Our calling to be like Christ is meant to be an overflow of His glory from what He is doing in our own lives. God's glory will flow freely through our lives when we choose to remain in His presence.

PRAYER

Father, show me Your glory. Reveal Yourself to me. I want to know You.
I want You to change me. I want to be like Jesus. Amen.

Journal: Are you trying to be Christlike apart from spending time with God in prayer and in His Word? Are you asking God to fill you with the Holy Spirit each day?

—Susan Sowell

Transformation Takes Time

And we, who with unveiled faces all reflect the Lord's glory,
are being transformed into his likeness with ever-increasing glory,
which comes from the Lord, who is the Spirit.
2 Corinthians 3:18

The Spirit of the risen Lord changes us from glory to glory, but sometimes it feels as if we are stuck between the glories. On November 23, 1986, when I asked Jesus to be Lord of my life, I experienced my first taste of His marvelous glory. I had been away from the Lord for 18 years, but He had never been away from me. At once, I began to experience His glory as He delivered me from smoking, foul language, my tendency to frequent bars, and so many other pieces of baggage that I had acquired.

The one thing I couldn't seem to get deliverance from was my addiction to food and laziness. I kept asking Him to help me, but it just wasn't happening. I felt as if I were totally stuck between glories. I kept asking God, "How long will it be until I get the victory?" Twelve years later, I began taking baby steps to gain victory over my food addiction when I came to First Place.

Sometimes, it may seem as if we've been waiting a long time, but when God is doing the transforming, it takes a while to get it the way He wants it for our lives. Although at times it feels like we are stuck between His glories, we have to remember it is all in His timing. Tick-tock on God's clock, not ours.

PRAYER
O Lord, I strive to be like You in every area of my life. I thank You,
Father, for changing me from glory to glory.

Journal: Reflect on your walk with the Lord and write down a time when God just wasn't moving fast enough to suit you. Tell about how glorious it was when He "finally" came through.

—Beverly Henson

Reflecting His Glory

And we, who with unveiled faces all reflect the Lord's glory,
are being transformed into his likeness with ever-increasing glory,
which comes from the Lord, who is the Spirit.

2 Corinthians 3:18

When new members join First Place, they often feel a little scared not knowing what is to come during the 13-week session. They may also feel intimidated by others, especially if everyone else is an extrovert and they are introverts. Some of these new members are like those who have veiled faces—they don't let others see the real person.

But slowly, as time passes, the unveiling occurs. The layers are peeled back as these members become more confident and more assured of who they are in Christ. During the sessions, as we get to know members a little better, we get to see their strengths and weaknesses.

During the First Place sessions, I often have the privilege of seeing people's lives transformed and renewed by God. It is always great to see members understand and use the Commitment Records and the Live-It plan and work through the memory verses and the Bible study. In further sessions, these members typically help others to understand the things with which they were once not familiar.

By the end of the program, they are not the same people they were when they first began First Place. Their testimonies are unique and special. God has truly transformed them into His likeness.

PRAYER
Lord, may Your glory be reflected on those who are
being transformed into Your likeness. Thank You that they are
beginning to live the life that You would have them live.

Journal: Write out some of the issues that you have hidden in your life so that you can begin to be transformed into His likeness and reflect God's glory to others.

—Barbara Lukies

Shining Through

And we, who with unveiled faces all reflect the Lord's glory,
are being transformed into his likeness with ever-increasing glory,
which comes from the Lord, who is the Spirit.

2 Corinthians 3:18

Henry is not only special in my life as an adopted son and prayer warrior, but he is a taxidermist as well. He takes the hides of animals and makes them look as if they are alive. Depending on what the animal is going to be used for, the finished product can either have the appearance of an animal in the wild or as someone's cherished pet.

Henry is a true artist in every sense of the word. I've seen him create animals that looked as if they were snarling and make others appear as if they were smiling. I've even seen him make some look as if they were locked in combat with a foe! Through his artistry, Henry can give these animals a variety of different appearances.

Of course, all the makeup and artistry in the world cannot create the look of Christ's love on our faces. No, that only comes when we are genuinely glowing—when we are truly reflecting what is in our hearts. Christ's love in us will show through and be revealed to others whether we are in a packed church or alone scrubbing the floors on our hands and knees. Time spent with God through prayer and Bible study is the best way to guarantee Christ's love will shine through!

PRAYER

Abba, Father, may Your love show on my face 24/7.
Thank You for loving me even when I'm not always showing
Your love to those around me.

Journal: How much time do you spend in prayer and Bible study? Do you spend time listening for His voice? Remember, it is the quality of the time that counts!

—Betha Jean Cunningham

Healthy Boundaries

Introduction

Too many of us struggle with what it means to establish healthy boundaries in our lives. I think that's why the First Place Bible study *Healthy Boundaries* has been so popular. Elizabeth Crews, who wrote the study, is an addictions counselor with firsthand knowledge of what happens to people who have poorly set or nonexistent boundaries.

You will find Elizabeth's devotionals right after mine in this section, and also in the next three sections of the book. Elizabeth has lost 92 pounds during the last 30 months of being a part of First Place. As she has been obedient to God in the area of establishing appropriate boundaries in her life, He has used her to write four powerful Bible studies for His glory and for the benefit others.

Every Bible verse in this section gives clear direction about how to form and maintain healthy boundaries. For example, John 8:32 tells us that before we can repair the broken boundaries of our lives, we must first know the truth about them. Knowing the truth will open the door to freedom. After God reveals the truth to us, we come to realize that, as Isaiah 59:1 teaches us, God is the only One who is able to rebuild our broken-down boundaries.

If you have a particular weakness with maintaining healthy boundaries in any of the four areas of life—physical, mental, emotional, spiritual—don't miss the steady progression of the 10 verses in this section. Each verse was specifically chosen to encourage you to learn what it means to build strong, healthy boundaries.

Starting Point

Then you will know the truth, and the truth will set you free.

John 8:32

Scales terrify some people. I guess the single worst part of a First Place meeting for some is the first few minutes when they get on the scale to weigh. I have known some to step on the scale backward and ask their leader not to tell them how much they weigh. Others refuse to weigh in for the first few weeks until they build a trust relationship with their group leader. The only people I know who love the scale are those who are staying on the Live-It plan and filling out their Commitment Record. Why is this? Well, they seem to know that the scale is going to show the evidence of all their hard work.

You see, a scale tells the truth. How does knowing the truth have the power to set us free? Well, when we know the truth, we can make a decision. We can decide to act upon the truth and change our lifestyle, or we can decide to do nothing different and keep gaining weight each week. Knowing the truth is always a starting point.

God's Word is truth, and when we know the truth, the truth will set us free. This is why the First Place commitments all work together to set us free. Once we know the truth, we are ready to take the next step to becoming truly free.

PRAYER

Dear Lord, I want to know the truth, the truth of Your Word and the truth about myself. Help me change as I learn the truth.

Journal: Are there areas of your life that need the illumination of truth? List those areas in your journal, asking God to reveal the truth to you.

—Carole Lewis

F.E.A.R.

Then you will know the truth, and the truth will set you free.

John 8:32

Many years ago, I heard motivational speaker and author Zig Ziglar use an acrostic for "fear": False Evidence Appearing Real. Since that time, I have used that acrostic as I teach on the subject of fear. Students are always enlightened to learn that many of their fears have no basis in fact—they are only figments of their imagination.

One day last year, as I was giving a presentation on fear to a group in an inpatient alcohol and drug recovery program, I learned another acrostic that addresses fears that do have a basis in fact. When I put F.E.A.R. on the board and asked if anyone knew what it meant, one young man replied, "Face Everything And Recover." Almost simultaneously another voice from the back of the room responded, "Forget Everything And Run." As we discussed the three acrostics, it became clear that whether our fear is based on false evidence or we're in real danger of harm, we have one of three choices. We can face the problem, we can deny that there is a problem, or we can turn the other way and run. Of those three options, only one—facing the problem—offers hope of recovery.

Jesus came to tell us the truth, not to frighten us or discourage us, but to set us free from the bondage of those things that strip us of joy, hope and peace with God. Today, ask yourself, *What am I afraid to surrender to Jesus so that His truth can set me free?*

PRAYER

Gracious God, You sent Jesus into the world so that I no longer
need to live in the bondage of addictions triggered by fear and doubt.
Today I will trust in You and allow the truth to set me free.

Journal: Which of the three F.E.A.R. options do you use when it comes to your relationship with food? Why?

—Elizabeth Crews

Obedience to Truth

Then you will know the truth, and the truth will set you free.

John 8:32

It seems like such a simple verse: "Then you will know the truth and the truth will set you free." We often hear that second half of the verse quoted: "The truth will set you free." When we are truthful, we are released from the bondage we have created for ourselves with lies. What a blessing truth is for those of us who have spent time trying to cover up our inadequacies by pretending to be something or someone we are not!

Dig a little deeper. What is truth? The Greek word for "truth" means "corresponding to reality" and is derived from two words meaning "to not keep secret, to not escape notice, to not be hidden, to not forget." Truth is all about taking our lives out of hiding and bringing them into the light of Christ. This is what sets us free!

But we're only halfway there. What about the first half of the verse, "Then you will know the truth"? Let's look at the context of those words. Jesus was speaking to the Jews in the Temple. The Pharisees were questioning the validity of His testimony. They were asking who He was and who He claimed to be. When some Jews put their faith in Him, Jesus told them, "If you hold to my teaching, you are really my disciples. Then you will know the truth and the truth will set you free" (vv. 31-32).

Here's the key: *If* we study and apply Christ's teaching to our lives (hold to His teaching), we are His disciples. *Then* we will recognize, acknowledge and understand the truth (reality). We will be set free from sin's oppression. Our freedom is dependent upon our initial obedience, and then God blesses us with an understanding of the truth.

PRAYER

*Gracious Father, I confess that I am often disobedient, and yet I still expect to
be blessed with wisdom. Please help me to change, to hold to Your teaching, so that
I may be blessed with the truth and be set free from the oppression of sin.*

Journal: In what ways has God blessed you with an understanding of the truth through your obedience? How has this understanding set you free?

—Susan Johnston

Coming into the Light

Then you will know the truth, and the truth will set you free.
John 8:32

In today's world, we have to search hard to find the truth. We are continually bombard-ed with all kinds of information about diets, food, exercise, medications and surgeries that promise us success in losing weight and looking great. But First Place is different. It is first of all about learning God's truth. The emphasis is on studying His Word and learning how to listen to the Holy Spirit's voice. By spending quality quiet time alone with our heavenly Father, we learn to hear and discern His voice from all the other voic-es that try to lie to us and distort the truth.

I love the balance this brings to all areas of life—not just to the spiritual, but also to the physical, mental and emotional. God works in every person's life in a unique way, but we have to know the problem—the sin or the bondage—we're dealing with before we can work on that area. God works first on the area that needs repair the most.

I believe that God has told me, and shown me, many times during my walk in First Place that if I will listen to Him, I will know the truth regarding how to take care of His temple—my body. The Spirit of truth will guide me through all the noise and deception that surround the topic of weight loss.

If I follow the nine commitments faithfully, wholeheartedly and am 100 percent invested for His glory, I will be successful, because this is the truth that God has given me. When we know God, we can know His plan and His desires for us.

PRAYER
Lord, please help me to keep my eyes focused on You.
Thank You, Lord, for revealing Your truth.

Journal: As you prayerfully consider the nine commitments (see the introduction of this book), evaluate and record what you need to work on.

—Janet Kirkhart

God's Favorite Child

Surely the arm of the LORD is not too short to save, nor his ear too dull to hear.

Isaiah 59:1

There is nothing sweeter than watching a dad with his much-loved child. The child falls down and the dad scoops her up in a flash. The child wants to tell him something and the dad leans in to hear every word. This picture is sweet because the two have a relationship built on love and trust, and the relationship will continue to grow as the child grows.

This father-child description is the kind of relationship our Father God wants to have with all of His children. He wants to protect us, listen to us and form a love relationship that is so strong that nothing—absolutely *nothing*—can convince us that we are not His favorite child.

The four spiritual commitments—Scripture reading, Bible study, Scripture memory, and prayer—are the keys to having this kind of love relationship with God. As we learn about and experience the character of our God, we will learn to love and trust Him. In First Place, the one thing I hear over and over again is, "Oh, the weight loss is great, but the spiritual benefits have been life-changing for me."

PRAYER
Dear Lord, I want to have this kind of relationship
with You. Help me, I pray.

Journal: Write about the kind of relationship you would like to have with God and then ask Him for it.

—Carole Lewis

Keeping Vigil

Surely the arm of the LORD is not too short to save, nor his ear too dull to hear.

Isaiah 59:1

When my children were infants, I kept them right next to my bed at night in a small wooden cradle. They were close enough that I could hear them when they cried and reach for them when they were in distress. Like most new moms, I often slept with one eye open as I kept vigil over a fretful baby during the dark hours of the night.

That's the image Isaiah 59:1 brings to my mind. At times, when I feel small and helpless and in need of tender loving care, I picture myself safely snuggled close to the God who never slumbers or sleeps, where I am protected and secure. He is the all-powerful, all-knowing, ever-seeing Lord of heaven and Earth. Yet He is tender and kind and loving and gentle. Isaiah assures me that "a bruised reed he will not break, and a smoldering wick he will not snuff out" (Isaiah 42:3). When I am most vulnerable, He is most vigilant.

Now that my four grown children have long outgrown those little wooden cradles, I find another type of comfort in the God whose arm is not too short to save, nor ear too dull to hear. On those fretful, anxious nights when I lay awake worrying about my brood, I know that God, who loves them more than I do, is keeping vigil over them, and over me too. I praise God that He holds us all in His tender loving care.

PRAYER
*Loving Lord, thank You for assuring me that You will
never leave me nor forsake me. You are my comforter, my protector
and my provider. How grateful I am for Your love!*

Journal: Write about an image from Isaiah 59:1. If you would prefer, you can draw an image rather than use words.

—Elizabeth Crews

Loving Discipline

Surely the arm of the LORD is not too short to save, nor his ear too dull to hear.
Isaiah 59:1

The prophet Isaiah had a lot to say to the Jews during a time of great turmoil in their lives. But rather than coddling the people into false security, Isaiah reminded them that God is holy. He is separate, set apart and pure. In fact, that is the way in which Isaiah most frequently refers to God—as "the Holy One."

When I'm in turmoil, the thing I want most is to be comforted. I cry out to God, knowing that He can and will hold and protect me. I know that His arm can reach me wherever I am, that His ear can hear me no matter how muffled my cries. But I need to remember, too, that God is holy. If my pain is caused by my own sin, I need to repent and seek forgiveness before God is going to comfort and restore me. Isaiah 59:2 says, "But your iniquities have separated you from your God; your sins have hidden His face from you, so that He will not hear."

It has taken me a long time to learn this truth; but now that I understand it, I see a loving Father's perfect parenting in my life time and again. As long as I keep sinning, He keeps letting me feel the pain of the consequences. But when I change my heart, change my actions and seek His forgiveness, He is quick to hear and comfort me.

PRAYER
Father, You are the most loving parent! Thank You for caring enough about me to let me feel pain when I need to make changes. Thank You for putting my eternal well-being above my immediate comfort. Thank You for consistently and patiently guiding me closer to You.

Journal: If you are in turmoil today, search your heart and ask God to show you whether your distress is due to your own sin. If it is, what do you need to change in your actions to stop this sin?

—Susan Johnston

Holding Back a Flood

Surely the arm of the LORD is not too short to save, nor his ear too dull to hear.
Isaiah 59:1

If we are strong-willed and independent, it's hard to admit weakness. We think we have to solve our own problems. And then, there comes the day when we have to admit that we're not able to handle something ourselves.

In June 2001, tropical storm Allison came ashore on the Texas coastline and dropped 30 or more inches of water on parts of Houston. Water was everywhere. During the daylight hours the rising water was frightening enough, but after dark it was even worse. At 3:00 A.M., after more than 12 hours of heavy rainfall, I opened our front door to find water standing 4 inches deep on the front porch. One more inch and the water would be inside the front door! I was home alone with my 81-year-old mother. There was no way we could stop the water, and I couldn't be sure that I could handle both the water and my mom!

That's when I turned to the Lord and prayed. I told Him that I knew He had parted the Red Sea for Moses and the Israelites; therefore, I knew that He could hold back the water from flooding our home. And do you know what? He did! It rained steadily and hard for another two hours, but that water never rose that last inch. I was at peace, and I actually slept until daylight.

I know now that God's arm will always be there to save me, and He will hear me when I call out to Him. I just need to humble myself before Him and trust Him with all my heart. God is ever near!

PRAYER
Lord, I can rest, knowing that You are there for me when I call.
Fill me with Your peace in trying moments and help me
remember to give You all the glory.

Journal: What impending dangers hover at your door, waiting for the opportunity to flood your life? Call out to God and turn these things over to Him!

—Pat Cook

Tried God Lately?

Like a city whose walls are broken down is a man who lacks self-control.
Proverbs 25:28

I will never forget the man who walked up to me at a Christian Booksellers Convention. We were doing body composition testing at our booth that day, and this man, who weighed close to 400 pounds, said to me, "Why do I need to lose weight? If I die, I'll go to heaven to live with Jesus." I tried to lovingly tell him that death was the very best-case scenario he could hope for.

This verse in Proverbs is a word picture of what a life lived without self-control looks like. I am saddened when I see a person rolling an oxygen tank around because of years of smoking; or a person in a motorized chair because his legs can no longer support his excess weight; or a person who is paralyzed from a stroke because she refused to acknowledge her high blood pressure; or a diabetic who loses a leg because the disease has gotten out of control.

God is the only One who can produce the fruit of self-control in a life broken down by lack of it. And He wants to help us, but we must first admit that we have failed miserably and ask Him to take over.

If you've tried everything else, why not try God? He is the One who can rebuild the walls of your body and make it strong and healthy again.

PRAYER
Dear Lord, I have tried to have self-control and failed.
Come in and take over, I pray.

Journal: Where are your walls broken down? Write a letter to God, asking Him to do the necessary rebuilding.

—Carole Lewis

Boundary Rebuilding

Like a city whose walls are broken down is a man who lacks self-control.
PROVERBS 25:28

When Carole Lewis asked me if I would consider writing a Bible study for First Place, my answer was an immediate yes. The answer to her next question, "What would you like to write about?" was just as easy—boundaries. For years I had lectured on personal boundaries at several local alcohol and drug treatment centers. The patients even called me the "Boundary Lady." But more than from my professional experience, my desire to write about boundaries came from my own personal healing journey. Like many others when they begin the boundary rebuilding process, I began this important task at a below-ground-zero level. Not only did I have crumbled boundaries, but years of living in shame and defeat had also eroded the soil of hope on which strong walls could be built.

Learning to set and maintain healthy boundaries was the most difficult work I have ever done. It was also the work that allowed me to set healthy limits and goals and to apply the self-control needed to stay on track in my daily walk with God. When I began, I was truly like a defenseless city. Raiding parties came in and out at will, stripping me of all hope for a better tomorrow.

If you are beginning this boundary rebuilding work at subzero level too, take heart! God has given us the book of Nehemiah as an example to encourage us, and I am also with you as your guide and companion. Together we will rebuild the walls so that we will no longer live in shame and disgrace.

PRAYER
Lord, You are the rebuilder of my broken dreams and the healer of my inner hurts. Thank You for showing me how I can restore my shattered boundaries so that I can live a life pleasing to You.

Journal: How does a lack of healthy boundaries keep you from practicing self-control?

—Elizabeth Crews

Reality Check

Like a city whose walls are broken down is a man who lacks self-control.
Proverbs 25:28

None of us likes to admit that we're broken, but until we do, we can't begin to rebuild the boundaries that are meant to protect us. I experienced this just yesterday. I found myself, once again, bingeing on sugary foods. Why? I couldn't come up with a good answer, except that they were available to me. Through the years I have put refined sugar into my pantry and refrigerator, knowing full well that sugar is what I want when I'm tempted to eat unhealthy foods. I have been in denial about my brokenness. But as long as I remain in denial, I won't clear my home of all the foods that are unhealthy for me, even though they might be okay for other family members. And I'll make excuses about not becoming too extreme. I'll lie to myself that it's okay to have the food around, and that I won't be tempted by it. The result is that I remain in denial, I remain broken and I remain defenseless.

When we live in denial, it is not due to a lack of knowledge. At some level, we know the truth. Rather, denial is an unwillingness to accept (it's even a defiant rejection of) reality. Nehemiah understood this and made a point of accurately assessing the condition of the walls of Jerusalem before beginning the rebuilding project.

Following Nehemiah's example, I took stock of my broken walls this morning and found many hidden areas of weakness. Once I began reading labels in my pantry, I found that many of the foods on which I binge contain added sugars. I decided to accept reality and donate those foods to charity. I am no longer willing to remain defenseless and without self-control. I am admitting my brokenness to my heavenly Father, changing my heart, changing my actions, asking for forgiveness and accepting responsibility for my body.

PRAYER

Gracious Father, You know my weaknesses, even if I'm in denial about some of them. Thank You for Your steadfast love. I know that I can trust You to shine light on my weaknesses so that I may repair my broken walls of self-control.

Journal: Ask God to reveal to you any hidden areas of weakness in your self-control boundaries.

—Susan Johnston

Keep Your Defenses Up

Like a city whose walls are broken down is a man who lacks self-control.
Proverbs 25:28

In the days when city walls kept outsiders out and insiders safe within, walls were the major defense of city dwellers. City walls were where the lookouts stood and where defensive maneuvers took place. To capture a city—to capture a people—the enemy had to first stealthily approach and then breach the walls that totally encompassed the city and kept it safe.

God has shown me through Proverbs 25:28 that when I lack self-control in any area, I am giving the enemy a grand opening into my life and my heart. I am told to be alert, because the enemy prowls around like a lion, looking for someone to devour (see 1 Peter 5:8). He is looking for me to be defenseless. He is just waiting for his chance to get inside! Rather than allowing the mighty fortress of God to shield me from all harm, my lack of self-control blinds me and breaks down my walls of protection. I walk around at the mercy of whatever the enemy may use to attack me with. I literally hand him an invitation to attack! Any unbridled passion in my life—for me that means food and spending—leaves me blind and defenseless.

God tells me that I have not been given a spirit of fear or timidity, but of power, love and self-discipline (see 2 Timothy 1:7). When I choose lack of self-control, I negate power, love and self-discipline. So daily I must choose to keep my defenses up by choosing to be self-controlled—by choosing to receive from God and refusing whatever the devil has to say or offer.

PRAYER
Glorious heavenly Father, keep me ever in Your hand of safety, power and love. Forgive the times when I have chosen the destructive path of self-indulgences and lack of self-control. Reveal to me where I allow the enemy entrance, and help me to repair wherever there are breaches in the walls of my heart, mind and actions. I bless and thank You. May I live according to Your Word, by Your Power and for Your glory. Amen!

Journal: Ask the Holy Spirit to reveal to you in what place and at what time you are particularly vulnerable to lack of self-control. How can you be more alert and better prepared?

—Tammy M. Price

Hope Restored

But you are a shield around me, O LORD; you bestow
glory on me and lift up my head.

Psalm 3:3

A woman who joined my class last session could barely lift her head during the first few meetings. She was so beaten down and hopeless about her excess weight that she actually had trouble holding up her head during our class. Yet the most amazing thing happened when she actually started doing the First Place commitments. As she began the Bible study, she began learning the truth of her situation. And as she started the Live-It plan, she began losing weight. When she started walking, she began to feel better about herself.

Even though she didn't actually begin doing the commitments until week 7 of the 13-week session, she lost 11 pounds during the last 6 weeks. The change in her countenance was remarkable. By the end of the session, her head was held high and she had a smile on her face. God was the One who had caused the difference. He had restored her hope and He was the lifter of her head.

PRAYER
Dear Lord, thank You for the truth of this verse.
Be the lifter of my head today.

Journal: Write about a time that God became a shield around you and lifted up your head.

—Carole Lewis

Safe from Doubt

But you are a shield around me, O LORD; you bestow
glory on me and lift up my head.
Psalm 3:3

Over a generation ago, Walt Kelly used Pogo to humorously declare, "We have met the enemy, and it is us!" In Psalm 3:2, David tells me the same thing about my many foes. My enemy is not a hostile army; it is my own internal voices, which say to me, "There is no help for you in God." At times, these old negative tapes repeat themselves over and over again in my head. Granted, their poisonous message varies depending on my circumstances, but the bottom line is always the same: "There is no help for you in God." There is absolutely no outside enemy that could ever damage my safety and security as surely as those inner enemies that convince me God will not protect, deliver and provide for me. The moment I doubt the truth that God is bigger than my circumstances and more powerful than the enemy's most lethal weapon, I have yielded to the internal enemy that keeps me in doubt and despair.

Not only does David help me identify my many foes, but he also gives me the solution to my dilemma: The Lord is a shield around me. My challenge each day is to live in the security of His protection so that the negative voices don't convince me that I am without hope. Reading God's Word and spending time in meditation and prayer each morning ensure that the Lord's shield will be in place, keeping me safe. Today I will be faithful to surround myself with His unfailing love and protection.

PRAYER
O Lord, You are a shield of protection around me when I am
faithful to read and study Your Word and pray.

Journal: Identify one negative voice that tells you there is no hope for you in God. Write a prayer, asking God to surround you in His love in that area today.

—Elizabeth Crews

Shielded by His Love

But you are a shield around me, O LORD; you bestow
glory on me and lift up my head.

Psalm 3:3

If you're anything like me, you've spent lots of time comparing yourself with others and coming up on the short end of the stick! Because of our ongoing struggle with body image and excess weight, we often hear negative voices inside our head—voices that tell us we're not beautiful, talented or worthy of love. Insecurity overwhelms us with fear, shame or depression. When I find myself engaging in the comparison game, I need to quickly remember that my confidence and acceptance are not found in approval from other human beings, but from God, my heavenly Father, who created me in His perfect love.

A shield is a piece of protective armor carried on the forearm and used to conceal or protect a person from harm. That's what God's love does for us: It surrounds us with protection from the voices that tell us we are not good enough to be a child of God!

But when we turn to God in prayer and lift up our head to our heavenly Father, His love will protect our heart and mind from the negative influences of the world. When we give our burdens to the Lord Jesus Christ, and we call out His name and allow Him to be a shield around us, His truth will set us free.

PRAYER

Father, protect me when the voice of destruction tries to bring me down and tries to keep
me from having a sense of my true self-worth. Shield me with Your precious love and
teach me to love who I am through Your perfect grace. Amen.

Journal: Do you look at yourself in the mirror with critical eyes? Seek the Father before you look in the mirror and you will see yourself clearly.

—Karen L. Duffy

Trusting His Timing

But you are a shield around me, O LORD; you bestow
glory on me and lift up my head.
Psalm 3:3

We were on week four of the *Healthy Boundaries* Bible study when my blood disorder recurred. Three years earlier, I had been found to have low blood platelets, which meant I was in danger of a spontaneous hemorrhage, and should an injury occur, bleeding would be difficult to control. The prior episode had been treated vigorously for about 18 months. At that point, I was able to get off all medication, and my platelet count remained in the normal range. I asked my doctor if I would ever have the problem again. He said, "Possibly; it may be 5 or 10 years, or never." So it's an understatement to say that I was extremely disappointed when it recurred only 18 months after I stopped taking the medication!

I had prayed to God for 36 years that I would be able to outlive my daughter, who has Down syndrome. I always felt that I could adjust to losing her better than she could adjust to losing me. I had always had faith that God would grant me this request. Then, when a potentially life-threatening illness occurred, and then recurred, I began to doubt. I do believe God knows best, but I always felt that He had given my daughter to me as one of my life's missions and that He would agree with me that I needed to be around for her.

Psalm 3:3 meant so much to me when I noticed for the first time that God is a shield around us! When the words sank in—that His shield extends all the way around me—I received great comfort from this thought.

My platelets are in the normal range again and I hope to eventually get off the medication. For now, I rest in the promise of that shield.

PRAYER

Most Holy God, thank You for being a shield all around me. You are my protector, my comforter and my life. May I walk in Your ways and never stray from Your watchful care.

Journal: Write about what God has done for you in the way of protection and care.

—Sara Toles

Transparency with God

But you are a shield around me, O LORD; you bestow
glory on me and lift up my head.

Psalm 3:3

Psalm 3:1-2 says, "O LORD, how many are my foes! How many rise up against me! Many are saying of me, 'God will not deliver him.'" How many times I have started my mornings with that kind of thinking! Sometimes it's accurate thinking; other times I'm exaggerating a bit. Either way, I am being honest with God about my feelings.

I like to call those mornings "show up" mornings because I will often write in my prayer journal, "God, today I'm just able to show up." I'm neither ready nor willing to pray the way my God deserves. I'm empty. No praise, no thanksgiving, not even any requests. Just empty. But do you know what? Those mornings God lovingly wraps His arms around me, and the Holy Spirit whispers to my heart that everything's going to be okay. He's in control. He will protect and comfort me.

Pretty soon, I find my head lifted a little higher, my heart a little lighter. God is a shield around me against all my problems and anxieties.

PRAYER
Father God, thank You for loving me so much that I can be myself with You.
I don't have to pretend to be "good." You don't rebuke me for being honest with You.
You shield me, comfort me and lift up my head.

Journal: Be honest with God about your feelings today. Then watch and see how He lovingly responds!

—Susan Johnston

Giving Over Control to God

Humble yourselves, therefore, under God's mighty hand,
that he may lift you up in due time.
1 Peter 5:6

There is nothing that will humble a person more than failure. A gambler who loses his entire paycheck is temporarily humbled. An alcoholic who loses his family is temporarily humbled. A woman who steps on the scale and sees that she needs to lose 50 pounds is temporarily humbled. The problem with this type of humbling is that the situation is the thing that humbles the person. When we get humbled by a mess that we have made, the humbling usually doesn't last. And before we know it, we've messed up again.

If we want to rebuild broken-down boundaries, we must first humble ourselves under God's mighty hand. When we humble ourselves, we give up control of our situation and ask God to come in and take over. When we humble ourselves, we give God permission to come in and help us change—permanently. The problem with situational humbling is that it just doesn't last.

PRAYER
Dear Lord, teach me what it means to humble myself under Your
mighty hand so that You may lift me up in due time.

Journal: In what areas of your life do you need to give over control to God?

—Carole Lewis

The Good Shepherd

Humble yourselves, therefore, under God's mighty hand,
that he may lift you up in due time.
1 Peter 5:6

Although the words "God's mighty hand" are used in Scripture to describe God's power, protection and provision, the image of a mighty hand was anything but comforting to me. I grew up in a less-than-nurturing family. My dad's harsh hand was the law. So the idea of humbling myself under a hand, even if it was God's hand, brought back humiliating memories of cruel punishment. Cowering in fear was certainly not what Peter had in mind when he penned the words found in 1 Peter 5:6. But in my mind, a mighty hand equaled being smacked down, not being lifted up!

Hanging on my bedroom wall is a reproduction of a classic painting "The Lost Sheep" by the British artist Alfred Söörd. In that picture, the Good Shepherd is leaning over the side of a large crevice, staff in one hand, the other hand extended down the slope toward a frightened lost sheep. Large birds of prey circle overhead, just waiting for the defenseless sheep to perish.

As I looked at that painting one morning during my quiet time, the meaning of 1 Peter 5:6 became clear to me. God's mighty hand was there to rescue, not punish; it was there to lift up, not humiliate. It was almost as though I could hear Jesus say, "I opened up my arms on the cross for you, so why are you still afraid that I will harm you?" At that moment, joyful thanksgiving was the only appropriate reply.

PRAYER
Precious Lord Jesus, You stretched out Your arms so that I could have eternal life.
When I was lost, You came looking for me. Today I will humble myself under
Your mighty hand, trusting that You will never do anything to harm me.

Journal: Write about a time when the Holy Spirit explained a difficult-to-understand verse to you, and how that revelation changed your attitude toward God.

—Elizabeth Crews

He Is Faithful

Humble yourselves, therefore, under God's mighty hand,
that he may lift you up in due time.

1 Peter 5:6

Mary was a type A (make that triple A) personality, career-minded, Dean's List over-achiever. After she and Dave were married, she soon became pregnant. Dave already had a three-year-old son, Dylan, so a family of four was in the making from the outset. With a preschooler and a baby on the way, they prayerfully determined that Mary would stay home and raise the children. Her financial savvy helped in working out a potential budget for a family of four. They remained committed to God's instruction, in spite of the income loss from Mary's job.

When baby Thatcher was two months old, Dave was given an opportunity to apply for a promotion at work. Many prayers were said, requesting God's favor—and also favor from the big-shots making promotion decisions. This advancement in Dave's position would almost completely make up for the loss of Mary's income in their household budget.

Before Dave received word about whether or not he would receive the promotion, he shared with an unsaved family member that he only wanted to glorify God in all things, and the decision on the promotion was up to the Lord. As he told me about that conversation, I told him that he was already glorifying God in what he had said to this family member.

Later that same day, he was notified that he had received the promotion. Despite the hard times of waiting, and as a result of their faithfulness and obedience, Mary and Dave have seen God's mighty hand lift them up in due time.

PRAYER
Dear God, thank You for Your mighty hand that lifts us up more times than we can
remember. Thank You for Your faithful, loving care.

Journal: Are you anxiously awaiting God's mighty hand to lift you up? Thank Him for the "unseen" things He has already worked out on your behalf. How can you glorify Him today, in word or deed, to show that you are under His mighty Hand?

—PJ Bahr

Humility, Not Humiliation

Humble yourselves, therefore, under God's mighty hand,
that he may lift you up in due time.
1 Peter 5:6

I read this verse with trepidation. Humble myself? Mighty hand? At first, fear and rebellion welled up in my heart. I have spent so much of my life thinking of myself as less than others. Everyone else was prettier, smarter, funnier, wealthier, you name it! How much smaller did God want me to make myself?! What was He planning to do with that "mighty hand" once I made myself so vulnerable?

Then I began to study the word "humble." I realized that I had been confusing the meaning of "humiliation" (disgrace, shame, embarrassment) with "humility" (modesty, compliance, deference, submission). God doesn't want to shame me! On the contrary, since I am His child, He wants me to thrive! He wants the very best for me! But to receive these blessings, I need to comply with His commandments, defer to His will and submit to His loving discipline.

Because God is not a tyrant, but rather a loving parent to us, we can trust Him to protect us with His mighty hand as we humble ourselves. Like a father who rests his hand on his child's head to keep that beloved one close, God places His hand over us to keep us safe. As long as we don't run away, His mighty hand covers us. Psalm 63:7-8 says, "Because you are my help, I sing in the shadow of your wings. My soul clings to you; your right hand upholds me."

But wait, protection isn't the only thing God offers us once we humble ourselves. He will also lift us up! Do you remember the joy you felt as a child when an adult who loved you scooped you up and snuggled you? I think God does that for us when we humble ourselves and stay close under His mighty hand.

PRAYER

Abba, calm my fears about humbling myself. Teach me the joy of submitting to Your
will so that I may enjoy Your mighty protection and abundant love.

Journal: What misconceptions might be stopping you from humbling yourself and enjoying God's protective care?

—Susan Johnston

Living in His Will

Humble yourselves, therefore, under God's mighty hand,
that he may lift you up in due time.
1 Peter 5:6

Humility is such a hard trait to develop. As humans, we are all inclined to think that our achievements are due to our own ingenuity and perseverance. We like to take all the credit for our successes and cast away blame for our failures. However, God wants us to accept the blame for our failures and give Him the credit for our successes. But when we give credit to ourselves, we've been giving credit to the wrong person, and we've certainly been trying to avoid accepting any of the blame.

God has a perfect plan for each of us. When we surrender to a life centered in His will, He can work that plan for our good. With God's blessing, all of our endeavors will succeed. But with success, we can get into the loop again of trying to take back the driver's seat so that we can drive our life *our* way! When we do that, we are destined to fail. God wants to do the driving! God wants first place in our lives.

So in humility, we need to seek His face, His will and His way. We need to seek shelter under the strength of His hand. And when His time is right, He will lift us up and honor us with success. Every victory is His! Resolve to start each day by saying, "Today I will give Him glory for my success and work to overcome the pride that keeps me in defeat and despair."

PRAYER

Father, help us bow to Your will in our lives. Keep us on our knees before You,
Lord, so that we can reap the blessings of humility according to Your will and
Your timing. Mold our will to Yours, and bless our efforts to follow You.

Journal: Ask God what He wants for you today, and then wait. The psalmist reminds us in Psalm 46:10, "Be still, and know that I am God."

—Pat Cook

Praying in the Midst of Change

Devote yourselves to prayer, being watchful and thankful.
Colossians 4:2

I am in a place of change right now. Kay Smith, one of my best friends in the whole world, is no longer employed by First Place because of a policy change that all full-time employees must live in Houston. Kay lives in Roscoe, Texas. How do you fill a hole left by a person who has been with you for 17 years? We are in the second month of life without Kay, and I am practicing this verse every day.

The first thing I did when I knew that Kay would no longer be with us was to go to God in prayer. I prayed for Kay and her family. I prayed for a new job for Kay. I began watching to see how God would work out this awful situation. Why did I know He would work it out for Kay's good? Because I know that God loves Kay more than I do. And Kay loves God more than she loves First Place.

As I continue to pray about who will replace Kay, I thank God for the years we were able to work together. I thank God for providing a new job for Kay. I thank God that He hasn't forgotten those of us left here in Houston. I thank Him that in due time, He will provide someone to fill the hole left in our organization.

How about you? Have you recently lost something precious to you? Make your first thought one of prayer and thankfulness for what God is going to do.

PRAYER
Dear Lord, teach me what it means to devote myself to prayer over the situations of my life.

Journal: Is there an area of your life that calls for devotion to prayer right now? Write a letter to God today and begin the process of watchful, thankful praying.

—Carole Lewis

Prayer as Work

Devote yourselves to prayer, being watchful and thankful.
COLOSSIANS 4:2

In my usual task-oriented, accomplishment-focused, goal-directed manner, I listed each of the verses for which I would write a devotional across the top of a 3 x 5-inch card. Then I read over the cards, making notes about stories that applied to each verse. My plan was that by the time I sat down at the computer, I would be ready to write.

But as I began to read through the verses, something caught my attention. Whether I was writing about establishing healthy boundaries, choosing thankfulness, celebrating victory or stopping destructive behavior, there was a common thread woven through my writing: prayer. Because communication is very important to me, I wasn't surprised to discover that conversing with God was high on my memory verse priority list. But what I discovered next did surprise me: Prayer is not just a thread that I had woven through my writings; prayer is the baling wire that holds my life together! Rather than being a writer who prays, I am a pray-er who writes. Often, the words that I scrawl across the page are prayers made visible so that I can share them with others.

Because I tend to view my usefulness in terms of accomplishment, I used to wonder how the apostle Paul could ask us to devote ourselves to prayer—after all, prayer wasn't about productivity! Today I realize that prayer is the most productive activity I can possibly engage in, because prayer puts me in communication with the Creator and Sustainer who, while working to reconcile a lost and dying world to Himself, invites me to join Him in His work.

PRAYER

Father, when my prayer becomes my work, my work becomes a prayer.
Thank You for the privilege of being able to communicate with You, no matter what
else I find myself doing as I go about the work You have called me to do.

Journal: Make prayer your priority by writing a prayer of thanksgiving to the God who calls you to devote yourself to prayer.

—Elizabeth Crews

Past, Present, Future

Devote yourselves to prayer, being watchful and thankful.
Colossians 4:2

Being watchful means living in anticipation of opportunities in the future. Being thankful means recognizing blessings of the past. Both watchfulness and thankfulness are part of a balanced prayer life. But sometimes my prayer life becomes so focused on the present that I forget to reflect on where I've been and how God has been faithful throughout my life. Whether I have succeeded or failed, God has never left my side. His love is unconditional and is not based on my success or failure. That fact is something for which I can be very thankful, and my prayers—my conversations with God—need to reflect that!

Similarly, I often neglect to look up from my daily tasks long enough to scan the horizon for new opportunities to serve God. Is God calling me to do something new or to do something in a new way? Is there someone in my life I could serve more lovingly? Is there a way that I can help others? Can I minister to my family in a way that better reflects Jesus? Is there something I need to lay aside so that I can add something new? No matter what the situation, prayer is the prism through which we can look ahead without worry and behind without guilt as we face today's challenges with confidence because we are watchful, thankful and surrounded by God's love.

PRAYER
Lord God, keep my feet firmly planted in today and my prayers timeless.
Teach me to learn from the past and joyfully anticipate the future, knowing
You always have been and always will be by my side.

Journal: Make a list of things in your past for which you want to thank God (these experiences might not have brought you joy at the time, but perhaps brought you wisdom today). Now list your concerns for the future and ask God to help you see the opportunities that lie within each area of concern.

—Susan Johnston

Conversations with God

Devote yourselves to prayer, being watchful and thankful.
COLOSSIANS 4:2

Although prayer has always been important to me, even when I was a teenager, it's only been since joining First Place that I've kept a prayer journal. I have grown greatly by putting pen to paper. I love having a written record to clearly see how God has intervened in my life and the lives of those around me.

Before I started keeping a prayer journal, I'm sure there were countless times when God provided, but I can't remember them all. But I do clearly remember one time in college, when I sat in my car waiting for a parking spot. After an hour, I prayed, "Lord, when possible, I'd really like to see Jami again. She's had a difficult time lately, and I just want to know she's okay. Also, I could really use a parking spot. I'm late for class." Almost immediately, Jami walked up and we chatted briefly. It turned out that she was headed for her car and said I could have her parking spot! I ran all the way to class laughing while thanking God for His sense of humor.

If you want to capture all the times when God has lovingly intervened in your life, try keeping a prayer journal to chronicle your experiences and see how God directs and protects you.

PRAYER
Dear Lord, thank You for the gift of prayer. What a privilege to come
to You at any time with any need. Help me to be vigilant in
bringing my concerns to You. Thank You for always hearing
my prayers and knowing what is best for me.

Journal: In what areas do you have a special need for God's guidance today? Take a few minutes to review your journal and note those prayers that have already been answered.

—Becky Sims

Only You!

You were running a good race. Who cut in on you and
kept you from obeying the truth?
Galatians 5:7

Galatians 5:7 is one of my favorite verses. I guess the reason is because I have lived it so many times. I can easily run a good race for a couple of weeks, but the daily routine of running finally gets to me, and I stop running. The truth is that I am basically undisciplined. I like the idea of living a disciplined life; I just don't like the hard work it takes to achieve it.

I love a clean closet, but that means I must pick up my clothes and shoes every single day. I love a clean desk, but that means I must handle paper only once, which is extremely hard for me to do. I love a clean car, but that means I must dispose of the trash I seem to collect. I love to see that I've lost weight when I get on the scale, but that means I must watch what I eat and write it down every day.

Well, you get the picture. I'm the only one who can run my race, and you are the only one who can run your race. Who keeps cutting in to keep us from obeying the truth? I suspect the answer is a simple one—me and you!

PRAYER
Dear Lord, I want to run a good race to the finish line.
Help me to keep from cutting in on myself today.

Journal: In what way are you your own worst enemy? Pray about a race that you need to re-enter.

—Carole Lewis

Staying on Track

You were running a good race. Who cut in on you and
kept you from obeying the truth?
Galatians 5:7

During the Summer Olympics of 2004, the world watched in disbelief as a man came out of the bleachers, ran onto the track and pushed one of the runners out of his designated lane. As I watched the scene unfold, the words of Galatians 5:7 flashed through my mind. Paul, who had himself watched the Greek Games, used that specific illustration to ask his readers who had cut in on them and kept them from obeying the truth. When I thought of the fate of the unsuspecting runner who was thrown off course through no fault of his own, I was humbled, because most of the things that throw me off track are neither surprising nor unexpected! When I examine my life, I find that I sin in such a consistent manner: same place, same people, same circumstances, same sin—usually the sin of overeating.

It is my own failure to eliminate those things that predictably lead to disaster that keeps me from running the good race. I drive by the donut shop that I will stop at in very predictable fashion. Or I push my cart down the ice-cream isle instead of shopping the perimeter of the store. Or I agree to go to lunch with friends who have traditionally been "eating buddies."

First Place invites me to do things differently so that I can press on toward the prize and not be thrown off track right when I begin to run the good race. With God's grace, I can stay the course!

PRAYER
Gracious God, You are so patient with me. Thank You for
giving me Your Word to show me the folly of my ways.

Journal: Talk to God about the things that keep you from running the good race.

—Elizabeth Crews

Leave the Past Behind

You were running a good race. Who cut in on you and
kept you from obeying the truth?
Galatians 5:7

Often it is our past that cuts in on us and attempts to squeeze us out of the race. In Philippians 3:13-14, Paul tells us to forget what is behind and strain forward toward what is ahead. Before I can forget the past, I actually have to name it and claim it as my own. I realized that what is behind me is close to 40 years of diet-hopping and yo-yo dieting begun in my early teens. In trying so many surefire, quick and easy weight-loss programs, and gaining and losing hundreds of pounds, I remember making thousands of pie-crust promises.

Today I shake my head with disbelief but not in disillusionment. God, my hope for today, gives me the strength to press on.

I read in Oswald Chambers's *My Utmost for His Highest* that God allows the memory of our past in order to turn the past into a ministry of spiritual culture for the future. God reminds us of the past lest we become complacent in the present. Chambers refers to God as our rearguard, always watching to keep us from past failures. God is also our security for today, ever before us as we press on to "leave the irreparable past in His hands, and step out into the irresistible future with Him."

PRAYER
Lord, thank You that You are before me, encouraging me to press on
in the good race to which You have called me. Thank You for using my past
to shape my present; but please continue as my rearguard so that I do not
revisit the past to make the same mistakes and failures.

Journal: What is a positive area in your life in which you feel God is encouraging you?

—Judy Marshall

Battling for Balance

You were running a good race. Who cut in on you and
kept you from obeying the truth?
Galatians 5:7

How many times have you felt as if you've got it all together when, seemingly out of nowhere, chaos hits and things fall apart again? For me, this is a familiar cycle. Just when I begin to balance my life through the nine commitments of First Place, illness, relationship troubles, stress or busyness throws me off balance again.

For years, I have felt helpless in the face of this maddening cycle that has kept me from reaching many of my goals. But when I began to look more closely at Galatians 5:7, I found that the one who "cut in" was often me! I realized that I become overconfident when things are going well, and I soon let Christ slip out of first place. Then I neglect to encourage my loved ones and friends, I become lax in my exercise and food choices, and I commit to things that distract from my work for God. I have sabotaged myself over and over through the years this way. Ignoring the cycle of renewed commitment and increased temptation has caused me to flounder needlessly.

Today, I am seeking increased awareness about these and other areas in which I am likely to be increasingly tempted.

What about you? Is there a familiar pattern to your struggle for balance?

PRAYER
Abba, thank You for Your Word that illuminates my blind spots.
Help me to run a good race and avoid the pitfalls of temptation.

Journal: List the areas in which you repeatedly get sidetracked from obeying the truth. How can you avoid falling into the same pattern again?

—Susan Johnston

Master of Deception and Distraction

You were running a good race. Who cut in on you and
kept you from obeying the truth?

Galatians 5:7

I *know* the truth. God has shown me what He wants me to do, and He has given me all the tools I need to accomplish my goals. Then why do I get sidetracked? Why do I allow circumstances and other people to keep me from obeying God and following His plan for my life?

I have found that even though I have greatly improved in my ability to keep healthy boundaries, I still have some boundary areas that are damaged. For instance, I allow the needs of others, especially my family's, to throw me off course. My biggest temptation to get off track is when my family wants me to do something for or with them, and I have planned to exercise or not to eat out. I need to know when to stop and do things with them and when I need to say no. I need to remember to go to God to ask for wisdom and discernment in knowing His will and His truth.

Satan knows my soft spots and weaknesses, and he knows yours. He is the Father of Lies and never plays fair. He will do anything to sabotage your plans to follow your commitments. He will get you so busy doing "good things" that you can't easily discern the best things that God has called you to do.

Since you and I know the real enemy and are aware of his schemes, we must constantly be on guard. We must daily seek God's help by spending more time in His Word and listening to His voice.

PRAYER

Lord God, I pray that You will give me wisdom and discernment to know
when Satan is a threat. Especially help me to recognize when Satan is trying to
distract me and keep me from doing what You have called me to do. I thank
You and praise You for Your protection and Your amazing love.

Journal: Make a list of the things or the people Satan uses to try to sidetrack you from your goals. Ask God to help you recognize Satan's tactics.

—Janet Kirkhart

God's Waiting Room

Never be lacking in zeal, but keep your spiritual fervor, serving the Lord.
ROMANS 12:11

For the last few months, I have been sitting in God's waiting room. All of us have been here at one time or another. We wait expectantly in the beginning. But the longer we wait, the more likely we are to lose our zeal and fervor.

The term used for this feeling in today's vernacular is "burnout." We begin to doubt if God is going to act on our behalf. Even though we know that He has the power to act, we sometimes doubt that He will. If we are confident that He will act, we get fidgety wondering when. That's where spiritual tenacity comes in. Oswald Chambers wrote, "Tenacity is more than endurance; it is endurance combined with the absolute certainty that what we are looking for is going to transpire. Tenacity is more than hanging on, which may be but the weakness of being too afraid to fall off."

Today, if you find yourself sitting in God's waiting room needing an answer and needing it now, the answer for you (and for me) is found in the last three words of Romans 12:11. God calls us to keep serving Him while we wait. As we serve Him through prayer and through our daily activities, our zeal and spiritual fervor will stay white hot.

PRAYER
Dear Lord, fill me with zeal and spiritual fervor today as I serve You.

Journal: Write about your "waiting room" experiences.

—Carole Lewis

All About Balance

Never be lacking in zeal, but keep your spiritual fervor, serving the Lord.
ROMANS 12:11

Those who know me well would never accuse me of lacking zeal. As a matter of fact, my unbridled zeal is often the reason that my spiritual fervor is dampened and my ability to serve the Lord hindered. I believe it was C. S. Lewis who said that good is the worst enemy of best. In my life that statement has been proved true way too many times.

When a volunteer is needed, I am the first to raise my hand. If a committee needs a member, or a chair person, then I'm there to fill the need. No teacher for the Sunday School class? No need to fear. I'll stand in the gap. Problem is, in all my zeal and enthusiasm, I often forget to consult with the Lord. In my haste to serve, I do the very things that keep me from *effectively* using the talents and gifts He has given me. Worst of all, in my serving-for-the-sake-of-service frenzy, my spiritual fervor grows lukewarm and then cold. Before long my prayer life is dull, my Bible study flat and my zeal has turned to bitter resentment because my efforts, no matter how well intentioned, are not bearing any fruit.

Romans 12:11 reminds me that life is about balance. I need to have zeal, but I must also limit my enthusiasm so that my spiritual fervor is not diminished and my service is focused on the Lord.

PRAYER
Gracious and loving Lord, serving You is my joy and my heart's delight. Help me stay balanced and focused so that I can always give You my best.

Journal: How is your zeal to do good keeping you from using your best talents and gifts in the Lord's service?

—Elizabeth Crews

Taking Jesus to Jail

Never be lacking in zeal, but keep your spiritual fervor, serving the Lord.
ROMANS 12:11

I was not enthused about going into the jail to teach women. I had asked God to enlarge my territory, like Old Testament Jabez had prayed, but this certainly was not the type of expansion I had envisioned!

The first night I was there, I saw how hungry the girls were for the Word. As I returned week after week, they began to accept me when they realized this was not a social outing for me. I had other things I could do. Some nights I would almost drag myself to the jail; but soon God would take over and the girls would give their hearts to Christ and hang on every word I spoke. I would come out of the meeting on a spiritual high and feel ashamed that my zeal had been lacking at the beginning of the evening.

I call those girls my little birds. They sit perched on a bench, leaning into the words and stories I tell. I carry tissues because hardly a night goes by that they don't cry. They so want to get free of the strongholds in their lives—the addictions to alcohol and drugs.

It has been three years since I started my new ministry at the jail, and I am excited about serving the Lord there. The girls know me only as Granny Bev and that I hug them and share Jesus with them. If I think about not going to my weekly meeting, I am reminded that there may be a woman waiting to give her heart to Jesus, and so I go.

PRAYER
*Thank You, Father, for showing me Your heart of love
so that I can share it with others.*

Journal: Do you only do what you like to do, or are you making an effort to give your will over to God? Talk to God about it.

—Bev Schwind

Saying Yes to God

Never be lacking in zeal, but keep your spiritual fervor, serving the Lord.
Romans 12:11

Today could have been like any other day. But today was different. Today I did something in a different way—not something new or even difficult. Today I took a deep breath and said yes quietly, but still it was heard. And today I found "yes" to be contagious. Soon the word popped out more assuredly—I even shouted it. In fact, I was feeling vibrant and alive. Now, that's not to say that I was not tempted to say no. In fact, I had said no just the day before. And yet today I said yes. But yes to what?

I agreed to *listen* to God. I did not only talk to Him as I sometimes do—a one-sided conversation in which I say all the right things I have learned to say. Instead, I truly listened. Some people are good at listening to God. But others, like me, may struggle at times with taking the time to listen, and more specifically, with following through on His plans. Out of fear, I put off trying new things, even when God urges me forward. But today, in the quietness of the morning, I said yes to obeying God's plans for me; yes to stepping out of my comfort zone and serving Him in the way He chooses; yes to trusting Him to meet my needs as I take on new challenges. And suddenly, I was alive and fired up with the knowledge that God has a special need for me. Today I said yes.

PRAYER
*Dearest Lord, today I am saying yes to You. Today I long to be alive
once again, zealously serving You as You would have me to serve.
May Your will be done as I serve You with a joy-filled heart.*

Journal: What are some ways that you can keep yourself willing and able to say yes when God calls?

—Susie Duren

Down in the Dumps

Never be lacking in zeal, but keep your spiritual fervor, serving the Lord.
ROMANS 12:11

Have you ever been down in the dumps? Satan sure likes to keep us on the discouragement track, because he knows that when we're discouraged, we will stop running the race God has set before us. We will sit down and wallow in self-pity and determine that someone else can run the race better than we can.

As a First Place leader, I find it easy to become discouraged if I focus my attention on what I should be doing for my class and forget to focus on what I should be doing for the Lord's service. I get bogged down with class preparation and trying to be the super leader in every way, and I fail to ask the Lord what *He* wants me to focus on. Then when I finally run out of steam and discover that in my efforts to be a super leader I have managed to gain weight instead of losing it, the discouragement overwhelms me and I want to give it all up.

God wants me to keep my zeal through spiritual fervor, not by being driven by self-worth. God wants me to seek His spiritual truths and teach my First Place group to love immersing themselves in His Word. He wants all of us to take our eyes off of self-accomplishment and focus them on His work—doing everything as unto the Lord. If we keep our lives focused on His spiritual truths, we will find the joy of a servant's heart.

PRAYER
Lord, give me clearer vision. Focus my eyesight on the things that are important to You. Give me a zeal for Your Word and Your truth, and fill me with a spiritual fervor that will allow me to serve You well.

Journal: Ask the Lord to put Scripture verses on your heart that will lift you out of discouragement and renew your enthusiasm for His service. Write the verses in your journal.

—Pat Cook

God and God Alone

Above all else, guard your heart, for it is the wellspring of life.
Proverbs 4:23

My personality is such that my life is pretty much an open book. Because of this, when I'm happy, angry or sad, everyone around me knows it. My batteries get recharged by being with people. I absolutely love people! I love getting feedback from others and talking things out.

There are times, however, when I find it necessary to guard my heart. These times are when I am fervently seeking God's face for help or direction in my personal life or for the ministry of First Place. These times are so few and far between that each one sticks out vividly in my mind.

What I know for sure is that guarding the heart means that you and I must learn to follow God and only God.

It has been said that the heart is the seat of our emotions. Guarding the heart is simply learning how to not be swayed by our emotions or the emotions of others when we're seeking answers from God. He will never allow us to stumble or fall if we keep our eyes on Him.

PRAYER
Dear Lord, teach me what it means to guard my heart so that my emotions don't get in the way of doing Your will.

Journal: Write about how something you are going through right now makes guarding your heart of the utmost importance.

—Carole Lewis

Early Warning System

Above all else, guard your heart, for it is the wellspring of life.
PROVERBS 4:23

An ominous message flashed on my computer screen. A virus-infected file had been detected trying to enter through my e-mail system. The culprit was disguised in a bogus attachment. The suspect had been captured by my antivirus software and was being held in quarantine. What did I want done with the contaminated file? Without hesitation, I selected the "delete" option—and with a click of the mouse the enemy had been destroyed.

That brief episode left me wondering, *Why can't I be as diligent when it comes to zapping the pollution that threatens to invade my heart?* Why can't I zap the contaminants that threaten to sneak into my soul and pollute that sacred space where the Holy Spirit dwells? I would like to tell myself it is because I don't have an early warning system to tell me I'm in danger. But in truth, God has given me a powerful virus shield: His unfailing, inerrant Word. He invites me to hide His Word in my heart so that when enemy invaders try to infiltrate my mind, the warning alarm will sound so that I can quarantine and destroy those infected messages before they spread and destroy.

My computer antivirus program is only effective if I install and run it. The same is true of God's Word. It won't work unless we install it in our hearts and minds. But when we do, it's the greatest protection system possible against the wiles of the evil one.

PRAYER
O Lord, You will never leave me to face my problems alone.
You have given me the all-powerful truth of Your Word so that I can
keep my heart pure and make it a holy place for You to dwell.

Journal: What virus threatens your sacred heart space, and what Scripture passages can you hide in your heart so that you can resist the devil's wiles?

—Elizabeth Crews

Be True to Your Heart

Above all else, guard your heart, for it is the wellspring of life.
PROVERBS 4:23

My heart—my thoughts and feelings—determines who I am. I have learned that I cannot go through life with my heart completely hidden. When I try to hide who I am, when I try to hide my thoughts and feelings from others, sooner or later my true heart comes to the surface—usually in stressful circumstances, and often at the most inopportune time.

I have found that if I live true to my heart regardless of what is happening around me, I can be who God created me to be! Then, when trying times come along, I won't try to stuff down my feelings with food. That won't be necessary, because I have been honest with myself and with others all along. They'll know where I stand, and I won't have to pretend.

Most important, if I'm living true to my heart, I must guard it carefully, because that is what the world is going to see and know about me and about the God I serve. According to James 1:27, the religion that God accepts as pure and faultless is this: to look after orphans and widows in their distress and to keep ourselves from being polluted by the world. Today I will be true to my heart so that the love of God can shine in and through me.

PRAYER
Father, show me how to be true to the heart with which You have blessed me.
Teach me to protect my heart from the impurities of this world.

Journal: Are you living in a way that is true to your heart? If not, why not? How is the Holy Spirit prompting you to protect your heart today?

—Susan Johnston

Heart Health

Above all else, guard your heart, for it is the wellspring of life.
Proverbs 4:23

Heart disease runs in my family. So two years ago, when I was diagnosed with a mild heart condition, my doctor urged me to lose weight, eat healthy and exercise to guard against future heart disease. But I'm concerned about more than the health of my physical heart. God's Word also urges us to "above all else" guard our hearts. We need to guard our spiritual hearts. Some of the things that block the arteries of our spiritual hearts are selfishness, pride, worldly desires and the lusts of the flesh.

When our hearts are filled with God's Word and His truth, they will spring up and overflow with love, joy and peace. We will be able to love others fully. Our greatest desire will be to please God and obey His Word rather than seeking to fulfill our own selfish desires.

What we choose to put into our hearts is what will spring up out of our hearts. We must be careful to fill our hearts with God's Word and guard our hearts against anything that blocks our spiritual arteries. If we neglect to guard our hearts above all else, it won't be long before we have a spiritual heart attack!

PRAYER
Father, forgive me for those times when I left my heart unguarded
and allowed the things of the world to creep in and take up residence.
Help me to guard my heart above all else and to walk in
obedience to Your Word. In Jesus' name, amen.

Journal: Write down what you need to do to guard your heart. Then write a prayer committing your plan to God.

—Joni Shaffer

Reducing Pollution

Above all else, guard your heart, for it is the wellspring of life.
Proverbs 4:23

While studying Proverbs 4:23, I was reminded how important it is to guard our hearts against negative thoughts and people. I find that when I am continually around negative people, I begin to think that what they're saying is true. Satan uses their negativity to pollute my mind. Guarding the heart against such intrusion is important if we are to serve God wholeheartedly.

My Bible concordance defines "heart" as "the vital center of one's being, emotions, and sensibilities." My commentary goes on to tell me that "our heart—our feelings of love and desire—dictates to a great extent how we live, because we always find time to do what we enjoy." Scripture teaches that the heart is the dwelling place of the Holy Spirit living within us (see 1 Corinthians 6:19).

That's why I love singing praise and worship songs and hymns. They can bring me into the presence of God like nothing else can and purify my heart from the negative thoughts that have found their way inside. The Lord has spoken to me through the music in a worship service so many times. Scripture tells us that the glory of God filled the Temple when the singers and musicians praised God. I find that it is almost impossible to be negative or think negative thoughts while praising God.

We are God's temple, and what comes out of our mouth reveals who resides in our heart.

PRAYER
Lord God, I thank You and praise Your wonderful name. Lord, You have given us limitations and commandments for our protection and as a guard to our hearts, Your dwelling place. Help me learn to obey Your commands and to always sing Your praises.

Journal: Ask God to show you people or places that undermine your work in order to rebuild healthy boundaries in your life. Listen to His voice as He gives you His instructions and His plan.

—Janet Kirkhart

Value of Silence

Then a cloud appeared and enveloped them, and a voice came from the cloud:
"This is my Son, whom I love. Listen to him!"

Mark 9:7

We know that we're developing spiritual maturity when we can listen to God without having to talk. In Mark 9:7, Peter had not yet developed the art of listening. He was so caught up in the splendor of the moment that all he could think to do was talk. I know; I've been there. How about you?

For some, listening comes easy. They love to listen to others more than they love to talk. People like me, however, have a hard time with what the media calls dead space. Only God can teach us that every silent moment doesn't need to be filled with words.

Last week, I was listening to a young woman teach the Bible. Since I had never heard her before, I was listening not only to what she said, but also to how she said it. Later that day, as I was thinking about her presentation, I realized that what stood out in my mind the most was when she would pause and let the truth of her words sink in.

Those of us who feel the need to fill every moment with words will only learn to listen to God by being quiet and still before Him. I know this may seem like a waste of time to those of you who are like me, but you must try it before you'll learn to like it.

PRAYER
Dear Lord, help me sit quietly before You today.
Speak, I pray, to my listening ears.

Journal: Write about some things you have talked about over and over again with God. After you finish writing, listen for His voice.

—Carole Lewis

Ignoring God's Voice

Then a cloud appeared and enveloped them, and a voice came from the cloud:
"This is my Son, whom I love. Listen to him!"

Mark 9:7

God speaks to all of us in different ways that correspond to the unique learning style He created as part of our being. Since I am a verbal-linguistic learner, God primarily speaks to me through His written Word. So Scripture reading is very important in my spiritual walk. Many times, as I have been headed down the wrong path at the wrong time and at the wrong speed, God has sent a Word messenger to my mind as a warning to *stop* what I'm doing, turn around quickly and get back on the right path.

The amazing thing is not that God speaks to me—God has spoken to His people throughout salvation history. What continues to amaze me is the fact that even though I know He speaks to me, and I have learned to recognize His voice, I still choose to ignore what He has to say! God, the sovereign Lord of the universe, stoops to Earth and speaks to me, and I hear but don't really listen. I choose my way over His Word.

Even though God's Word tells me repeatedly that I am the temple of God's Holy Spirit, that I was bought at a price, I do not care for my body as though it belongs to Him. Why do I call Him Lord and yet not do what He asks of me? Probably because I don't realize how very precious I am to the One who loves me with an everlasting love and who invites me to listen to His amazing plan for my life.

PRAYER

Gracious God, I am without excuse when I fail to listen to You. You speak to me in so many ways so that I can understand. Today help me to be responsive to Your Word so that I can listen to Your Son, Jesus, the living Word.

Journal: Write about the primary way God speaks to you, and explain why you are not a better listener.

—Elizabeth Crews

The Promised Land

Then a cloud appeared and enveloped them, and a voice came from the cloud:
"This is my Son, whom I love. Listen to him!"

Mark 9:7

This verse of Scripture follows the verse that recounts how Peter had the bright idea of building three tabernacles on the Mount of Transfiguration—one for Moses, one for Elijah and one for Jesus. God had a different idea and spoke through a cloud to Peter, telling him to get a grip and listen to Jesus, the eternal Word of God, rather than build earthly tents.

I can relate to Peter as I recall how many bright ideas I have had to help me lose weight—and lose it fast! I have always known that God wants me to be healthy and lose weight, and I have often taken it upon myself to "help" Him out by finding a new pill or belt to jiggle the pounds away. I went through years of trying diet things rather than just listening to the Son. Whenever a new diet center would open in my town, I was one of the first visitors to that new place! I can truly say that I have been there and done that to every diet plan, pill and "miracle" on the market.

When I came to First Place, the Lord spoke to me and told me that I was about to walk into my promised land. It didn't require having a Joshua go in and destroy the enemy; it had King Jesus, who had already shed His blood and possessed the land for me. God told me to listen to Him! No more diet gimmicks. This was the real thing.

PRAYER
Thank You, Lord, for giving me Your precious Son to
listen to as I dwell in my promised land.

Journal: List the times you went your own way and didn't listen to the Son. Then list the times you did heed His voice and how that affected your quality of life.

—Beverly Henson

Know His Presence

Then a cloud appeared and enveloped them, and a voice came from the cloud:
"This is my Son, whom I love. Listen to him!"

MARK 9:7

We cannot talk and listen at the same time. When a speaker wants an audience to pay attention, many times he or she will say, "Now listen closely." And when we need directions to travel to a specific location, we must concentrate on what we are hearing or we will get lost. Sometimes our lives get so busy that we don't think we can slow down enough to listen. But when we concentrate on getting the information we need, we can accomplish more in a shorter period of time.

What if we can't listen with our physical ears? When God said, "Listen to him," it was more than His telling us to give ear to what Jesus would say. The Father was telling us to heed Jesus' sacrifice on the cross, to pay attention to the fact that He loves us unconditionally and infinitely. To listen to Jesus is to feel His presence—to listen for Him in our inner person. The deaf do not need to hear to know His presence. They feel it and weep for joy.

God wants all of us to listen to His Son, just as He commanded the three disciples who were chosen to be with Jesus that day on the mountain. He wants us to listen to Jesus with our whole hearts.

PRAYER

Father, I'm sorry I don't take the time I should to listen.
Help me to be still and to hear and listen with my heart.

Journal: Write about the different ways you hear God.

—Bev Schwind

Rise Above

Then a cloud appeared and enveloped them, and a voice came from the cloud:
"This is my Son, whom I love. Listen to him!"

Mark 9:7

I am chaplain of the Boy Scout troop our church sponsors. While on a recent camping trip, we awoke to discover our mountaintop campsite was above the clouds! On the horizon we could see other mountain peaks poking above the clouds. During our service that morning, I shared the fact that our worldly activities are often shrouded in clouds; however, by accepting Christ in our life and following His teachings, we can rise above the world.

God has given us free will; but when we live like the rest of the world, we have the world's problems and stresses. And we often imitate the world's method of dealing with that stress: using food as a way to indulge our senses or to overeat.

In Mark 9:7, God asks us to listen to His Son. It is by obeying God and listening to Christ as He speaks to us through His Word that we can rise above the world as we build a healthy body, mind and spirit with which to serve Him.

PRAYER

Lord, You speak to us not only in Your Word, but also through the beauty of the world You have created for us. Thank You for the inspiration and dedication of godly leaders. I ask You to help me find time to be still and listen for Your voice.

Journal: Are you ready to rise above the world by obeying God and listening to Christ? How is His Word speaking to you today?

—Jack Dorn

Choosing Thankfulness

Introduction

Choosing to be thankful is a learned skill. The more we practice being thankful, the better we get at it. Perhaps you were raised in a negative, fault-finding home where thankfulness was not modeled or taught. If this was the case and you have not learned to practice the art of thankfulness, the Scripture verses in this section will be of great help to you.

The verses chosen for this section all relate to being thankful. Try to commit all 10 verses to memory and begin a Thankfulness Journal as you go through this section. Every morning, write down 5 things for which you are thankful, and every evening write 5 more. At the end of a month, you will be amazed at how gratitude and thankfulness are healing your heart and changing your life.

Bless you as you choose thankfulness as a way of life.

In Times of Sorrow

Give thanks to the LORD, for He is good. His love endures forever.
Psalm 136:1

Yesterday, I telephoned my 91-year-old aunt to see how she was doing. Her husband of 70 years died six months ago, and she has since moved into an assisted-living facility. As we talked, Aunt Blanche told me how much she misses Harold and how the only thing that comforts her is to sit and read her Bible. Blanche shared that she can read it for hours on end.

After we hung up, I began to think about what it must be like to lose your husband or wife after many years of marriage. Blanche said that it's as if a part of her is missing. I shared with her that the Bible says that when we marry, the two become one flesh, so a part of her truly is missing.

What a comfort for you and me to know that when we experience any kind of loss in this life, God is good and His love endures forever. The time to establish that up-close and personal relationship with God is right now. If we spend time with Him every day in prayer and Bible study, we will be ready when life's trials come. If we don't already have the relationship established, it will be much more difficult to get there when we find ourselves thrust into a position of grief and loss.

PRAYER
Dear Lord, I give You thanks because You are good.
Your love endures beyond the termination of earthly love.
Your love endures forever. Bless Your holy name.

Journal: Write about a loss you have experienced and how you found God to be good in the middle of it.

—Carole Lewis

Loving the Unlovable

Give thanks to the LORD, for He is good. His love endures forever.
Psalm 136:1

It was the day after Thanksgiving, and my oldest daughter, Sheri, left early for her power walk. It had rained during the night. The sidewalks were still slick and the dark clouds signaled more rain. With umbrella in hand, she strode out the door determined not to miss a day of exercise. Little did Sheri know that waiting outside for her was an abandoned dog in dire need of a loving home. That dog would not only become her walking companion that day but he would also teach us all a lesson about God's enduring love.

Although she is a purebred Shar-Pei, Zoë looked like anything but a royal breed as she followed Sheri home that morning! It was obvious that Zoë had been on the streets for quite some time and had probably been neglected long before her careless owner abandoned her. To say she was one pathetic-looking dog is an understatement! Her eyes were infected and her fur was falling out; she had a skin rash; she was dirty, smelly and emaciated; and she had a large gash down her back, the obvious aftereffects of a street fight. But even in her pathetic condition, Zoë won our hearts. We took her in, cleaned her up, took her to the vet for needed treatment and began to care for her like the royal princess she really is.

Two years later, Zoë is a treasured member of our family and a constant reminder to all of us that we too were poor, pitiful, pathetic and unlovable. Yet God, who is good, favored us with His enduring love that will last forever.

PRAYER
Today, O Lord, I give You thanks. When I was lost,
You found me. You are good and Your love will endure forever.

Journal: Write a letter to God expressing your thankfulness for His enduring love.

—Elizabeth Crews

Thankfulness Journal

Give thanks to the Lord, for He is good. His love endures forever.
Psalm 136:1

"Obedience is the cost of success" read the sign board in front of a local church, a poignant reminder that joyful obedience is the key that opens the storehouse of God's blessing. Now, if obedience were limited to my outer actions, I could pretend that I am living a life God can bless. However, God doesn't just look at the outer things—God sees my heart. He knows that cultivating a thankful heart is a continual challenge for me and that I often fall short of thankfulness.

Yes, I can recite all the Bible verses that tell me to give thanks. Certainly my head knows that in order to reap God's richest blessings—and repel the wiles of the enemy—I need to live a life characterized by thanks and praise. I can talk about being thankful; I can write about being thankful; I can sing about being thankful. But there are days when it feels so much better to grumble, complain and indulge in self-pity than to give God the thanks and praise He deserves. "Woe is me!" all too often takes the place of wonder and gratitude for God's perpetual goodness.

Keeping a Thankfulness Journal is the best weapon I have discovered in this battle I wage against negative thinking and the "poor me" attitude that goes with it. Only when I meditate on God's love, which will never end, can I give God thanks and praise, not because I feel like doing it but because it is the right-with-God thing to do.

PRAYER
God of all goodness and love, You are deserving of all glory,
honor and praise, no matter what else is going on in my life.
Your love endures forever and Your mercies never end.

Journal: If you are not already keeping a Thankfulness Journal, begin that practice today.

—Elizabeth Crews

Bread, Jam and Consolation

Give thanks to the LORD, for He is good. His love endures forever.

PSALM 136:1

I remained at my mother's bedside most of the night, listening to her shallow breathing. She had the flu, and since she was 96, I knew the illness was very difficult for her. I thought about all the times she had probably sat by my bed and lost sleep worrying about me. Now the roles were reversed, and I was the caregiver. Finally, in the early morning hours, I recalled the words of Psalm 136:1 and knew that my mother was in God's care, whose love endures forever.

The next morning, Mother's fever was gone. *Thank You, Lord, for watching over Mother,* I thought as I began making breakfast. I opened a jar of blackberry jelly we had bought at a festival. The Bible verse on the label caught my eye: "Surely the arm of the LORD is not too short to save, nor His ear too dull to hear" (Isaiah 59:1).

I called the phone number on the label. A young man in Kentucky answered and said that he was the maker of the jelly. I asked him who had picked the Bible verse on the jars.

"My father. He's gone to be with the Lord now, but we still use the verses he selected. I appreciate your call," he said. "I needed that today."

PRAYER
Thank You, Lord, for Your love—a mighty love that endures forever.
Today I thank You that You have arms that reach as far as the east is from the west
and that You can hear the slightest utterance of Your children.

Journal: Ask God to give you encouragement from His Word and then ask Him to bring someone to mind who could use the same encouragement. Pick up the phone or write a quick note and mail it today.

—Bev Schwind

A Thankful Heart

For the Mighty One has done great things for me—holy is his name.
Luke 1:49

My book *A Thankful Heart* was born out of the lessons I learned through some times of great loss. My husband, Johnny, and I have experienced financial loss, his cancer, and the death of our daughter Shari. We've also survived a fire in our home, which necessitated our moving out for three months. And once we woke up to find our house flooded after our washer got stuck on the fill cycle and water poured out of it all night.

As I thought of all these losses and challenges during the last 25 years, I realized that through it all, and in it all, every single event was a time when we learned more about God and His will for our lives. He has done great things for us, because we are His children. He restored our financial ruin and turned it into financial stability. He has sustained Johnny's life for eight years after the diagnosis that he might live for two years. He has helped my son-in-law Jeff continue to raise his three wonderful girls after the death of Shari in 2001. Cara, the oldest, is now married and expecting her first child. Christen is in college, and Amanda is a junior in high school.

Our God does great things for us because of His character. He is love, righteousness, holiness, patience, kindness, goodness, grace and mercy personified. Yes, God has done great things for me, and He has also done great things for you.

PRAYER
O God, You have done great things for me—holy is Your name.

Journal: Write about the great things God has done for you during seasons of loss. Thank Him for His love and care for you.

—Carole Lewis

Thankfulness in Uncertain Times

For the Mighty One has done great things for me—holy is his name.
Luke 1:49

As I wrote the *Choosing Thankfulness* Bible study, I spent some time thinking about Mary the mother of Jesus. Bible scholars tell us that she was about 16 years old, a poor peasant girl, engaged but not married. However, unlike modern-day engagements, Mary and Joseph's betrothal was a binding contract. Joseph might have divorced her. He could even have had her stoned to death for adultery. Mary didn't know what the future would hold when the angel announced that she would bear a son. She didn't know all the details. Yet in the uncertainty of the moment, Mary could only say that the Mighty One had done great things for her. How humbled I am each time I read her words!

It is so much easier to see the great things the Mighty One has done for us in hindsight. But there are also so many opportunities to proclaim the great things the Mighty One has done for us before we see the end results. It's been so long since I was at my ideal weight that I have no idea what that ideal weight will look like when I get there! Yet each day is an opportunity to proclaim God's goodness in faith and trust that He knows exactly what He is doing.

PRAYER
Lord, all too often I want all the answers before I can sing Your praise.
Just for today I will declare that You have done great things for me before
I see the results of the miracle You are bringing forth in my life.

Journal: What song of praise can you offer to the Mighty One today, even though you are not sure what He's doing in your life?

—Elizabeth Crews

Be Grateful in All Circumstances

For the Mighty One has done great things for me—holy is his name.
Luke 1:49

Although I have been a Christian since I was 11 years old, and over a period of years have completed many Bible studies, attended numerous conferences and listened to many sermons, I have learned more about having a personal relationship with my Lord and Savior since I have been in First Place than in all the other years combined. The nine commitments of First Place (see front matter) have taught me so much. Just as God provided His statutes and commandments for our protection and guidance, the nine commitments have given me protection and guidance too.

Before joining First Place, I had severe colitis. Four years before I could retire on full retirement, I had to go on medical disability because I could no longer teach music in the public school where I had worked for 26 years. After following the First Place program, God healed the colitis and I no longer have to take any kind of medication. I do not have attacks like I did before my eating was under control.

I could choose to be angry and upset with God because I didn't get to finish my 30 years of teaching. But I know God had a greater plan for me. I feel better now than I have in years. I have been able to use this experience as a testimony to the Mighty One who has done great things for me.

PRAYER
*Lord God, I choose to be thankful for everything in my life—
the good and the bad circumstances—because I know that You are
the Mighty One, the awesome, holy I Am. Thank You for all that You are
and for all that You have done in my life. I praise Your holy name.*

Journal: List all the great things God has done for you. Take time to thank Him and praise Him for His work in your life.

—Janet Kirkhart

Praise God Amid Tragedy

For the Mighty One has done great things for me—holy is his name.
Luke 1:49

"Nooooooo!" I screamed, as the driver ahead of me slammed on the brakes to avoid running into a group of darkly clad teenagers. My car, its tires unable to get traction on the wet pavement, plowed into the rear end of the other vehicle. I watched incredulously as the teens laughed and shrugged like it was no big deal that they had just caused a major two-car accident.

"I can't afford this!" I cried out, anxiety, shock and depression quickly overtaking me. I had just spoken at a very successful women's retreat and was about two miles from the home of my friend, who was riding in the car with me. We had gone from praising the Mighty One, who has done great things for us, to wondering why in the world this bad thing had happened.

My friend, being more spiritually inclined in that moment, said, "No one was seriously hurt. You have car insurance. We're okay." I didn't feel okay. I was angry. Finances were tight and I had a good-sized insurance deductible. Guess what I wanted to do? Eat. Yes, eat. Oh, and get mad at God. But as my friend kept rattling off her personal gratitude list, I felt convicted.

Letting go of my anger was a choice. Thanking the Mighty One, who has done great things for me, was another choice. Celebrating God in the midst of my seemingly tragic situation allowed me to see His goodness. I didn't have to eat my way out of my pain, but rather, I was able to praise my way out.

PRAYER
Dear Lord, thank You so much for everything. Just as Paul celebrated
Your goodness and grace while behind prison bars, help us to do the same. Lord, we bless
Your mighty name today. We love You. In Jesus' name, amen.

Journal: Do you only celebrate God when things go your way? Or do you praise Him in every circumstance? This very moment, no matter what might be happening in your life, praise Him.

—Carol Van Atta

Rescued—Again!

He brought me out into a spacious place; he rescued
me because he delighted in me.
Psalm 18:19

We had a Golden Retriever named Beau who couldn't swim! Our other Golden, Major, loved to swim, while poor Beau just stood at the water's edge and watched. One day, our granddaughter Katherine, who was visiting us at the Bay, was convinced that Beau could swim but wouldn't. So she pushed him off of the pier into the water. As Beau floundered in the water, Katherine could see that he was struggling, and she jumped into the water fully clothed to rescue him. Watching her holding this 100-pound dog, with all four legs flailing and kicking, and help him back to the shore and safety was a sight to see. You see, Katherine loved Beau and was not about to leave him in the middle of the Bay to drown.

God has rescued me on many occasions over the course of my life. When I have been caught in the trap of sin, He has snatched me out of the pit I dug for myself. When I have made really poor choices, He has taught me how to turn those poor choices into powerful life changes that have helped me grow. Why has He continued to rescue me over and over again? The simple fact is that God delights in me because of a choice I made as a 12-year-old to ask Jesus into my life. God will continue to bring me into a spacious place every time I get into trouble. And He will do the same for you. Why? Because He delights in you!

PRAYER
Dear Lord, thank You for rescuing me and for delighting in me.
I am Your child. What a glorious thought!

Journal: Write about a time when God rescued you and brought you into a spacious place.

—Carole Lewis

Act as If

He brought me out into a spacious place; he rescued
me because he delighted in me.

Psalm 18:19

"Even if you can't believe it's true, act as if you believe it's true until you can believe" are words I had said so many times to others that I didn't even stop to think about how I might need to become my own wise counselor. "Act as if . . ." was easy to say to others, but when it came to believing that God delighted in me, it was like putting on an ill-fitting garment. Struggle and survival by wit and tenacity felt so much better on this independent, self-willed body of mine, even though the extra weight I was carrying was woven into the very fabric of my persona. How foolish I must have looked to God, struggling under this self-imposed burden rather than accepting the love He longed to give me.

Being able to surrender to God's plan for me in the confidence and trust that He delights in me and longs to do good things for me is still an "act as if" proposition for me most of the time. Yet, as I am willing to act as if God delights in me by caring for myself in a way that brings Him glory and honor, I find it easier to let go of my need to struggle, and I simply surrender to His goodness and grace.

PRAYER

Gracious and loving God, today, help me to see Your goodness
and give me the grace to delight in You because You delight in me
and long to bring me into a spacious place, free from the bondage
of my destructive habits and thoughts.

Journal: What aspect of God's love do you need to act as if you believe until that truth becomes part of the fabric of your life?

—Elizabeth Crews

Escaping the Recliner

He brought me out into a spacious place; he rescued
me because he delighted in me.

Psalm 18:19

On February 8, 1998, the Lord rescued me from Lazy-Boy Recliner Land. Up to that time, my life was work, church and the Lazy-Boy. I had no social life, no friends and no plans for the future. The only thing I looked forward to each day was getting back to my Lazy-Boy, watching television and eating. That year the Lord truly picked me up and taught me to walk by taking baby steps. First I simply walked. Then I began riding a bike, followed by rollerblading, and then kayaking, and now my new thing, sailing. Yesterday the Lazy-Boy, today the world!

The enemy loved it when I stayed in that chair and didn't enjoy being with God's people. He loved it when I had no life. He loved it when I would go home on Friday and not leave the house until Monday morning.

What a different life I live today! Filled with friends and positive things to occupy my time. When I was in Lazy-Boy Land, even a trip to the mailbox was a long trip. But in the spacious place to which God has brought me, anything is possible. Through Christ Jesus, I am more than a conqueror.

PRAYER
Father, You know where I am now and where I need to be. Bring me into my own special, spacious space that You have set aside for me.

Journal: Have you ever felt boxed in? List the areas in which you would like the Lord to bring you into a spacious place.

—Beverly Henson

Have a Plan

He brought me out into a spacious place; he rescued
me because he delighted in me.

PSALM 18:19

When our sons were small, we took a trip to Washington, DC. They eagerly looked forward to their first camping trip. After packing the equipment, food and clothes in our VW bus, we headed north. Our campsite was a spacious place with trees beside a lake. While we unloaded our van, my husband set up the tent and heavily coated it with waterproof spray. Then we headed to the lake for a swim.

All at once, rain started pouring down. Fast as we could, we ran to the tent, dried off and changed into dry clothes. It was so much fun sitting inside the tent playing games, laughing and enjoying our family, until we began to feel our blue jeans getting wet! You see, while the outside of the tent had been waterproofed, the floor had not, and rain seeped in. We had to leave all our belongings and head for a motel for the night.

As I pondered this experience, I was reminded of my First Place goals and commitments. In order to succeed, I must coat all nine commitments with prayer and set aside a specific time daily to complete each one. If I leave off one or two, Satan will find a way to cause me to get wet with disappointment and discouragement.

PRAYER
Forgive me, Lord, when I make decisions to come out from
under Your umbrella of protection. Keep me within the boundaries of
Your love so that I may live in victory every day.

Journal: Are there any uncoated areas of your life today? Record what you could do to get them waterproofed.

—Barbara Brown

The Lord Hears Our Cries

He brought me out into a spacious place; he rescued
me because he delighted in me.
Psalm 18:19

Throughout Psalm 18, we learn that the Lord is our Rock, our Strength and our Shield of Protection. When we have come to the end of ourselves and we can no longer do it on our own, the Lord hears our cries. At that point, I believe that Abba Father, "Daddy God," reaches down from heaven and scoops us up into His loving arms and sets us down in "a place of safety" (*NLT*)—a spacious place.

This fall, I attended my first First Place National Conference in Ohio. This was a life-changing conference for me as I became more aware of God's power to heal me. I learned what a balanced-portion-sized meal is—I ate and I was content! I was challenged by Dr. Dick Couey's instruction to walk three miles a day. Within a month, the Lord put a brochure for a local 5K (3.10 mile) Run-Walk Race in front of me. I thought, *This is crazy!* But God answered back, "What better way to celebrate turning 46?"

Two days before the race, the Lord led me to Psalm 18. Yes, He had brought me to a place of safety (to First Place). He had rescued me with a new lifestyle of proper eating and exercise. Now He was giving me the battle plan (see vv. 30-36): His right hand would support me and He would give me a wide path for my feet. He would give me victory (see v. 43)!

PRAYER
Dear Lord in heaven, I pray that my testimony will encourage others
to exercise daily—and to walk with the Lord!

Journal: Be encouraged by the words of Psalm 18. Write down the nuggets of truth you find there.

—Janet Boyles

Heavenly Reminders

But the Counselor, the Holy Spirit, whom the Father will
send in my name, will teach you all things and will remind
you of everything I have said to you.
John 14:26

My assistant, Pat, and I committed to memorize 100 of our First Place memory verses in 1999. It took us a couple of years, because we only memorized one verse a week. By November 2001, when my 39-year-old daughter, Shari, was killed by a drunk driver, we had all 100 verses memorized and we recited every one of them each morning as we walked side by side on treadmills in our Christian Life Center at church.

I have experienced the truth of John 14:26 many times since Shari's death. The Holy Spirit is able to remind me of the truth of this verse and the others I have learned because He taught me the verses. All that Pat and I did was show up each day ready to saturate our minds with God's Word. So when I need peace, the Holy Spirit reminds me of 1 Thessalonians 5:23, which tells me that He is the God of peace. When I need hope, the Holy Spirit reminds me of Romans 15:13, which tells me that He is the God of hope.

We can only be reminded of what we already know. This is why the First Place Scripture memory commitment is vital to our growth in Christ. As we allow the Holy Spirit to teach us Scripture, He will be there to remind us of what we've learned when we need reminding.

PRAYER
Dear Lord, I am so thankful that You teach me Your Word
if I commit to learn it. I am even more thankful that You remind
me of the truth of Your Word when I need it most.

Journal: Write about a time when the Holy Spirit reminded you of something He had previously taught you.

—Carole Lewis

Getting Out of God's Way

But the Counselor, the Holy Spirit, whom the Father will
send in my name, will teach you all things and will remind
you of everything I have said to you.

John 14:26

All week long I have been reminding my oldest son of something he needed to take care of before the week's end. And all week long my words have fallen on deaf ears. When he has taken the time to respond to my reminders via e-mail, he has offered excuses. He is too busy to talk when I call him. "Mom, I know what I need to do," he has sharply replied. "But it's my job to remind you!" I have shot right back.

Yet there is a huge fallacy in my reasoning, because my son is no longer a child. He is 28 years old, and my job as a mother who reminds her small child still in training has long ended. My son prides himself on being independent, no longer dependent on me—except when he chooses to be irresponsible and gets himself in a jam. And when he finds himself in that uncomfortable spot, he expects me to come to his rescue. My reminders aren't welcome but the rescue efforts are.

Today there is only one reminder needed—that it is not my responsibility to remind or to rescue. As the mother of a grown son, my job is to get out of the way so that the Holy Spirit, working amidst the adverse circumstances God is using, can teach my son without my interference. Today I need to remind myself that God loves my son more than I do, and it's the Spirit's job to teach him and remind him of all truth.

PRAYER

O Lord, so often my reminders are really a form of control.
Help me today, dear Lord, to stay out of the way so that the
Spirit can do His work in the lives of those I love.

Journal: What reminder do you need to give yourself so that you don't get in God's way as He works all things together for good, according to His purposes, for those He loves?

—Elizabeth Crews

Seeking the Holy Spirit

*But the Counselor, the Holy Spirit, whom the Father will
send in my name, will teach you all things and will remind
you of everything I have said to you.*
John 14:26

Several years ago, I had a personal revelation about the role the Holy Spirit plays in our daily lives. I came to realize that He truly is our counselor, teacher, comforter and friend.

I had just begun my 160-pound weight-loss journey in 1998 as a First Place member. I was afraid to meet people I didn't know. I didn't want to go outdoors where people would see me working out. During this part of my journey, the Holy Spirit became my comforter and encourager.

I remember asking Him to help me with my food plan. I was so afraid that I wouldn't do it correctly. Knowing that advance preparation was essential to my First Place success, the Holy Spirit prompted me to prepare my breakfast and lunch the night before so that I wouldn't be tempted to eat at fast-food restaurants. Meal planning was an important part of my success!

I vividly recall one particular morning when the Holy Spirit and I were having an excellent quiet time together before I left for work. I felt as though He was enjoying being with me as much as I was enjoying being with Him. Just as I picked up my purse and opened the door to leave, I heard Him say to me, "You forgot your lunch." That's when I knew that God and I were truly in this thing together. My success in First Place was as important to Him as it was to me—maybe even more so!

PRAYER
*Thank You, Holy Spirit, for being my comforter and for reminding
me of all things. Thank You for helping me plan my menus.*

Journal: What are some areas of your diet, health and exercise in which you need to give the Holy Spirit permission to be your personal assistant?

—Beverly Henson

Relying on the Holy Spirit

But the Counselor, the Holy Spirit, whom the Father will
send in my name, will teach you all things and will remind
you of everything I have said to you.
John 14:26

When I began attending First Place meetings as a brand-new Christian, about 7 years ago, I wouldn't even try to memorize verses, although I was faithful in keeping all of my other commitments, and I lost 30 pounds in the first few months. I stayed at home, refusing to join a group. I was sure I'd never be able to do my memory verses and I didn't want to be embarrassed.

Thankfully, God reaches us where we are. He has allowed me to see that I was relying on His Holy Spirit to enable me to fulfill all my other commitments, so why not the commitment of memorization? If the Spirit could change me from a gym-class skipper to an exercise lover, then maybe He could help me with Scripture memory too. I gave it a try.

To my surprise, my Counselor not only showed me ways to memorize verses, but He also taught me how to let them take root. He even reminds me of them whenever I need them. I like the way the *New American Standard Bible* calls the Holy Spirit the "Helper." When I ask, God sends His gracious Spirit, and my Helper lives up to His name!

Now I memorize two verses a week. As I have kept the other First Place commitments, God has helped me lose 70 pounds. He has also turned His Word into a prayer ministry in my heart and helped me write five books, all about Him!

PRAYER
Heavenly Father, remind me to ask You daily to help me and to cleanse,
fill and teach me. Remind me of Your Word, and bear fruit with it in my heart.
Thank You for the gift of the Counselor sent in Jesus' name. Amen.

Journal: Are you remembering to ask God to send His Spirit to counsel, teach and remind you of His Word? Thank Him for the gift of His Spirit, and ask Him to reveal where He is working in your life.

—Tammy M. Price

God's Power Source

But the Counselor, the Holy Spirit, whom the Father will
send in my name, will teach you all things and will remind
you of everything I have said to you.
John 14:26

I was just too tired to start a new First Place group. Thoughts of canceling this second orientation meeting went through my mind as I watched the rain outside. At that moment, my co-leader, Kelly, suddenly had the nudging of the Holy Spirit to pray for me, and she obeyed. Hours later, she came into the meeting room and gave me a big hug and told me how she had prayed.

"That's why I didn't cancel the meeting!" I told her, as I prepared to get the orientation started. Suddenly the power in the building went out. Down the dimly lighted hall we could hear voices and laughter—one of the alumni had picked up two new people, and they were excited about First Place. Then more people came, all eager for First Place to begin. I realized that Kelly's prayer had ministered to me through the power of the Holy Spirit, and I knew that leading this group was God's will for me.

We sat around the table, using a big flashlight that gave off a gentle, candle-like glow. We simply shared from our hearts. The new women freely talked about their reasons for coming to the meeting, and the alumni spoke words of encouragement. I confessed my poor attitude—that I had forgotten that it wasn't about me, and the Holy Spirit had brought that thought to my remembrance. The group bonded that night in a special way. The power came back on as the meeting ended, and I laughed because we had not needed it. We had used the power of the Holy Spirit.

PRAYER
Thank You, Lord, that You did not leave us without providing the
Holy Spirit to direct our lives. We thank You that He reminds us of the truth of
the power of His Word and He promises to never leave us or forsake us.

Journal: When have you felt the Holy Spirit nudge you to pray for someone or to encourage him or her with a phone call or e-mail?

—Bev Schwind

Angelic Aid

What other nation is so great as to have their gods near them the
way the LORD our God is near us whenever we pray to him?
Deuteronomy 4:7

Dottie Brewer, the founder of the First Place program, was involved in a serious automobile accident one night when returning from a trip. This happened in the early 1980s when Dottie had driven to Dallas to talk with a publisher about publishing the First Place program. After she took the other lady home who had traveled with her, she was struck by another car. Her car was on fire and she was unable to open the car door. Dottie said that as she cried out, "God, help me," the door opened and a man dressed completely in white helped her out of the car and led her to safety. She said that a few moments later she looked around and the man was gone.

Dottie said later that she was thankful for two things that happened that night. The first was that she was on a first-name basis with God and it was natural to call out to Him when she was in trouble. "I was so glad that I had a daily time of talking to God and that when I cried out, I didn't hear, 'Dottie who?'" The second thing is that our God is powerful—He can and did send an angel to help her that night when she cried out to Him.

PRAYER
Dear Lord, I am so thankful that You are
always near to me when I pray.

Journal: Write about a time when you cried out to God and He showed Himself powerful on your behalf.

—Carole Lewis

Interactive Relationship

*What other nation is so great as to have their gods near them the
way the LORD our God is near us whenever we pray to him?*

Deuteronomy 4:7

There was once a time when I felt so unworthy that I could not even begin to imagine the privilege of knowing and experiencing God. And, of course, the problem stemmed from my thinking that I had to earn the right to be reconciled to God rather than accepting a relationship with Him as a gift freely given because Jesus died to bring me into a right relationship with the Father.

I have also learned that even though salvation is a free gift of God, grace demands a response. I do not work *for* my salvation; I work *from* my salvation. Part of that work is prayer. Deuteronomy 4:7 equates greatness with having the Lord near when I pray, for at the heart of all relationship is interactive communication. Rather than trying to earn God's favor, I am invited by God to develop an intimate relationship with Him by simply spending time in His presence, sharing my heart with Him and letting Him share His heart with me. Greatness is not about doing; it is about having a great God near to me when I pray.

PRAYER
*Sovereign Lord, it is hard for me to realize that You want to be
in relationship with me even more than I want to be in relationship
with You. But You sent Your Son, Jesus, to show me just how important
I am to You. Thank You for Your love.*

Journal: Write about what an intimate relationship with God looks like to you, and what you would need to change in your life to have such a relationship.

—Elizabeth Crews

Just Do It!

What other nation is so great as to have their gods near them the
way the LORD our God is near us whenever we pray to him?
Deuteronomy 4:7

I stood in the bookstore looking at row upon row of books on the subject of prayer. It seemed as if every Christian author had a different bit of you-need-to-know-this advice on how to pray. It suddenly occurred to me that the disciples didn't ask Jesus to teach them *how* to pray, but that they asked Him to teach them *to* pray—the discipline of prayer as opposed to the how-to directions of prayer. The sheer number of books on how to pray was a sad testimony to the fact that Christians would rather read about how to pray than just get down on their knees and do it! The very fact that I was standing there looking at the myriad of books on prayer meant that I too had succumbed to "how to-ing" instead of just doing.

Using the words "prayer" and "discipline" in the same sentence almost seems oxymoronic. It's so much easier to think of prayer as an option rather than a necessity. Yet unless I train (discipline) myself to pray, I will never get around to saying the words that bring the Lord my God near. Great prayers do not come from knowing how to pray. Prayer has great power because of the omnipotent God who invites me to pray and who promises to draw near to me when I draw near to Him in prayer.

PRAYER
O Great and Awesome God, teach me to pray! You aren't impressed
with form; it is faith that pleases You. May I never again be guilty of
substituting how to-ing for just doing when it comes to prayer.

Journal: Write a heartfelt prayer to your Father in heaven, confident that as you draw near to Him, He will draw near to you and hear the earnest prayer of His beloved child.

—Elizabeth Crews

My Prayer Journal

What other nation is so great as to have their gods near them the
way the LORD our God is near us whenever we pray to him?
D e u t e r o n o m y   4 : 7

Ready, set, pray. "Dear Lord, thank You for this day . . . (*wait—gotta feed the dogs*) . . . Sorry, Lord, please bless my husband and please protect our children . . . (*did I take the meat out of the freezer?*) . . . Okay, then; also, Lord . . . (*what's that noise?*) . . . and thank You for hearing my prayers."

When I joined First Place and learned about the prayer journal commitment, I was scared to death. Who has time to do that? What if someone found the journal and read it? Reluctantly, I bought a $2 school notebook, determined to write at least one sentence a day. That would fulfill one of the nine commitments, and I could carefully word my prayers in case someone found it!

That was four years ago. Today my journals have become a powerful visual witness to my family. They now share their prayer requests because they have seen my stacks of filled prayer journals. I still purchase inexpensive notebooks, but I decorate them with stickers. It's fun to change the look when starting a new journal.

I write something every day—sometimes a sentence, sometimes a paragraph, or even five pages. Has anyone ever read them? Is it time-consuming? Those questions don't matter to me anymore. What is important is that my mind no longer wanders. My mind is focused on the God who is near to me when I pray to Him.

PRAYER
Dear Lord, thank You for the blessing of a prayer journal to keep me
consistently communicating with You. Please bless my families—
my God-given family and my First Place family. In Jesus' name, amen.

Journal: Ask God to show you ways that you could use your prayer journal as a record of His faithfulness.

—PJ Bahr

Living in the Light

You, O LORD, keep my lamp burning; my God turns my darkness into light.
PSALM 18:28

My husband, Johnny, and I have experienced the truth of this verse during the last eight years as we've lived under the cloud of stage-four prostate cancer. Johnny's diagnosis was a dark one—one to two years to live. For a few days, we were plunged into the pit of despair. Little by little, we moved into the sunlight when we began to realize that this dark cloud was nothing but a cloud, and after it moved, the light would come back.

God turned our darkness into light by taking away our fear of dying. All of us are going to die; God just gave us advance notice so that we wouldn't waste a lot of time worrying about the small stuff of life. Our marriage grows sweeter every day because we don't waste time being angry with each other. We make time for each other and always kiss hello and good-bye. We have a huge advantage over many other married couples, because we will have no regrets when we're no longer together on this earth.

We have also learned that cancer is a chronic disease and that Johnny is not going to die until God is ready to take him home. Today we live in the light of faith and trust in God, rather than in the darkness of fear and uncertainty.

PRAYER
Dear Lord, I have learned what it means to give thanks in everything because You are in everything that happens to me. Today, I thank You for the dark times of life, for You are the One who turns my darkness into light.

Journal: Write about a time when you were plunged into darkness and God turned your darkness into light.

—Carole Lewis

Ask the Right Questions

You, O LORD, keep my lamp burning; my God turns my darkness into light.
Psalm 18:28

Living with a chronic autoimmune disease is rather like tinkering with an old car. No sooner do you get one thing fixed than something else goes wrong! When I was diagnosed with rheumatoid arthritis in 1990, I felt as though my world had come to an end. Pictures of gnarled, deformed hands raced through my mind. I sobbed as the rheumatologist outlined the course of treatment. My heart's desire was to be a writer. Why had God dealt me such a cruel blow!

Later that evening, I called a trusted spiritual advisor to pour out my lament, hoping for sympathy. What I heard on the other end of the phone sent me reeling. "Use this as an opportunity to learn to ask the right questions. Don't waste your time asking 'Why me, God?' Instead, ask God to show you how you can use what seems to be a setback for His glory." Several days later, the Holy Spirit gave me Psalm 18:28 as God's solution to my dilemma.

Yes, I still have flare-ups—days that are more about pain than pleasure. But 15 years later, my hands are not deformed, and God has even used the changes necessitated by this debilitating disease to usher in a lifestyle that allowed Him to make my dream of writing a reality. When I ask the right questions, God is always faithful to keep my lamp burning and turn my darkness into light.

PRAYER
*Even in my darkest hour, I can trust that You will keep my
lamp burning and turn my darkness into light, O Lord. Thank You
for Your faithfulness and love.*

Journal: What situation in your life is inviting you to ask the right question? Ask God how He can use this apparent setback for His glory.

—Elizabeth Crews

Trimming the Lamp

You, O LORD, keep my lamp burning; my God turns my darkness into light.
PSALM 18:28

August 15, 2005, my precious, healthy 19-day-old grandson, Andrew, died from SIDS (sudden infant death syndrome). I'd never felt such grief. The previous month, I had, after prayerful consideration, begun leading my first live First Place group at our church. Now this tragedy began to undermine my resolve to follow through on my commitment. The evil one seized the opportunity to flood my mind with negative thoughts: *Why did I agree to do this? Why did I think First Place was something my church needed?* I was convinced that the 24 people in my First Place group didn't need me. I surely didn't need *them*! My distorted thinking even told me that if I had not agreed to lead this study, Satan would have left me alone—and my grandson would still be alive.

I doubted my faith, my Lord, my Christian walk, my conviction and my dedication to First Place. Then, one Thursday during a study, a class member said, "PJ, how lucky you are that God brought you to us!" I looked at her incredulously. What could she possibly be talking about? This was a nightmare! She continued, "God obviously knew you were going to be walking through this deep valley, so He brought 24 people to you, in this class, to hold you up in loving prayer through this dark time!" That night God turned my darkness into light in a dramatic and powerful way. And He has kept my lamp burning.

PRAYER
Dear God, thank You that even when life's events threaten to blow out my burning flame of faith, You are my light.

Journal: Are you walking through a dark time? Ask God to shed light on your circumstances to show you that He is keeping your lamp burning.

—PJ Bahr

Facing Dark Days

You, O LORD, keep my lamp burning; my God turns my darkness into light.
Psalm 18:28

Four years ago, I lost my husband after a brief time in the hospital. He became ill on Christmas day and was buried one day after my birthday in January. After this kind of grief-filled experience, how do you face these special days each year? Psalm 18:28 gives us the answer.

God used the First Place staff and the members of my class to see me through my dark days. The strength I have gained from my years in the First Place Bible studies and from being in God's Word make it possible for me to put one foot in front of the other and continue my life's journey.

My husband and I often talked about being together in our senior years, and it's difficult to face these years without him. The one thing I do know is that my God has been and will continue to be with me every step of the way.

PRAYER
Heavenly Father, You are so awesome. Without You, I am nothing and can do nothing. With You, all things are possible. Thank You, my Father, my God, my All, for turning my darkness into light. In the sweet name of Jesus, amen.

Journal: If you are walking through dark days, write down what you are feeling—bad or good. Pour it all out and let Him comfort you and bring light to your darkness.

—Mary Etta Jackson

Take Aim and Pray

You, O LORD, keep my lamp burning; my God turns my darkness into light.
PSALM 18:28

It had been a rough day. I got out of my car, slammed the door and prayed—"Abba Father, give me something to turn the day from darkness to sunlight!" Before I could walk the few steps to the gate, God answered my prayers. Where I had just been tearful, He suddenly turned my tears into laughter! Had there been anyone with me, that person would have been convinced that I had totally lost it. And I had! I had lost the dark clouds! For the remainder of the day, I laughed and giggled like a young teenager—and I had fun! It was a memory that God pulled from the deep part of my soul that kept the sun shining in my life long after the sun had set that night.

Sending up arrow prayers to God in times of need is often all it takes to change an entire day. Try it—you may like it as much as I do.

PRAYER
*Thank You, Abba, that You are so in tune with me that an
arrow prayer is often all that is needed. Teach me to thank and
praise You as often as I ask You for help.*

Journal: How many things can you thank God for that show how He cares for you? Keep it simple. For example: the smile of a child, playful kittens, the song of a bird.

—Betha Jean Cunningham

Trust in God, Not in Riches

I rejoice in following your statutes as one rejoices in great riches.
Psalm 119:14

More than 20 years ago, Johnny and I were so broke that the requirement for doing something fun was that it had to be free. We learned to rejoice while sitting side by side on a big flat rock, eating a sack lunch and watching the sailboats in Galveston Bay, or watching the beauty of the sunrise or sunset, or the full moon on a starlit night. Even though we had never been poorer financially, we learned what it meant to be rich, really rich. We were rich because we had our health, a wonderful family and we could still work.

More than that, God taught us to follow Him and not the riches of this world. We learned how to manage our finances and how to give back to God that which was already His in the first place. We learned that the most important things—love, family and good health—had nothing to do with money. We learned that if we would follow God instead of trying to do things our way, He would take care of us.

Today, because we have learned what it means to follow His statutes, God has richly blessed us with a home on the water. I believe that He gave us this home because He knew we had learned what it means to follow Him and we would use the home to bless others. How about you? Are you trying to do things your way, or have you experienced God's blessings as you follow His wise laws?

PRAYER

Thank You, Lord, for teaching me what it means to follow Your statutes. Thank You for the hard times when I learn the most about You and Your ways.

Journal: Write about a hard time when God taught you what it means to trust Him and follow His statutes.

—Carole Lewis

What Money Can't Buy

I rejoice in following your statutes as one rejoices in great riches.

Psalm 119:14

Psalm 119:14 is one of those Bible verses that are easy for me to memorize but very diffi-cult to apply. As a matter of fact, I am so much a product of our consumer-oriented, have-it-your-way culture that I seldom think of following God's statutes as something to rejoice in, let alone a way to experience His riches. Following God's statutes runs against my nat-ural inclinations that consider riches as things that give me immediate gratification.

The key to unraveling this "obedience is great riches" riddle is found in what I per-ceive the world's riches can do for me. Jesus called the world's riches Mammon—that in which we put our trust. When I think of riches as things I put my trust in, I can begin to see how following God's statutes is great riches. The first memory verse I learned after joining First Place was Matthew 6:33: "But seek first his kingdom and his righteousness, and all these things will be given to you as well." When I made a list of "all these things" that I thought God might add to my life if I put Him first, it gave me great insight into what I considered to be riches!

Now I look at all these things that God has given me as a result of putting Him in first place in my life and I see a list of things the world's riches could never buy.

PRAYER

O Lord, help me this day to see joyful obedience as the key
that unlocks the storehouse of Your vast riches.

Journal: Make a list of all the riches you have received by putting God first in all things. Be creative, and don't limit your list to the things the world values.

—Elizabeth Crews

Trusting God with Our Finances

I rejoice in following your statutes as one rejoices in great riches.
Psalm 119:14

"If money was not a limiting factor, what would you do in the kingdom of God?" No matter how many times I asked myself that question, the answer was always the same. I would want to write in a way that would illuminate God's truth to give new understanding and produce changed lives. But my practical mind always short-circuited my heart's passion by reminding me that money was a limiting factor. No matter how great my God-given dream, the physical reality of my circumstances held me down. I found myself saying, "Yes, Lord, I know You are calling me to write, but right now I just can't afford to do that. One day I'll feed Your flock, but for right now there are bills to pay and children to feed and a career to pursue. Please excuse me, Lord; I have others things to do."

Then one day during my quiet time, Luke 5:11 hopped off the page and right into my lap: The disciples "pulled their boats up on shore, left everything and followed him." They left the security of their income source and obeyed Jesus' command. The Spirit was telling me that I needed to do the same. Once I said, "Yes, Lord," a series of events that only God could have orchestrated began to unfold. Today I am living my heart's passion and writing it down, because obeying God's statutes became more important to me than the illusion of the financial security the world calls riches.

PRAYER
O Loving and Gracious Lord, how faithful You are once I stop making
excuses and begin to do all You ask of me. Thank You for inviting me to pull
my little boat up on the shore, leave everything, and follow You.

Journal: Write about what you would do in the kingdom of God if money were not a limiting factor.

—Elizabeth Crews

Rich in the Lord

I rejoice in following your statutes as one rejoices in great riches.
Psalm 119:14

My home library is filled with volumes penned by the English preacher Charles Haddon Spurgeon, and I refer to them often. One of his works, now out of print, has a title that is almost longer than the book itself: *The Cheque Book of the Bank of Faith*. It consists of promises arranged for daily use. And yet that little gem continues to have a big influence in my life.

When I first acquired the book, I was a single mom, working full time to support four children. This was before laws were adopted to ensure that fathers contribute to the support of their children after divorce splits a family unit. So the task of providing for my children's daily needs fell squarely on my shoulders. At times the burden seemed more than I could bear. By the world's standards, there was barely enough money to cover our monthly expenses, let alone provide for the extras that children consider necessities!

It was during those lean years that the very great and precious promises of God made huge deposits into my bank of faith. Often, they were the only thing that got me from one payday to the next. Today, I rejoice, confident that when I make God and the riches of His Word enough, what started out as lack ends up with more than enough, and even provides leftovers!

PRAYER
Because You, O Lord, are my Shepherd, I have everything I need.
I rejoice because of Your faithful provision and great and precious promises that
contain a treasure that is more than sufficient for my every need.

Journal: When has God's great and precious promises provided for your needs in a way that seemed impossible?

—Elizabeth Crews

Forgiven and Restored

He who did not spare his own Son, but gave him up for us all—
how will he not also, along with him, graciously give us all things?

ROMANS 8:32

I work out in the weight room of our Christian Life Center at my church each morning and have made so many wonderful friends there. One friend has shared some of his life story with me on occasion about a painful divorce and separation from his two sons. Recently, he shared an incredible story of God's mercy and grace.

It seems that he was separated from his sons because there was a warrant for his arrest and he was hiding from the law. He told me that God impressed on his heart that he needed to face what he had done, so he asked for time off from work and went to the city where the warrant had been issued. He thought he was facing 10 years in prison for some felony offenses but found they had been dismissed over the years. As it turned out, he only had a misdemeanor warrant, for which he was given 18 months of probation and a fine of a few thousand dollars in restoration.

We praised God together that God had graciously forgiven him and restored his relationship with his sons, who have also forgiven him.

PRAYER
Thank You for giving up Your one and only Son so that we
could have eternal life. Thank You for graciously giving us all things
when we walk in obedience to You.

Journal: Are you hiding from something or someone? Write about it and ask God to give you the grace to do the hard work to make it right.

—Carole Lewis

The Rest of the Story

He who did not spare his own Son, but gave him up for us all—
how will he not also, along with him, graciously give us all things?
ROMANS 8:32

A few months ago, a friend came to my office and broke down as he shared "the rest of the story." He told how he had lost his sons, his family and friends because of a gambling addiction. After losing his job and his wife, who he said was "my best friend and the love of my life," he turned to gambling for comfort instead of seeking God.

The night before he came to my office, he had gone to the horse track and lost his entire paycheck, which was to last him for the next two weeks. His rent was due and he would be evicted if he didn't pay it that evening. I am not a person with the gift of mercy, but God spoke to my heart strongly and told me to give this man a certain amount of money. It was clear to me that it was not to be a loan but an unconditional gift of God's gracious love toward him. We prayed together and asked God to set him free from this gambling addiction.

I gave my friend a Scripture verse and asked him to learn it. A week later he proudly recited the verse to me in the weight room where we all work out. I knew that God's Word in his heart was the only thing that was going to heal this powerful addiction.

PRAYER
Dear Lord, since You have graciously given me so much,
help me graciously give back to Your children.

Journal: Do you have an addiction? Could it be food, shopping or the need for approval? Ask God to free you.

—Carole Lewis

The Heart of the Matter

He who did not spare his own Son, but gave him up for us all—
how will he not also, along with him, graciously give us all things?

Romans 8:32

When I came back to exercise after Christmas break, my friend with the gambling addiction shared that the school where he works as a custodian invited him to lunch on the last day of school before the holidays. After lunch, when he was ready to leave, one of the teachers said, "Don't go; we have something for you." They had found out that his TV had gone out and they presented him with a gift card for $120 to buy a new TV. I was so excited when he told me about this generous gift. But my friend said, "That's not all; there's more."

He shared that on the Friday before Christmas, one of the parents at the school called and asked him if he had used the gift card yet. He said that he had, and she replied, "Well, take the television back. I told my husband about you, and he wants his car dealership to give you a television." She asked him if he had a DVD player and said they wanted to buy one for him. She also asked for his clothing and shoe size because they were going to purchase a coat and shoes for him.

My friend was so overjoyed that he took the money from the return of the TV and purchased groceries to make Christmas dinner for the six men who live in his apartment building.

PRAYER

Dear Lord, thank You for graciously blessing my friend.
Help me bless others today as You have so graciously blessed me.

Journal: Is there someone who needs a blessing from you? Write his or her name in your journal and explain what you intend to do for this person today.

—Carole Lewis

Will There Be Enough?

He who did not spare his own Son, but gave him up for us all—
how will he not also, along with him, graciously give us all things?
Romans 8:32

On the bookshelf next to my prayer place there is a small picture of a crown of thorns. I keep it there to continually remind me of God's gracious provision for my every need— even those needs I am not aware of. With Paul, I can boldly declare, "While I was still a sinner—and totally unaware of my true condition—Christ died for me" (see Romans 5:8). And then, of course, Romans 8:32 follows that bold statement with a simple question: After God so graciously gave His Son on the cross, how can I doubt His provision for all those needs that don't cost Him the life of His son?

I am a product of the "not enough" mentality that came out of the Great Depression. Raised by parents who had experienced those lean years, I was reared in a home characterized by a scarcity mentality. Even now, Satan uses the fear of economic disaster to keep me from enjoying God's blessing. "Will there be enough?" is the haunting fear I continually battle. Even today, most of my concerns have their root in a deep-seated financial insecurity rather than in confident expectation of God's faithful provision.

Each morning, when I look at the picture of the crown of thorns and recite the words of Romans 8:32, I am reminded to trust that God will provide for all my needs, no matter how large or small.

PRAYER
Gracious and loving God, You did not spare Your own Son,
but gave Him up so that I might have eternal life.
Help me stop doubting and start trusting in Your love for me.

Journal: How does the fear of economic insecurity impact your life, and what symbol of God's love can you use to help overcome this fear?

—Elizabeth Crews

Unfathomable Love

He who did not spare his own Son, but gave him up for us all—
how will he not also, along with him, graciously give us all things?

Romans 8:32

Do you have anyone in your life that you love so deeply that you would die for that person? I do—my 18-year-old daughter, Ali. Since she was a little child, Ali has been obedient, sincere, hilarious and fun. Obedience and fun go a long way with me.

As I was trying to compose a prayer for a Bible study assignment, I happened to glance at a picture of Ali and the word "sacrifice" popped into my head. Would I allow my precious daughter to be tortured, mocked, abused and weighed down with the burden of the world's sin to save other people? No! And yet, did God love Jesus any less than I love Ali? Was it any easier for God to allow His precious Son to take that long walk up the hill, bearing an unfathomable burden so that you and I could live forever?

And what about Jesus—obedient, delightful Son, so loved by the Father? An innocent Lamb. He was butchered by those for whom He willingly and selflessly gave His life.

God loved each of us so much that He allowed His precious, obedient, innocent Son to bear unspeakable horrors. Which sacrifice was greater, the Son who paid the price—or the Father who had to watch?

PRAYER
Lord, You are a Father who has made the ultimate
sacrifice for me. How, then, can I doubt that You will also walk
with me through all the changes I need to make in my physical
and spiritual life? Increase my faith and trust in You, Lord.

Journal: Reflect on the sacrifice the Father and Son made for you, and then write about how it motivates you to make needed changes.

—Barb Lee

Teachable Moments

Therefore, since we are receiving a kingdom that cannot be shaken, let us be thankful, and so worship God acceptably with reverence and awe.
Hebrews 12:28

I have learned so much about God's character since the death of our daughter, Shari. I wrote the book *A Thankful Heart* because of all the things God has taught me. I am the most teachable in times of hardship, grief and loss. When life is going well, I just seem to coast, oblivious to what God might want to teach me.

One of the greatest things I have learned is that this life is not *it*! This life is but a blip on the radar screen. Our real life is found in heaven when we go to be with Him.

I have learned that the things that happen to me are not about me at all. Everything that happens is all about God and bringing glory to Him during those times.

I also have learned that others are watching to see if God is able to bring me through these hard times victoriously, just as I have looked for the same thing in the lives of others.

I have learned that thankfulness in the midst of a bad situation is the way I can worship God and show Him how much I love and trust Him to carry me through the painful times.

PRAYER
Dear Lord, thank You for teaching me about You and Your ways. Help me stand firm when the trials of this life try to shake my faith and trust in You.

Journal: Write about a hard time in your life and what you learned about God through it.

—Carole Lewis

Unconditional

Therefore, since we are receiving a kingdom that cannot be shaken, let us be thankful,
and so worship God acceptably with reverence and awe.

H e b r e w s   1 2 : 2 8

According to Henri J. M. Nouwen, the world's love is and always will be conditional. There will always be a requisite "if . . . if . . . if . . ." Because people place their identities in conditional love, they will become enraputured in the world's harsh and endless cycle of trial and failure.

Hebrews 12:28 reminds me that in sharp contrast to the "ifs" of the conditional love offered by the world, there is the "therefore" of God! I am receiving a Kingdom that cannot be shaken. This conditional, iffy world is not my home. And because I am not dependent on the world's agenda that tells me I am not enough, I am free to be thankful and to worship God acceptably.

I must admit that the word "acceptably" makes me squirm. I would like to think that I can worship God on my own terms. This is especially true when it comes to keeping the nine commitments of First Place. I find great joy and delight in the so-called spiritual commitments. But eating and exercising and keeping a CR (commitment record) are another story. The world's conditional "ifs" tell me that I can eliminate the things that don't suit me. God's "therefore" tells me that I cannot, because I am receiving a Kingdom that cannot be shaken. I am to worship God acceptably, and that means no "ifs," "ands" or "buts."

PRAYER
Sovereign Lord, You are worthy of all glory, honor and praise.
Today I will worship You acceptably to the best of my ability.

Journal: Explain how you are still hooked to the world's "ifs" rather than accepting God's "therefore" that frees you to give Him acceptable worship.

—Elizabeth Crews

Three Cs

*Therefore, since we are receiving a kingdom that cannot be shaken, let us be thankful,
and so worship God acceptably with reverence and awe.*
Hebrews 12:28

"I'm so fat." "I can't do anything right." "Today is going to be another awful day." "You-know-who always gets her way." The dreaded three Cs—criticism, condemnation and complaint—occupy my thinking too much of the time, causing hours of discontent and emotional distress.

Just the other day, I had fallen short of my health goals. Instead of choosing to be thankful for all the progress I'd made, and the fact that I was alive and breathing, I chose to criticize myself, condemn others and complain about everything. After a short time of this negative thinking, I found myself wallowing in the pit of despair. Somehow, I remembered that no matter what's happening right now, my future lies in a Kingdom that cannot be shaken.

God's eternal truth is the greatest reason to choose thankfulness any day, under any circumstance. No matter what the scale says or how the stock market performs, my kingdom in Christ remains steadfast. So today is a perfect day to worship God with reverence and awe. Nothing less is acceptable in light of His love, which He so freely extends to me. When I maintain an attitude of thanksgiving and worship, I wipe the dreaded Three Cs right off my lips. Thank You, Lord!

PRAYER

*O mighty God, You alone are holy and just. Your ways are perfect.
Your goodness is unfathomable, and You alone are worthy to
be praised. It is in Your Son's name I pray. Amen.*

Journal: What are some of your triggers that lead you to the Three Cs? Now, list all the things you are grateful for.

—Carol Van Atta

Glimpses of Kingdom Beauty

Therefore, since we are receiving a kingdom that cannot be shaken, let us be thankful,
and so worship God acceptably with reverence and awe.
Hebrews 12:28

Living in the country has definite advantages to living in town. We do not have street lights to subdue the beautiful sunrises, sunsets and full moons. Each evening, I hurry with whatever I'm doing so that I can witness what God has to offer in His sunset! There are never two alike—the colors are different as well as the design. Some nights He will put thin wisps of clouds in His artwork. Strange as it may seem, dust and smoke often provide some of the most beautiful sunsets. Just when I think nothing can top God's sunsets, I witness an amazing sunrise. I have been known to be late to an appointment because I stood on the front porch and watched God's handiwork as He began the day in spectacular color.

The nights that I seem to sleep the best are when a full moon shines and lights up my room. Sometimes I get out of bed to watch the critters move in the moonlight—especially if there is a light covering of snow on the ground.

As I enjoy each sunrise, sunset and full-moon-lit night, I stand in awe and reverence to think that as beautiful as each event is there will be no need of it in heaven, where His brilliance will outshine anything I have seen on His earth.

PRAYER
Abba Father, almighty God—thank You for the beauty of Your created
world displayed in the sun and moon. Thank You that as beautiful as they are,
what You have waiting for us will be even more breathtaking!

Journal: Use what you see in a sunrise, sunset or full-moon night as a time of worship of the Artist who created this beautiful world.

—Betha Jean Cunningham

Failing the Test

Always giving thanks to God the Father for everything,
in the name of our Lord Jesus Christ.
Ephesians 5:20

It seems there is always a time after I finish a book that God requires that I walk out the truths about which I have written. After finishing *A Thankful Heart*, Johnny and I went to California to see Johnny's oncologist. After the medical appointment, we drove up to Ventura for a meeting at Gospel Light, our publisher. While in Ventura, Johnny had a two-day bout of intense stomach pain but was better when it was time to fly home. Two weeks later, it happened again, and Johnny woke me at 2:00 A.M. asking to be taken to the hospital.

He had acute pancreatitis, necessitating removal of his gallbladder. During this harrowing time, I found that I totally failed to take the advice I had given in the book. Instead of giving thanks, I lived with the fear and dread that this illness was brought on because Johnny's cancer had spread to his gallbladder. In my mind, I played out having a hospital bed in our bedroom and went through the scenario of saying good-bye.

The gallbladder was removed, and Johnny healed nicely and hasn't had any more problems. Even though I failed the test, giving thanks was still the answer to my dilemma.

PRAYER
Thank You, God, that even when I fail to practice
what I preach, You still love me. Help me learn that giving thanks
is the answer to fear and anxiety.

Journal: Write about a time when your imagination ran wild. How did God bring you through it? Thank Him for His faithfulness.

—Carole Lewis

Lifestyle of Thankfulness

Always giving thanks to God the Father for everything,
in the name of our Lord Jesus Christ.
Ephesians 5:20

"Before I begin to sit down to write, I must first stand up and walk, and then kneel down and pray," reads the poster next to my computer—my personal-application adaptation of a quote by Henry David Thoreau. I made that poster when I began writing the Bible study *Choosing Thankfulness*, because I was going to have to learn to live a lifestyle of thankfulness.

Carole Lewis was writing the book *A Thankful Heart* at the same time I was putting the Bible study together, and we often compared notes on how the evil one was doing his best to keep us from walking the walk we were writing about! The more reasons we found for thanking God in all circumstances, the more ways our archenemy found to tempt us to question God's goodness and fall into doubt and despair.

That's when the "kneel down to pray" part of my homemade poster became the backbone of my writing. If I was ever going to walk the thankfulness walk, I was going to first walk it on my knees! That was also when I learned the value of the word "yet." "Yet I will rejoice in the LORD, I will be joyful in God my Savior" (Habakkuk 3:18). No matter what was going on, I learned I could be thankful because God loved me enough to send Jesus to be my Savior—the only reason I could possibly need to choose thankfulness today.

PRAYER
Thank You, faithful Father, for sending Jesus as my Savior so that
I can praise You regardless of what else is going on in my life.

Journal: List five things you are thankful for, and then turn that list into a prayer of thanksgiving.

—Elizabeth Crews

Thanking God—In Advance

Always giving thanks to God the Father for everything,
in the name of our Lord Jesus Christ.

Ephesians 5:20

It was the Sunday before Thanksgiving, and I had been asked to share a message with the "guests" of the DeKalb County Jail in Atlanta, Georgia. As I drove through the gloom of that rain-threatened evening and approached the foreboding structure that housed prisoners facing a dismal holiday, my attitude was lousy. What do you say to people who have little for which to be thankful?

Then God reminded me of Ephesians 5:20: "always [give] thanks." So, I began thanking God in advance for the opportunity to minister. I thanked Him for people willing to hear the Word. I also thanked him for a "congregation" that understood their neediness and were eager for a Word from Him. What a night! God moved in a wonderful way. It was the highlight of my Thanksgiving!

In First Place, I found the value of thanking God in advance for keeping His promises. Now, when I don't feel like exercising, I thank Him for the benefit that such exercise would produce. When I am tempted by the wrong foods, I thank Him for the power to resist such temptation. Thanking God in advance helps me to rely on His power and trust in His promises.

PRAYER

Lord, I thank You in advance for not asking of me what
You didn't place in me spiritually. May my character
be one of always giving thanks.

Journal: Make a list of things for which you are thankful. Then make plans daily not just to be thankful after the fact, but also to verbally give thanks in advance.

—David Self

Always a Reason for Thanks

Always giving thanks to God the Father for everything,
in the name of our Lord Jesus Christ.
EPHESIANS 5:20

Sometimes we are so caught up in the daily events of our lives that we forget to give thanks for anything. Three years ago, our suburban county was under siege from a sniper attack. For days, we never knew where or when the sniper would attack. Many people were gunned down as they were going about their daily lives.

My husband is a school bus driver, and he leaves for work very early each day. After he left for his daily run, I sat at my computer struggling to prepare a lesson on thankfulness for my First Place class that night. Suddenly, the silence was broken by my ringing telephone. I was frozen in fear because my husband was out there in the danger zone. Then I heard my husband's voice say there had been another shooting. The latest victim was a county transit bus driver. I fell to my knees and thanked God that my husband was safe and for comfort for the slain victim's family.

That day, I learned to give thanks as never before. The lesson I was preparing flowed with thankfulness as I recognized there is always something to be thankful for, even on the worst of days.

PRAYER
Heavenly Father, let me never forget to be thankful for
something each day. No matter how bad things seem,
let me recognize Your good works. In Jesus' name, I pray.

Journal: Where has God placed you today, and what can you learn from this situation? Make a list of things you are thankful for.

—Kathy Geehreng

God Things

Always giving thanks to God the Father for everything,
in the name of our Lord Jesus Christ.
Ephesians 5:20

I used to groan and moan about my weight struggles. I'd complain about every pound and every mistake I made along the way of my weight-loss journey. Every time I complained or wanted to beat myself up for a single bad choice, I opened the door to the enemy. I was allowing the devil to keep me knee-deep in despair and focused on my problems.

Now I choose instead to be thankful for everything. I see things not as good or bad things, but as God things—which He will use for my good and His glory, as He promises us in Romans 8:28. I'm thankful now that He used my weight to bring me to First Place and used First Place to teach me more about Himself. I remain focused on the good choices I make and don't dwell on the bad (or surely I would repeat them). When I choose to be thankful, God, in Christ, is given access to my heart. As He transforms my heart, He changes my actions and circumstances as well.

PRAYER
Heavenly Father, thank You that I can come in Jesus' name.
Forgive my anger, impatience, complaining, discontent and disbelief.
Give me a thankful heart and help me see all things with Your eyes;
change me from the inside out! In His Mighty name, amen.

Journal: How you act is based upon what you believe. What do your actions say about what is in your heart?

—Tammy M. Price

Celebrating Victory

Introduction

For some of us, the only time we celebrate is once a year on our birthday. This section is about celebrating the abundant life found in Christ Jesus. As the old hymn says, there is "victory in Jesus."

Our prayer for each of you reading this book is that you will begin to celebrate every moment of every day. Every morning you can celebrate that you are alive, that you have a roof over your head and food to eat. You can celebrate that you are able to work at a job and that you have a car to drive. As you celebrate the everyday things of life, you will begin to see all of life as one big celebration.

First Place reached its twenty-fifth anniversary in 2006, celebrating the thousands of lives changed through God's work in them. This section is based on the Bible study *Celebrating Victory* through Jesus, written by Elizabeth Crews. You can find Elizabeth's devotionals immediately following mine for each of the 10 verses in this section.

Victory is available for each of us today!

It's All About God

Not to us, O LORD, not to us but to your name be the glory,
because of your love and faithfulness.

Psalm 115:1

January 2006 was the kickoff month for a year of celebrating the twenty-fifth anniversary of the First Place program. We had many plans for the year—participation in the Houston Marathon on January 15 was the first planned event.

God, however, had bigger things planned than we could ever dream or imagine. My new book *Stop It!* came out the first of January, and my publisher hired a publicist to secure interviews on radio and television. The very first week of January, First Place was contacted by the PTL program and *Geraldo at Large* for a feature story.

Assuming that the publicist had arranged the interviews, we were shocked to learn they knew nothing about the contact from either program. You see, God knew all about our twenty-fifth anniversary, and He planned a year of celebration that would bring Him glory.

The greatest error we can ever make is to think that anything good that happens in our lives is because of us. Our God owns everything in this world, and He has the power to manipulate the affairs of humanity to give us whatever He desires. Our job is to remember that it's never about us, and always about Him.

PRAYER

Dear Lord, help me remember that You desire to bring glory to
Yourself through my life. Use me for that purpose, I pray.

Journal: Write about an experience that you know was caused by God and God alone. Give Him glory for His love and faithfulness to you.

—Carole Lewis

He'll Take It from Here

Not to us, O LORD, not to us but to your name be the glory,
because of your love and faithfulness.

Psalm 115:1

Several years ago, I was waiting to give a presentation to a group of esteemed religious leaders on the spiritual implications of addiction. But all I could think about was my stupidity in agreeing to address such a scholarly group! Sensing my distress, the program organizer came over and gave me a bit of much-needed advice: "Just remember, dear," she whispered, "whoever gets the glory carries the burden. If you want the glory, then keep on fretting about the results. But if you want to give the praise and glory to God, He will carry the burden for you." And of course, she was right. Once I took my mind off my own ability and began thinking about the One who is worthy of all glory and praise, the butterflies subsided. I knew I would not be giving that talk in my own strength, but in the power of His Holy Spirit. It was not about the eloquence of my words; it was about God's Word that would flow through me with power that day.

When I make my success in the First Place program dependent on God's love and faithfulness, rather than on my own ability to do it right, the same truth applies. All I am asked is to do the work and leave the results in His capable hands.

PRAYER

Sovereign Lord, You are faithful! All glory and honor
belong to You. Help me this day to be willing to give You the glory for
my success, knowing that You will do for me what I cannot
do in my own strength and power.

Journal: What needless burden are you carrying because you're not willing to give the glory to God?

—Elizabeth Crews

Sing His Praises

Not to us, O LORD, not to us but to your name be the glory,
because of your love and faithfulness.

Psalm 115:1

I love the book of Psalms! Having been a music teacher most of my life, praise and worship music speak to my heart in a very special way. I love beginning my quiet time each morning with psalms, praise songs and hymns. They express my feeling for God in a way that my own words cannot.

Psalm 115:1 is special to me because it sings of the desire of my heart. My prayer is that everything I say and do—all that I am or ever will be—will glorify God. Whenever I sing or speak or share with people, I pray that they will see God's love in me. He has done so many miraculous things in my life through First Place that it would take a book to share it all. But one of the things I love about the ministry is that our number-one goal is to put Christ first in every area of our lives and in everything we do.

His love is so amazing that we can't begin to comprehend its magnitude. He is always faithful. We can always depend on Him and His love to get us through whatever circumstances we face.

To God be the glory!

PRAYER
Lord God, I praise You; I love, honor and worship You.
May my life be pleasing to You and may You receive all the glory
for all You have done and are doing in my life today.

Journal: God loves to hear our praises. Write a song of praise to God in your prayer journal.

—Janet Kirkhart

Look to the Lord

Not to us, O LORD, not to us but to your name be the glory,
because of your love and faithfulness.

Psalm 115:1

I am always so amazed at the things God does. There have been many times when I've thought, *Wow, what an amazing way to answer that prayer! I would not have thought of that or been able to do that on my own!* Psalm 115:1 helps me focus on where all good, great and amazing things come from—God Himself.

Because of God's love and faithfulness in the past, I can look for Him to do great things for me in the present moment. When I remember His faithfulness and love, my faith remains in Him, not in my own ability or my circumstances. This renewed hope allows me to be filled with His Holy Spirit and remain in His Presence, where He promises to fill me with all good things. As I contemplate His glory, my joy breaks out into praise, and I desire to share with others all the great things He has done in my life! When I remember to give all the glory to God, I no longer expect to be filled with the world's elusive joy that comes from food, shopping or earthly relationships. Instead, I look to God, who deserves all glory and praise—He is the source from whom all good, great and amazing things flow!

PRAYER

Heavenly Father, today I praise You for all the amazing things You have done,
are doing and will do in my life. You are my giver of joy.

Journal: Is the fruit of the Spirit evident in your life? How might you be grieving the Holy Spirit?

—Tammy M. Price

Source of Our Significance

Not to us, O LORD, not to us but to your name be the glory,
because of your love and faithfulness.

Psalm 115:1

"Let not the wise man boast of his wisdom or the strong man boast of his strength or the rich man boast of his riches, but let him who boasts boast about this: that he understands and knows me, that I am the LORD, who exercises kindness, justice and righteousness on earth, for in these I delight," declares the Lord in Jeremiah 9:23-24. With those words, God continually invites us to examine the source of our significance.

It's so easy for me to fall back into the pit of self-sufficiency and the self-indulgent pride of boasting in my accomplishments and abilities. How quickly I forget that my personal relationship with the true and living God is the only thing I have to boast about—and even that relationship is not based on my ability or accomplishment but on God's love and faithfulness.

What is the source of my significance? Each morning, I ask myself that question so that I will never forget the One who deserves all honor, glory and praise. I did not choose Him; He chose me. And He calls me to bear fruit that will last as I daily die to self-sufficiency and sinful pride and remember who and what I would be were it not for God's faithful love at work in my life.

PRAYER

O sovereign Lord, I humbly acknowledge that even my ability to
understand and know You are a gift from You. It is only in and through
You that I can be a witness to Your faithful love, and exercise the
kindness, justice and righteousness that give You pleasure.

Journal: What is the source of your significance? Write down your answer.

—Elizabeth Crews

Losing It

So whether you eat or drink or whatever you do, do it all for the glory of God.
1 Corinthians 10:31

It puts a whole new spin on our daily activities when we begin thinking about whether or not they bring glory to God. For example, we are in the process of selling a lot that is attached to our property. One day our realtor e-mailed me for some information. I asked her to call me so that we could talk about the problem. She e-mailed me back and said that we could just handle it by e-mail and for me to e-mail her the answer.

I was furious and wrote a scathing e-mail back to her that, fortunately, I decided not to send. But I continued to be angry. Two weeks later, when she finally called me, I just let her have it over the phone. When I got off the phone, I was shocked at the level of anger I had displayed, and I was grieved that my conduct had not brought glory to God.

After receiving an e-mail of apology from the realtor, I had the opportunity to write back asking her to forgive me for my behavior. I am still grieved, and I'm praying that God will ultimately receive glory out of my loss of self-control.

PRAYER
*Dear Lord, my desire is to bring You glory today in
whatever I do. Remind me when I am tempted to eat, drink
or say something that won't bring You glory.*

Journal: Write about a time when something you said or did failed to bring God glory. Make it right if you have the power to do so.

—Carole Lewis

Potluck Pitfall

So whether you eat or drink or whatever you do, do it all for the glory of God.
1 Corinthians 10:31

"Oh, Lord, bless the hands that have lovingly prepared this food for our enjoyment," prayed the pastor before we began to shuffle through the church potluck buffet line. Had the pastor, a man who needed to lose about 100 pounds himself, been honest in his words, his prayer would have been about the hands that prepared this dietary disaster for our self-indulgence. And while I'm sure the intent of all the women who brought a potluck favorite that night (me included) was meant to be loving, in truth preparing food laden with fat, sugar and refined carbohydrates is anything but an expression of love and concern for the well-being of the eater.

Somehow a church potluck doesn't seem like the proper place to put on my prophet's robe and preach repentance! And yet I feel called to proclaim the truth of God's Word that tells us to eat and drink and do whatever we do to the glory of God. Faith and fitness continue to challenge the church of Jesus Christ, especially those of us who choose to make health and fitness part of the faith that puts Jesus Christ first in all things.

PRAYER
O Lord, You call me to eat and drink and do everything
I do to Your glory. Help me to be faithful to Your Word, even when
circumstances make it challenging to do so.

Journal: Think of some ways you can remain faithful to living a healthy lifestyle and still enjoy fellowship when it is centered around food.

—Elizabeth Crews

What's Your Motivation?

So whether you eat or drink or whatever you do, do it all for the glory of God.
1 Corinthians 10:31

After a weight loss of 60 pounds, I just stopped exercising, and my weight loss came to a standstill. I prayed, cried and even tried kicking and screaming a few times, but nothing worked. I felt as if my passion and power to make good choices and continue toward my 100-pound weight-loss goal was slipping out of my hands. I wanted to do it, but I just couldn't get myself going!

When I started First Place seven years ago, my motivation was to lose weight and be healthy. Although that did happen, somewhere along the way God replaced my desire to look good with the desire to be good and to know and please Him—through His power, of course. My motivation turned away from me and toward glorifying Him.

Yet now I couldn't find the will to exercise because I had somehow slipped back into my old thinking. As I stood in my kitchen one day, choosing my afternoon snack, I spoke 1 Corinthians 10:31 out loud. Then I asked myself whether an apple or a slice of Thanksgiving apple pie would glorify God. Like I even had to ask, right? As I sat down with my apple, it was as if the Spirit lit up this verse again. I am thankful that God uses our desire to lose weight to bring us to First Place; but once we're here, the ability to continue with the lifelong commitment must be fueled with the desire to glorify Him.

PRAYER
Heavenly Father, help me make good choices, stay committed and
have victory in every area of my life! May everything that I eat, drink, do,
say and think bring glory to Your name. Amen.

Journal: Ask God to convict you of any areas in which you need to refocus your desires and motivations to be about Him.

—Tammy M. Price

You're Being Watched!

So whether you eat or drink or whatever you do, do it all for the glory of God.
1 Corinthians 10:31

It seems that in First Place we think and talk a lot about what we should or should not eat and drink. Now, don't get me wrong; I know this is important to our health and physical fitness. It is also important to God that we take care of our body, His temple and dwelling place. However, 1 Corinthians 10:31 reminds us that it is important to God that *everything* we do should be for Him and for His glory. How we treat our bodies, how we treat other people and how we treat God show our love for Him. He wants our love for Him to be the motivation for all we do for His glory. Putting Christ first in everything will give Him all the glory.

We need to remember that others are always watching us to see if we walk the talk. Is everything we do and say bringing honor and glory to the Lord as people watch? My prayer today is that I will eat and drink and do all that I do in a way that brings glory and honor to God—my Creator, Sustainer, Redeemer and Friend.

PRAYER
Lord, I pray that people will see You in my life.
I want to honor You and bring glory to Your name.
May I always do "my utmost for Your highest."

Journal: Ask God to show you how to honor Him in your actions as you go throughout your day.

—Janet Kirkhart

Quoting Chapter and Verse

So whether you eat or drink or whatever you do, do it all for the glory of God.
1 Corinthians 10:31

Long before I joined First Place, Scripture memory was part of my spiritual discipline. Being a word person, it was easy for me to remember the actual Bible verses. I could even picture where the words were on the page of the Bible I regularly use for my study and Scripture reading. However, since I am not a numbers person, remembering the "address" for the verse was not easy for me. As a result, I had to use a concordance to find the verses the Holy Spirit brought to mind when writing or preparing to teach a Bible lesson.

Determined to find a way to tie the address to the verse, I decided to create a story or rhyme that would make remembering the address a word process too. First Corinthians 10:31 is an easy verse for me to associate with a story, mainly because "10:31" reminds me of Halloween (on 10/31), and Halloween is not a day when folks eat and drink and do all that they do for the glory of God. Now, instead of associating 10/31 with ghosts and goblins and jack-o-lanterns filled with candy, I remember that as a Christ-follower, I am called to eat and drink and do whatever I do to the glory of God.

PRAYER
Thank You, Gracious Father, for giving me Your Word.
When I hide Your Word in my heart, I am able to live my life in a way that
brings glory to You, rather than conform to the world's style of living.

Journal: Think of a story or rhyme that will help you tie the address (chapter and verse) to the words of Scripture you are currently learning.

—Elizabeth Crews

Only Through His Power

Finally, all of you, live in harmony with one another; be sympathetic,
love as brothers, be compassionate and humble.

1 Peter 3:8

First Peter 3:8 is one of those verses that hurts all the way through! Is it possible to live like this? I'm sure it is or this teaching wouldn't be in the Bible. The biggest problem I have in living out this verse is *me*! The older I get and the more I learn about myself, the more I know that it is absolutely impossible for me to live this way without God's help. But God can live this way through me!

If (and "if" is a big word) I give God control of my entire day, which includes my words, attitudes and actions, He is powerful enough to accomplish this verse in my life. On those days, I am astounded at how pleasant I can be!

Each of us, if we know Jesus, can choose to live a victorious life played out like the verse above. The Holy Spirit wants to help us when we are weak so that we can live in harmony, be sympathetic, love others and show compassion and humility. It just won't happen on a regular basis until we realize that we have no power in and of ourselves to do it alone. Praise God, He's bigger than we are!

PRAYER
Dear Lord, I'm asking You to take over and make
this verse real in my life today.

Journal: Write down the five attributes listed in the verse above and select the one you have the most trouble with. Tell God all about it and invite Him to come in and take over.

—Carole Lewis

Gift of Self

Finally, all of you, live in harmony with one another; be sympathetic,
love as brothers, be compassionate and humble.

1 Peter 3:8

One of the hardest lessons I have learned in my Christian walk is the difference between compassion and pity. Pity feels sorry for; compassion suffers with. Pity is about feeling superior; compassion acknowledges a common humanity that leaves me vulnerable to the same pain. Pity is being like the Pharisee who looked down at the tax collector and thanked God that, as one who religiously kept the law, he was exempt from the sins common to man. Compassion recognizes that we are all sinners before God. Compassion is humble enough to say, "Lord, have mercy on me a sinner," knowing that it is God's grace and not anything we have done that saves us.

What I have found is that when I can be compassionate and humble, I am much more effective than when I pity others and put myself in a position of superiority. Compassion requires that I love, that I enter into the other's pain. Pity allows me to judge from a distance. Pity sends a check; compassion joins in the suffering.

God didn't observe my plight from afar. When Jesus took on human flesh and entered into the human experience, He became our role model for living on Earth. We are to do the same for our brothers and sisters. Giving of self is hard work, but that's what you and I are called to do.

PRAYER

O Lord, it is by Your grace that I am saved. Help me to
extend the love of Christ, who entered into the process, to my
brothers and sisters in Christ today.

Journal: Think about a time when you confused pity with compassion, and talk to God about what you need to do differently in the future.

—Elizabeth Crews

Tears of Joy and Sorrow

Finally, all of you, live in harmony with one another; be sympathetic,
love as brothers, be compassionate and humble.

1 Peter 3:8

Both my daughter and daughter-in-law were pregnant during the summer of 2005. It was so exciting to learn they both were carrying boys and expecting delivery within one to two months of each other! Mandy delivered a beautiful, healthy boy, Andrew John Hassett, on July 21. There was so much love and celebration in our home, including many conversations about "the boys" as we anticipated Mary's delivery of the baby she carried. When Andrew died on August 15, it was emotional upheaval in our home.

Everyone mourned for Andrew, yet they also felt indescribable hope at the anticipation of another baby in the family, proving that life does go on and God is alive. We received that blessed assurance on September 21 when Thatcher Robert Van Den Hemel was born.

Our family is very close knit, compassionate and humble. However, this life-changing loss has altered the family dynamics in many ways. I pray that our family will one day soon be able to live in complete harmony with one another as we remember Andrew yet joyfully watch Thatcher grow up.

PRAYER
Dear God, thank You that even when we don't understand
Your ways, we can understand that You are faithful and give us
the strength to live in harmony with one another.

Journal: Do you need to show compassion to someone? How can you reach out in God's love and strength and be a living example of 1 Peter 3:8?

—PJ Bahr

Loving When It's Tough

Finally, all of you, live in harmony with one another; be sympathetic,
love as brothers, be compassionate and humble.

1 Peter 3:8

Twelve women of all ages and temperaments trying to get along in close quarters is not an easy task. Add to that the fact that these women were together in jail because of their drug and alcohol abuse and crimes.

I see these women every week. New ones come and go, but many are there for months. I have used 1 Peter 3:8 to challenge them to fill their otherwise boring days with reading and praying. I have told them how they can walk miles right there in jail and do workouts to expel some of their pent-up emotions. Six of the women responded to an opportunity to be baptized in jail. The week after the baptism, they came for Bible study. They were all smiles and told me how they had gotten together and made a paper Christmas tree and put it on the wall. One woman confessed that she had never had such good friends as those in jail; and although she was anxious to be released, she valued their love.

First Peter 3:8 speaks to all of us. We are to live in harmony in our churches and in our families and in our workplaces, showing one another sympathy, compassion and humility, regardless of our circumstances or individual situations.

PRAYER
Lord, I ask for harmony among the churches and the leadership
of our country. Help me to be humble and kind, forgiving others as
You have forgiven me. Help me to be more compassionate toward
people who are difficult for me to love.

Journal: Do you need to humble yourself toward someone and say "I love you" or "I'm sorry"?

—Bev Schwind

Behaving Like Adults

How good and pleasant it is when brothers live together in unity!
Psalm 133:1

Our grandson, Carl, just celebrated his twenty-first birthday. As I was thinking about how it seems like just yesterday that he was a baby, I remembered a time when he and his sister Katherine were riding in car seats in the back seat of my daughter Lisa's car. The two of them were just 17 months apart, and even though Katherine was the younger of the two, she had no desire to live in unity!

Carl started to cry. When Lisa asked him what was wrong, he said, "Katherine said she doesn't love me." Lisa said, "Carl, Katherine loves you; don't you, Katherine?" To which Katherine replied, "No, I don't!"

I know that many times, in God's eyes, we must look like those two toddlers. We know how to live in unity—we just don't want to do it! The only thing is that it's not nearly as cute when we're all grown up and still acting like babies.

Last week, a neighbor called and asked me to pray with her. She called a few days later to report that a miracle had taken place in her family. I was amazed at what God had been able to do when one of the people involved asked for help to bring unity to their family.

PRAYER
Dear Lord, I want to be a person who brings unity to every situation
in my life. Make me an instrument of Your peace today.

Journal: Write about an area in your life that needs peace and unity. Ask God to work through you to bring it about.

—Carole Lewis

Pleasing God, Not Men

How good and pleasant it is when brothers live together in unity!
Psalm 133:1

Being a people pleaser by nature, it's easy for me to read verses like Psalm 133:1 and see those words as a call to sacrifice God's truth in the name of pleasant fellowship and harmony. When I buy into that deception, I am living in a type of peace with my brothers and sisters, but I'm not living a life worthy of my calling. God first calls me to unity of purpose with Him; then He calls me to unity of purpose within myself; and finally to unity with my brothers and sisters in Christ who are also desirous of doing God's will. All too often I try to reverse that order. When I do, all my attempts at unity, no matter how well intentioned, end in discord and dissension. My allegiance cannot be split, even in the name of peace.

When given a choice between being a God pleaser or a people pleaser, it is so easy for me to fall back into my old codependent ways! It takes great effort to remind myself that my relationship with God *is* my first priority. Until I am faithful to God's plan and purpose and His present-day assignment for me, I am double-minded and divided—at odds with God and with myself! Only by being faithful to my calling in Christ Jesus can I have unity with other like-minded brothers and sisters.

PRAYER
O Lord, I confess that it is so much easier to be a people pleaser than a God pleaser. Today I will take up my cross and follow You, even though it is not the polite, popular or politically correct thing to do.

Journal: Write about a time in your life when you chose to be a God pleaser rather than a people pleaser.

—Elizabeth Crews

Conflict and Food

How good and pleasant it is when brothers live together in unity!
Psalm 133:1

Being Nana to 11-year-old twin grandsons is a continual challenge, and I am amazed at how different identical twins really are. It is indeed good and pleasant when Christian and Daniel are living together in unity. My grandsons have also taught me that living in a house characterized by chaos and discord is not conducive to healthy eating! Like many others who eat impulsively, I learned at an early age to manage anger and frustration by stuffing those unpleasant emotions with food. Rather than look for constructive ways to resolve conflict, my natural inclination is to reach for something to numb my emotions and soothe my jangled nerves. However, being faithful to the Live-It plan is dependent on my ability to deal with conflict in a God-honoring way.

Yes, it takes more time to stop what I am doing and work to bring peace, but in the end it is time well spent. Creating an atmosphere in which brothers and sisters live together in harmony is part of my daily commitment to eat and drink and do whatever I do to the glory of God (see 1 Corinthians 10:31). When I am a peacemaker rather than a conflict avoider, I am really taking care of the inner conflict that sets me up to sabotage my peace with God.

PRAYER

*Gracious God, help me to bring peace where there is discord so that
I will not be tempted to manage stress with food.*

Journal: What emotions are you stuffing down with food rather than working for peace and harmony that will bring glory to God?

—Elizabeth Crews

An Unforgiving Heart

How good and pleasant it is when brothers live together in unity!
Psalm 133:1

My friend was distraught as she talked about her dysfunctional family. One son had an unforgiving heart toward his only sister. The problem was his attitude, and although the son thought the problem was strictly between him and his sister, and that it didn't hurt anyone else, his unforgiving heart affected the entire family.

My friend went on to explain how she could never have all her children, grandchildren and great-grandchildren together at a family gathering. The unforgiving spirit kept them from enjoying good and pleasant times. And if the stress during good times together was noticeable, the stress was even more pronounced at funerals.

The son's bad attitude made the whole family suffer. What made the situation even more bizarre was the son's puzzlement that his sister's children were not as warm and friendly toward him as they used to be. The son was blind not only to how his attitude affected the family but also to how loyal his niece and nephews were to their mother. Where there is disunity in a family, everyone suffers.

All I could do was assure my friend that I would pray for her son to find not only peace and happiness in his life but also that his willingness to forgive would allow the rest of the family to enjoy a great family reunion!

PRAYER
Abba, Father—true happiness comes only from You.
Open my eyes to see that an unforgiving heart will prevent me
from receiving Your forgiveness.

Journal: When has unforgiveness caused disruption in your life and in the lives of others?

—Betha Jean Cunningham

Personal Pollution

Do not defile the land where you live and where I dwell,
for I, the LORD, dwell among the Israelites.
NUMBERS 35:34

We hear a lot today about the pollution of our environment and the carelessness and greed that destroy our rivers, lakes, streams and land. Even though most of us don't intentionally pollute, we, and the generations to follow, will bear the consequences.

Bringing this verse a little closer to home makes us think about areas of our lives that we do have control over and the ways we pollute our own personal space. The same two things that pollute our land pollute our bodies. We exhibit carelessness when we refuse to exercise regularly, eat right or make time to spend with God. We exhibit greed when we eat or drink too much of anything that will pollute our bodies.

After Tamara Fisher lost 140 pounds in a year, she said, "I did all the First Place commitments every day, because I wanted to prove that the program would not work for me." Instead of failing like she had done so many times before, she found that she began having victory. As she ate healthy foods and exercised, her body became healthier. As she spent time with God every day, her soul prospered. Today, Tamara has a brand-new body and a restored environment, because she made the decision to stop being careless and greedy.

PRAYER
Lord, I want to stop polluting this body of mine. Help me, I pray, to fill
my body with only those things that will stop the pollution.

Journal: Write about your personal pollution problem. Is it food, drink, cigarettes, sex or polluted relationships? Ask God to restore your personal environment and give you victory.

—Carole Lewis

A Pleasing Aroma

Do not defile the land where you live and where I dwell,
for I, the LORD, dwell among the Israelites.

NUMBERS 35:34

My early morning quiet time was shattered by what sounded like a fight between two cats; however, the pungent smell that immediately filled the air quickly told me that one of the creatures was not one of the neighborhood cats! A frightened skunk had left its mark in a very powerful way. Not only had it sprayed the air, but it had also sprayed our wooden deck and the back wall of the house.

Days later, I was still trying to get rid of the smell. Room deodorizers didn't cover up the stink. Washing the deck and exterior walls with plain water didn't eradicate the odor. Only after several thorough scrubbings with bleach did the stench begin to subside.

How often are we as offensive as that frightened skunk when we feel our safety and security are in jeopardy? We defile the place where God dwells by using language and actions every bit as offensive to God as the odor of a skunk is to us. Yes, we are trying to defend our territory. We feel that our personal boundaries have been violated and we must defend ourselves against the intruder. Yet God calls us to be a pleasant aroma, a fragrant offering (see Numbers 28:8). Only when we trust Him to be our shield and defender can we spread the good news, not a defiling stench, in all we say and do.

PRAYER

O sovereign Lord, when I trust in You, I do not need to
be rude and offensive. When I trust in You, I can be a pleasant aroma,
even when I am surrounded by things that threaten my peace.

Journal: Talk to God about your need to trust in Him so that when your safety and security are in jeopardy, you do not defile the place where He dwells.

—Elizabeth Crews

Lord, *Close* My Lips

Do not defile the land where you live and where I dwell,
for I, the LORD, dwell among the Israelites.
NUMBERS 35:34

When I came back to the Lord at the age of 34, I brought with me plenty of baggage. Jesus tore down many of the strongholds in my life; I was able to stop smoking and cussing, and I shook my worldly ways and attitudes. The only thing I couldn't get the victory over was my weight and my food addiction. I knew there was a root deep in my soul that needed to be uprooted.

When I came to First Place and began to dive into the Scriptures, the Holy Spirit revealed the root. One of my problems was what was coming out of my mouth. Being critical of God's people polluted the land instead of bringing health and healing. My critical mouth placed an enormous amount of stress on my spirit. Then I used food as my drug of choice to ease the stress caused by my critical mouth.

My mouth had become a swinging door—an entrance for food and an exit for the harsh, critical spirit that caused me to overeat. When the Spirit revealed the truth to me, I began to use my mouth to pray. I asked the Lord to go to the bitter root of criticism and destroy it with the blood of Jesus. Over a period of time, praise the Lord, I was given the victory.

PRAYER
Help me, O Lord, with my mouth. My prayer today is that
I will use my mouth only to bless others.

Journal: Do you find yourself standing at the refrigerator looking for a food fix after your mouth has gotten you in trouble? Ask the Lord to reveal the root of bitterness in your soul and help you uproot it.

—Beverly Henson

God's Cleanup Crew

Do not defile the land where you live and where I dwell,
for I, the LORD, dwell among the Israelites.
Numbers 35:34

Partygoers flock to San Diego beaches on the Fourth of July. But the next day, the results of the patriotic celebration are bottles and cans and garbage left behind by careless folks who thought only about the pleasure of the moment. It takes work crews and volunteers longer to restore the beauty of God's creation than it took for the partygoers to defile it!

It's easy for my judgmental self to exclaim, "How could they possibly do such a thing?!" It's always easier to see the speck in someone else's eye than to take the log out of mine! But when I look closely at myself, I am guilty of the same crime. Before coming to the First Place program, I defiled my body, this place where God's Holy Spirit dwells, through careless eating and neglectful self-care. Rather than considering the consequences of my out-of-control eating, I thought only about the pleasure of the moment. Rather than taking the time to exercise and spend quiet time with God, I focused on what gave me temporary relief.

I am cleaning up the mess those careless years produced. Praise God it will not take me longer to undo the damage than it took for me to defile what God created and called good.

PRAYER
Sovereign Lord, thank You that You have given me an opportunity
to restore the damage created by my foolish actions. Forgive me for defiling the
place where You live by out-of-control eating and negligent self-care.

Journal: What are you doing that defiles your body? What can you do today to begin repairing the damage?

—Elizabeth Crews

Letting Go of Chocolate

Do not defile the land where you live and where I dwell,
*for I, the L*ORD*, dwell among the Israelites.*

NUMBERS 35:34

I typed the words of Numbers 35:34 and then went to get some hot tea and have a little talk with Jesus about what He might have in store for me to write. Seems that Jesus had a little talk with me when I got caught, literally, with my hand in the chocolate can! Yes, I have a large can of chocolate in my kitchen. Now, chocolate is allowed in reasonable amounts, but it seems that today the reasonable amount became unreasonable. So God took my detour to the can of chocolate and decided to teach me a valuable lesson. I was reminded that I came from dirt—a top grade of dirt—and I was not taking care of the land from which I was created! Ouch! I had not been prepared for that!

As a result, I have spent the last hour asking forgiveness and trying to be more conscious of what I'm doing. I have indeed polluted the land! God used the story I was going to write as a story I needed to live. The can of chocolate will be moved from the small table in the kitchen, and I will have a few extra pounds to shed by sweating and proper eating!

PRAYER
Abba Father, thank You for loving me so much that You sometimes
correct me on the spot! Thank You for making me aware in the strangest
of ways when I need to take better care of myself.

Journal: In what ways are you neglecting to take care of yourself?

—Betha Jean Cunningham

Come as You Are

Come, let us bow down in worship, let us kneel before the LORD our Maker.
Psalm 95:6

Kneeling has the same effect on me as journaling; it is impossible to forget that I am praying when I do either one. When I kneel to pray, the pressure on my knees reminds me of why I'm there. When I journal my prayers, the pressure of the pen on paper does the same thing.

For some, the idea of kneeling creates a feeling of dread and raises the questions, If I get down on my knees, will I experience tremendous physical pain? Will I be able to get back up?

I believe this verse is talking about the attitude of our heart more than the position of our bodies. God wants us to meet with Him every day so that He can become our friend. He created us, and He alone knows the mess we can make of our lives. God invites us to come to Him in an attitude of worship so that He can meet us there and heal our hearts.

Today is a brand-new opportunity to worship God our Maker. It doesn't matter how we come. It only matters that we come.

PRAYER
Dear Lord, I acknowledge that You made me and You know me well.
I want to worship You because You are worthy of my worship.

Journal: Tell God about the areas of your life that need a more personal relationship with Him.

—Carole Lewis

Worshiping God by Caring for Our Bodies

Come, let us bow down in worship, let us kneel before the LORD our Maker.
Psalm 95:6

Many Christmases ago, I spent a lot of hours making life-sized Raggedy Ann dolls for my two young daughters. Loving stitches went into the clothes, and I spent hours stuffing and forming the arms, legs, torsos and heads. I carefully braided the yarn hair and embroidered the facial features. By the time I put the finishing touches on those two dolls, I felt as though I had given birth to two more children. As a matter of fact, being pregnant took a lot less time and energy that the crafting of those Raggedy Ann replicas!

Yet, at ages two and three, my daughters did not understand what a labor of love those dolls were. Consequently, they left Raggedy Ann lying around, sometimes outside in the yard. They pulled their dolls' hair, took off their pretty ruffled dresses and stuffed the dolls in places they were never meant to go. In less time than it took me to put the dolls together, my little "dolls," Sheri and Lauri, managed to destroy the work of my hands.

While their childish carelessness was understandable, I am without excuse. I fail to acknowledge God as my Maker when I refuse to care for His precious handiwork—the body He knit together to accomplish His plan and purpose for me. A major way that we can kneel before God is by caring for the body He created and called good.

PRAYER
Creator God, You are my Maker. Today I will bow down and worship You by humbly acknowledging that I am Your handiwork and that self-care honors Your creation.

Journal: Think about a time when you made something special for someone, only to have that person carelessly destroy your handiwork. How do you think God feels when you don't care for your body?

—Elizabeth Crews

OCTOBER 26

Worship—It's About Him!

Come, let us bow down in worship, let us kneel before the LORD our Maker.
Psalm 95:6

A few years ago, I was seated in the Sunday morning contemporary service with a critical attitude. Although my intent when I got up that morning was to fully participate in corporate worship, somehow in the short distance from my house to the church, there had been an unholy shift in my heart. I had gone from being a worshiper to a worship critic. That morning, there was something wrong with everything! The band was out of sync. I didn't like the song selection. The PowerPoint operator was too slow changing the words on the screen. The soloist was off key. You name it, I criticized it. Finally, I said to the Lord, "Lord, this music is not doing anything for me." I will never forget what He so clearly spoke to my heart: "It's not for you."

You see, I had missed the point! Worship is to God and for God. He is the focus. He is the center of attention. He is the audience. Worship is ascribing to God the glory and the honor due His name, declaring His worth, His power and His might. Worship is praising Him for the works of His hands and thanking Him for His faithfulness, His undeserved favor, His tender mercies and His unfailing love. When we worship God, everything else fades from view as His holy glory blazes like fire before our eyes.

PRAYER
Right now, Lord, in this place, we worship You. We exalt You.
We magnify You. We declare Your name and rejoice in Your righteousness!
You are the holy One. We fall down at Your feet and proclaim together,
"You are worthy, O Lord, our God, to receive glory and honor
and power, forever and ever." Amen.

Journal: Have you had a similar "worship critic" experience? What did God reveal to you?

—Eulalia King

Bow Down in Spirit

Come, let us bow down in worship, let us kneel before the LORD our Maker.
Psalm 95:6

The book of Revelation is full of accounts of the saints, the four living beings and the angels falling down to worship our Lord. While on Earth, we have a perfect time to practice what we will get to do in heaven. But let's be practical about falling down to worship. Ever get the feeling that you wanted to fall down and worship while driving on a crowded freeway or in the mall when you witnessed something that made you want to shout and praise God? I have a feeling that if we are sincere in our praise and worship, we can bow down in our spirit and not actually fall face down.

I have had arthritis since young adulthood (many years ago now), and in the last few months, I have had vertigo. So believe me, falling down is all too easy, but getting up is another story! If I'm in the car or home alone, I belt out my songs of praises at the top of my lungs. But if I'm in a crowd, I hum or sing to myself. I enjoy practicing for the real thing now!

PRAYER
Abba Father, may my praise, whether in my spirit or out loud,
be acceptable to You as a dress rehearsal for heaven. Help me to worship
You with abandon, no matter where I am.

Journal: What verses or songs of praise do you need to memorize to worship your Maker regardless of where you are or what you are doing?

—Betha Jean Cunningham

Consolation of His Word

Speak to one another with psalms, hymns and spiritual songs.
Sing and make music in your heart to the Lord.
Ephesians 5:19

Scripture memory is one of the nine First Place commitments. We memorize one verse each week and say it when we get on the scale to weigh in. For many years, I only made the basic commitment. I memorized the verse enough to be able to say it when I weighed in, but I never thought about it again. I didn't get the verse to descend the 18-inch distance from my head to my heart.

Practice makes a song or a memory verse go to the heart. That is why the First Place Scripture memory CDs are so powerful. They use music to teach Scripture and music that stays with us forever. A friend gave me a set of four CDs that included all the old songs I had learned as a child. I was surprised that I still knew every word of those songs my mother sang more than 50 years ago!

Memorizing Scripture and listening to Christian music will plant spiritual truths deep in our hearts for God to use to bless us and to bless others. It's important to memorize Scripture and Christian songs when we are emotionally upbeat. Then, when we are down or even depressed, God can remind us of the truths of what we already know in our hearts.

PRAYER
Dear Lord, help me memorize Your Word and listen to music about You so that You can bring it to my remembrance when I need to hear from You.

Journal: Write about a time when God came to you through a Scripture or a song you had memorized.

—Carole Lewis

Careful Speech

Speak to one another with psalms, hymns and spiritual songs.
Sing and make music in your heart to the Lord.
Ephesians 5:19

According to the traditional English nursery rhyme, Little Tommy Tucker sang for his supper, but my CR (commitment record) would certainly look a lot different at the end of the day if I had to sing for my daily bread! Because I am always curious about the origin of quaint sayings and phrases, I went to the Internet to see exactly what "singing for supper" meant. It turns out this was a colloquial term commonly used to describe orphans who were often reduced to begging, or singing for their supper, in order to survive. How different those unfortunate children were from those of us who are called to speak to one another with psalms, hymns and spiritual songs because we have been adopted into the family of God!

And just as my CR would look a lot different if I had to sing for the food I eat, my life would look different if I was careful to observe the words of Ephesians 5:19. So much of my conversation with others, even with my brothers and sisters in Christ, is anything but "making music to the Lord." As a matter of fact, my words are all too often more off-key than the notes I try to sing. Just as I must closely watch what goes into my mouth, so I must monitor the words I speak. Both my eating and my speaking are part of my profession that Jesus Christ has first place in my life.

PRAYER
Thank You, gracious Father, for accepting me into the family of God. Today keep me mindful of the food I eat and the words I speak. May they be honoring to You.

Journal: Which is more problematic for you, the food you eat or the words you speak?

—Elizabeth Crews

Written on Your Heart

Speak to one another with psalms, hymns and spiritual songs.
Sing and make music in your heart to the Lord.
Ephesians 5:19

Caroline had a stroke when she was 85, and this former choir director and organist could no longer speak. I met Caroline when I worked as a nurse in the nursing home. She could not form words to carry on a conversation, but when we sang and played hymns, she automatically opened her mouth and the correct words poured forth. Caroline had the words stored in her mind from many years ago, and praising the Lord with her heart was an automatic response. A big smile would spread across her face as she "walked" in this familiar territory.

The deaf enjoy making music in their hearts as they read and sign the words to songs and hymns. They feel the beat of the music and smile as they praise God with their hearts.

Why does the writer tell us to speak to one another in this manner? Because there is nothing but a lifting and positive response when we do.

PRAYER
Father, I thank You for the written Word. Help me to hide it
in my heart so that in my waking hours, I can praise You.
And as I fall asleep, Your Words will be in my heart.

Journal: If you were unable to speak, would the voice inside you be able to think on the things of the Lord, on His Word? If not, start memorizing today!

—Bev Schwind

A Radical Commitment Record

Speak to one another with psalms, hymns and spiritual songs.
Sing and make music in your heart to the Lord.
Ephesians 5:19

Of the nine commitments in First Place, the most challenging one to me is the daily food diary. Having to write down everything I eat, whether it's half of a banana or an ounce of smoked turkey, requires focus and discipline. But I recognize the food diary's inherent value because it helps me see where I am and what changes I must make to get to where I need to be. But what would happen if in addition to keeping a diary of everything we put in our mouths, we had to keep a diary of everything that came out of our mouths—a virtual word diary that would detail the "who, what, when and where" of every murmuring word, every mean-spirited comment, every remark laced with sarcasm and every syllable soaked with pride?

So how do we speak to one another with psalms, hymns and spiritual songs? How do we sing and make music in our heart to the Lord? The answer is found Ephesians 5:18. We have to be filled with the Holy Spirit. He is the fountain of living water springing up in our souls. When we are filled with Him, He floods our heart with so much mercy and grace, healing and hope, strength and courage that we burst forth in psalms of praise and hymns of faith to God our Father—and to each other.

PRAYER
Oh Lord, even now, fill me with Your Spirit so that the words
of my mouth speak life and bring light!

Journal: During the last 24 hours, are there any words you may have spoken to a Christian brother or sister that brought death and not life? What is the Holy Spirit urging you to do?

—Eulalia King

In Times of Trouble

But thanks be to God! He gives us the victory through our Lord Jesus Christ.
1 Corinthians 15:57

I have a friend who is going through a time of trouble right now. Her husband is out of work. Their utilities are turned off more than they are on. This couple is behind on their bills to the point of losing their home. Her marriage is in trouble and her kids are struggling. Where is the victory in this situation? How can this family be thankful?

There is victory in the fact that all four people in this family know Jesus. Because the Holy Spirit lives inside of them, God's power is available to them. Their marriage can become stable again if they will both turn to God instead of looking at their circumstances. There is victory in the fact that they are all healthy. There is victory in living in a country where anyone can turn his or her situation around through hard work and prayer.

All of us can make a bad time worse by complaining and casting blame. But giving thanks for what we can starts us on the path to victory.

Jesus Christ is our victory, and for this we can be thankful. Times of trial and testing come to everyone, but our attitude about those trials is everything. No matter how hard the times we are going through, our God can bring us through them.

PRAYER
Dear Lord, help me look at my problems through Your eyes today.

Journal: Write about the trials in your life, thanking God that victory is certain because of Jesus Christ.

—Carole Lewis

Symbol of Victory

But thanks be to God! He gives us the victory through our Lord Jesus Christ.
1 Corinthians 15:57

As I write this devotional, it is Advent season, and my Advent meditation this morning invited me to place a wreath on my door as a symbol of the victory over sin and death that is mine in Christ Jesus my Lord. How strange that I had never thought of a wreath as a symbol of victory before.

Until this morning, I had thought of the wreath that graces my front door as a symbol of welcome to friends and neighbors and to the Spirit of the living Lord who, through the presence of others, would visit my humble home this Christmas. And while keeping the Advent tradition of lighting the candles on an Advent wreath has long been a part of my journey to the manger each year, now I will look at the wreaths in my home with new eyes.

I welcome Jesus Christ as the One who wears the victor's crown and who invites me to share in His triumph by trusting Him as the only One who can give me victory over sin and death—those things that separate me from God and destroy His desire to give me life in abundant measure.

PRAYER
*Jesus Christ, You came to give me victory and reconcile
me to the Father. Thank You for Your goodness to me.*

Journal: Draw a wreath and decorate it with victory medals, one for each victory you celebrate today.

—Elizabeth Crews

A Daily Deal

But thanks be to God! He gives us the victory through our Lord Jesus Christ.

1 Corinthians 15:57

Our victory was won through Jesus on Calvary and in the empty tomb. But before then, in Luke 9:23, Jesus commanded us to follow Him—but to death? Paul writes in Romans 12:1, "Take your everyday, ordinary life—your sleeping, eating, going-to-work, and walking-around life—and place it before God as an offering" (*THE MESSAGE*).

Oswald Chambers, in *My Utmost for His Highest*, wrote, "Not—I am willing to go to death with You, but—I am willing to be identified with Your death so that I may sacrifice my life to God." He tells us to give up the things that bind our lives to enter into a relationship with God and sacrifice our lives to Him.

Before First Place, I wanted to go directly from denying myself to following Jesus in victory; but I could never get there. I realized I had been trying to follow Him without the cross. I had expected victory without suffering, inconvenience or hardship. I learned that First Place is neither a quick victory nor a once-and-for-all plan, but a daily deal. Daily we are called to set ourselves apart from our old habits and replace them with healthy ones. This new life of victory through our Lord Jesus Christ becomes my daily offering before Him. Thanks be to God!

PRAYER

Lord, it is my desire to follow You, but first show me how to deny myself today. And help me to take up my cross daily so that I may follow You.

Journal: In what way do you deny yourself, and is it done as an act of worship?

—Judy Marshall

Victorious Finish

But thanks be to God! He gives us the victory through our Lord Jesus Christ.
1 Corinthians 15:57

When I participated in my second 5K (3.10 mile) run-walk race, it was a very cold December Sunday afternoon. A light snow fell, so fitting for a race called the Snowflake Sprint.

Although I had trained and eaten healthy foods in previous weeks, I felt that I had let God down. I had gained weight again. My legs and feet felt heavy and ached with shin splints and cramps. I talked to God and I prayed in the Spirit as my feet pounded the pavement. I didn't want to be in last place! I asked God to take away the pain so that I could continue. I asked God to make my feet fly, to quicken my walking pace.

Little did I know that 183 runners and 22 walkers had finished, and there were 4 walkers behind me. The Lord had answered my prayers! As the finish line clock came into view, I realized that I had just shaved 4 minutes off my personal time! And I was not last—I had just placed third in my age group. Yes! Thanks be to God, for He has given me *His perfect victory*!

PRAYER
Dear Lord, thank You for life and breath. Thank You for my personal victories that are possible only because of Your life in me.

Journal: Walking is a great way to enjoy the beauty of God's creation and a great time to have a chat with Him. After your walk or other exercise today, record your conversation with God.

—Janet Boyles

Learning Perseverance

But thanks be to God! He gives us the victory through our Lord Jesus Christ.
1 Corinthians 15:57

Trying to lose weight and get more physically fit is hard work! It's a daily battle for me—or maybe I should say a full-fledged war. But I am in this for life! I refuse to allow Satan to stop me as I seek God's strength and power for the victory.

My First Place story is about learning perseverance. I have been in First Place for 15 years, and I love the program. God has changed my heart and made me a different person from the inside out. He has worked in the emotional, spiritual and mental areas as He works to make me more Christlike. But the physical area has been the most difficult for me.

God has taught me so much during this time. I continue to thank and praise Him daily for the work He continues to do in my life. My journey has been one of losing, gaining and beginning again. But during all of this, God has been faithful. He has always been there, ready to forgive my disobedience and give me another chance to begin again. My walk with my God has proven to me that I can trust Him and that even though I may lose a battle or two (and believe me I have), together we will win this war!

PRAYER
Thank You, Lord God, for the victory You promise to give me every day when I ask. Thank You for Your mercy and grace.

Journal: List the battle or battles for which you need victory. Give each one to God and allow Him to fight each battle for you.

—Janet Kirkhart

God Is at Work

The LORD has done great things for us, and we are filled with joy.

Psalm 126:3

Henry Blackaby, in his book *Experiencing God*, talks about spiritual markers—points in our lives when we've seen God at work. Henry says that when we don't see God's hand, we need to go back to those times when we recall how God blessed us, fought a battle for us or mightily answered a prayer, and our faith will be strengthened as we wait to see His hand again. Because He has done great things for us in the past, He is also working to do great things in our present and in our future.

I am filled with joy as I recall the great things God has done for me. He came into my life when I was a 12-year-old girl, and my life has never been the same. He rescued me from the pit of sin and self and restored my life, working miracle after miracle since the day in 1984 that I sold out completely to His Lordship in my life. He has strengthened me during times when I was weak, and He has filled me with hope and peace when I have been filled with grief and pain.

The Lord has also done great things for you. Even if you don't feel like that's true today, trust that it is and move forward in faith.

PRAYER
*Dear Lord, fill my heart with joy today as I go back to those spiritual
markers in my life when I saw Your hand at work.*

Journal: Write about the spiritual markers in your life.

—Carole Lewis

Discovering Hidden Places

The LORD has done great things for us, and we are filled with joy.
Psalm 126:3

When Carole Lewis asked me to write a devotional for each of the 10 memory verses in the four Bible studies I have written for First Place, I was hesitant to say yes. The problem with writing these 40 devotionals wasn't in the writing; it was in the content. These were to be personal-experience devotionals rather than my usual didactic teaching style. Sharing personal stories is not my forte!

In retrospect, I can see that the Lord has done great things for me as I have been faithful to do the task at hand. As my personal words have appeared on the page, I have seen parts of me that have been hidden from my sight. Much like I have when writing prayers in a journal and reading Scripture out loud, I have seen God interact in my life through these words, and I am filled with great joy as I reflect on what the Lord has done for me in the writing of my story. If you aren't already keeping a daily prayer journal, start today so that you can experience the great joy of growing closer to the Lord and reveling in how He meets you right where you are.

PRAYER
*O Lord, You have done great things for me, and I am
filled with joy. Thank You for always meeting me where I am
and for allowing me to watch You work in my life.*

Journal: Write part of your personal story and ask God to show you parts of yourself that until now have been hidden from your awareness.

—Elizabeth Crews

Putting the Scale in Its Place

The LORD has done great things for us, and we are filled with joy.
Psalm 126:3

When you step on the scale each week, do you roll your eyes, groan and begin making excuses if the number tells you you've gained weight? Do you let that number on the scale affect your mood for the remainder of the day? Is it affecting how you respond to your family members and coworkers? Are you letting the scale be the final judge about how well you have or haven't done during the past week in your journey to give Christ first place in your life?

As a First Place member for several years, I know how discouraging it can be to have the scale record a weight gain. As a new First Place leader, I wanted to encourage the members of my group when they faced the scale and give them a proper perspective about what should influence their attitude.

Instead of letting the scale determine your attitude, remember something from the previous week that filled you with joy. For example, did you exercise? Did you do your Bible lessons? Did you write in your prayer journal? Don't let the scale tell you that you've succeeded or failed. True victory is already yours in Christ Jesus!

PRAYER
Thank You, Father, that I can recall many wonderful things that
You have done for me. I look forward with joy to seeing Your hand in my life.
Thank You for being a God who loves me in spite of what the scale says.

Journal: Spend some time writing your thanks to God that in Christ Jesus, He has a different way of viewing your efforts.

—PJ Bahr

Attitude of Gratitude

The LORD has done great things for us, and we are filled with joy.
Psalm 126:3

Yesterday, I was wiped out. I was sad at the death of an elderly friend, discouraged at learning that another friend's cancer had returned and frustrated from trying to teach a class of students who had given me their silence and their attention for exactly 10 minutes. I hadn't followed my Live-It plan, and I was angry at myself.

When two friends came over to walk with me, I started to fill them in on my complaints. As I was talking, I listened to myself and felt ashamed. I had left all those issues at God's feet in my daily prayer time earlier that day. To change tack, I said, "Hey, let's take turns saying what we're thankful for." My friends were surprised and a little skeptical, but they decided to humor me. What started out slowly and hesitantly turned into spontaneous outbursts of gratitude and even some accusations of "Hey, you took *my* turn." "I'm thankful for a warm bed!" "Flannel sheets!" "Family!" "My Savior!" "Night sky!" "Prayer!" "Healthy eating!" "Opportunities to encourage others!"

As we rounded the corner toward home, I had once again gained God's perspective on my life. Thankfulness can do that to a person.

PRAYER

Lord, please forgive me when I focus on the complaints
of life rather than on the great things You have provided for me.
Cause me to have a grateful heart in all circumstances. Thank You for
the many ways You take care of my every need, Father.

Journal: Make a list of 10 things God has provided for you and then write a simple prayer of thanksgiving.

—Barb Lee

Wear Your Joy

The LORD has done great things for us, and we are filled with joy.
Psalm 126:3

"You say you're a Christian? Please let your face know!" I laughed when I read this on a church sign while driving home from the grocery store. Although meant to be humorous, the saying packs a powerful message for us. Does our joy in the Lord show on our faces? When unbelievers are around us, do they want what we have? Can they see our joy? Do we have thankful and grateful attitudes, or do we whine and complain about everything?

I used to be a chronic complainer. I often found myself joining in when my friends and family complained about everything from the weather to the high cost of prices at the grocery store. I realized through studying God's Word that ungratefulness has no part in a Christian's life. It's hard to be joyful while complaining about things. Likewise, I am learning that it's hard to complain while praising the Lord and being joyful!

We have so much to be thankful and joyful about! Regardless of our circumstances, the fact that we are saved by grace alone should be enough to fill us with joy. Add to that all of God's great promises and His blessings and provision for us. He has done great things for us and we should be filled with joy, simply because we belong to Him!

PRAYER
Father, You have blessed me with so many wonderful things.
Help me speak words of praise and thanksgiving and not complaint.
Give me a grateful attitude and a joyful spirit in all circumstances.
In Jesus' name, amen.

Journal: Write a prayer, praising God for the blessings He has given you.

—Joni Shaffer

Every Day Is a Gift

The end of all things is near. Therefore be clear minded
and self-controlled so that you can pray.

1 Peter 4:7

When my husband, Johnny, was diagnosed with stage-four prostate cancer in 1997, I was anything but clear-minded and self-controlled. The cancer had already spread to his lymph system and to his bones, and he was told that he would live one to two years.

Well, the doctors might as well have said one to two days, because I came unglued for a week. I couldn't stop crying and I couldn't pray. After several days of this kind of behavior, I realized that the end of Johnny's life was no more imminent than that of anyone else's. Our lives are all in God's hands if we know Jesus personally, and none of us is going anywhere until God calls us home.

It has been more than eight years since that diagnosis, and Johnny is still alive. He still has cancer, but we both face it clear-minded and self-controlled so that we can pray. Cancer has been a gift in many ways because when you have a disease that brings a diagnosis of imminent death, you start really appreciating every part of life—both the good and the bad.

Most of us take our lives, our loved ones, our possessions and our freedom for granted and only really know their worth when we think we could lose them.

PRAYER
Dear Lord, remind me of the things that are really valuable in life
and help me not to take anyone or anything for granted.

Journal: Write about what you value.

—Carole Lewis

Preoccupied with Food

The end of all things is near. Therefore be clear minded
and self-controlled so that you can pray.
1 Peter 4:7

Ironically, I find it is often the goal of accomplishing my to-do list that keeps me from being clear-minded and self-controlled so that I can spend quality time in prayer.

Before I joined First Place and kept a daily food record, thoughts of food kept me from spending time with God in prayer. I would wonder how much I was going to eat that day, what I needed to buy, when I would shop, how much time I needed to prepare all the items on my menu and how good it was all going to taste. Food had become my preoccupation, the thing that took up valuable space where God's Spirit longed to dwell. Food kept me from doing the one thing that had the power to break the vicious cycle: pray.

When I write down my food choices, I am free from the compulsion of thinking about food. Writing it down gets it out of my head and onto the paper and allows me to be clear-minded and self-controlled—so that I can pray! Instead of obsessing about my relationship with food, I have time to think about my relationship with God!

PRAYER
Gracious God, help me to keep You first in all things so
that I can focus on my relationship with You rather than obsess
about how to satisfy the desires of my sinful nature.

Journal: Talk to God about the things that keep you from being clear-minded and self-controlled.

—Elizabeth Crews

Be Prepared

*The end of all things is near. Therefore be clear minded
and self-controlled so that you can pray.*

1 Peter 4:7

Here I sit, propped up in bed wearing three layers of clothing, gloves, stocking hat and with several blankets on the bed. We had an ice storm last night and have been without electricity and telephone for six hours. We may have a few hours left on our cell phones. Although we don't have many ice storms in this part of the South, we do get alerts when winter weather could be approaching. I chose to ignore the alerts and failed to prepare this time.

I can see out across the fields of ice and white trees. Constantly I hear the crash of tree limbs—sometimes the noise is so loud that you know the limbs are hitting something besides the ground. In my yard are three large trees very close to the house. But their limbs are not a threat to our roof because they were recently pruned to nearly stumps. Thank goodness my husband prepared in advance for the possibility of an ice storm.

We know that it's more than a possibility that Jesus is coming. But because there will be no advance alerts when He returns, we are called to take seriously that His return is near and to live the disciplined life, watching and praying.

PRAYER
*Forgive me, Lord, for the undisciplined seasons in my life.
Thank You, Father, for the opportunities to learn the disciplined life.*

Journal: Are you all that you want to be when Christ returns? Talk to God about undisciplined areas of your life.

—Sybil D. Smith

Making Excuses

The end of all things is near. Therefore be clear minded
and self-controlled so that you can pray.

1 Peter 4:7

We are now nine hours into no electricity or telephone. The outside temperature is still 30 degrees, but the inside temperature is dropping. Freezing rain is falling again and blowing against my window. I no longer have a clear view to the outside. I continue to hear crashing tree limbs. It's getting darker, and I now have candles burning.

My husband has managed to get a vehicle out, chatted with neighbors and is thinking about our driving south to our son's house for the night. However, there are several iced inclines to navigate to the main roads. I need to prepare for staying here through the night and also for driving out of the area. Both options have serious risks.

This day is filled with uncertainty about creature comforts, but there is a much deeper uncertainty that everyone must face. People want to know that life has meaning. And they yearn to know what awaits them in eternity.

I wasn't prepared for the ice storm, and I'm living the consequences of not getting our supplemental heat source repaired. I can make excuses for not following through on healthy choices and delay reaching my goals. But dare I risk letting someone fail to prepare for eternity because I was their bridge to Christ and something in my life has kept them from seeing Him in me?

PRAYER
Lord, I have accepted Your Son as a gift. Let me give as
a gift what I have received as a gift. Remove from my life anything that
is preventing a clear vision of those perishing around me.

Journal: How does Jesus want you to live in preparation for His coming?

—Sybil D. Smith

Moment by Moment

The end of all things is near. Therefore be clear minded
and self-controlled so that you can pray.

1 Peter 4:7

As I started to gather some items for traveling to my son's house, I also placed candles and flashlights in strategic locations around the house.

Just as dusk was setting in, I looked out one of the windows toward a nearby town. Suddenly I saw three lights twinkle on. Up to that point there had been much uncertainty about staying or leaving for the night.

I marched to the other end of the house, and my husband came in from the garage to tell me he had the camp stove operating. He felt we should stay at home. Then the telephone rang!

Four hours later, our electricity came on. A newscast revealed that many people had been stranded on the roads, some stopped by trees that had toppled onto their cars.

Going through the ice storm was an hour-to-hour event. Some days, normal living is like that. Being diligent with our commitments moment by moment will bring protection for today as well as clear-mindedness and strength for tomorrow.

PRAYER
Thank You, Lord, for Your faithfulness to see us through
difficult days. Thank You for protecting us from harm when we
are unaware of what lies ahead.

Journal: What areas of your life need the protection that practicing a disciplined life can bring?

—Sybil D. Smith

Start Living

Introduction

The book *Stop It!* came about because of a Bob Newhart sketch I saw on television. Comedian Bob Newhart played a psychologist with a unique knack for solving people's problems. In this sketch, a woman came to him with a very troubled state of mind and told him she had a fear of being locked in a box.

Bob asked her if she had ever been locked in a box. "No," she replied. Bob then said, "If you've never been locked in a box, then you aren't going to be locked in a box. STOP IT!"

The sketch went on with each problem the woman had being answered with the same two words: "STOP IT!" After the sketch was over, I realized there is great power for all of us in the use of those two words.

We must first stop doing the things that are destroying our lives. After we stop destructive behaviors, we are then able to start doing the things that will propel us forward to victorious living.

Elizabeth Crews wrote the Bible study *Start Living* as a resource to help us stop our destructive behaviors that are keeping us stuck. The 10 Bible verses Elizabeth chose for the study are in this section. Elizabeth graciously agreed to write a devotional for each of these verses, and you will find her writing right after my devotional for the verse.

You will be blessed as you learn what it means to STOP IT! and start living.

Stop It!

*Blessed is the one who reads the words of this prophecy, and blessed are those who
hear it and take to heart what is written in it, because the time is near.*

Revelation 1:3

I had so much fun writing the book *Stop It!* It took a lighthearted approach to talking about the things we must stop doing before we can start doing the things that will propel us forward. The Bible is full of things we need to stop doing and things we need to start doing.

Today's verse tells us to stop putting off reading our Bible. Reading God's Word is the commitment I have struggled with the most since moving to Galveston Bay. I drive 45 miles into Houston every morning, and it seems that I am always running late when it comes to reading my Bible. I make time to do my Bible study and to pray, but reading my Bible is the way God speaks to me. If I miss it, I have missed a crucial component of my quiet time.

This year, I was able to purchase CDs of the Bible for half-price after Christmas, and I have been listening to the Bible on tape every day as I drive into town. What a blessing! As I have listened to the Gospels of Matthew, Mark, Luke and John, I have felt like I know the writers personally, because I've listened to the different way each one tells the same story.

If you, like me, are putting off reading your Bible, today is the day to *stop it!*

PRAYER
*Thank You, Lord, for giving us Your Word in written form
and for speaking to me when I read it.*

Journal: Write about a time when God spoke to you from His Word. What Scripture did He use?

—Carole Lewis

Reading Out Loud

*Blessed is the one who reads the words of this prophecy, and blessed are those who
hear it and take to heart what is written in it, because the time is near.*

REVELATION 1:3

One of the ways I use my God-given gifts at the church where I worship is by serving as
a liturgist, the one who reads the Word of God during the worship service. Before each
Scripture reading, I am instructed to say, "Listen carefully, this *is* the Word of God." After
a brief pause, I begin reading God's Word in a clear, expressive voice that allows the hear-
ers to take in the Word as it was meant to be taken in: through audible sounds that can
be heard with the ears of the heart.

As part of the training process to become a liturgist, I was asked to read Scripture
aloud for 20 minutes every day during the 6-week class I was attending. To my amazement,
I found that as I listened to myself read, words and passages that I had never "heard" before
became clear. And not only did my present moment hold awareness, but I also found that
my words echoed in my being throughout the day.

As a result of that experience, I now read Scripture out loud as part of my daily devotion time. I begin by saying the words, "Listen carefully, this *is* the Word of God." Then I
read out loud so that the words can go into my ears and be taken into my heart without
my mind running interference.

PRAYER
*O Lord, Your Word is truth. Today I will tell myself
the story of Jesus and His love.*

Journal: Write about how you can read, hear and take to heart the Word of God so that
it becomes a living reality in your life.

—Elizabeth Crews

Keep Your Eyes on Jesus

*Blessed is the one who reads the words of this prophecy, and blessed are those who
hear it and take to heart what is written in it, because the time is near.*

Revelation 1:3

Raising four children as a single mom was the greatest challenge God ever gave me. My continual challenge was finding ways to communicate so that they would listen to my words and take them to heart. Much like God's children who hear His voice and then do as they please, my children learned at a very early age to let my words go in one ear and out the other faster than I could speak them.

But there was one type of word they always listened to: the way I lived my life before them. The nonverbal messages I gave Sheri, Lauri, Jeremy and Zachary back in the days when I was struggling with my own Christian walk impacted them more than all the good lessons I tried to verbally teach them! How it grieves my heart to see my children falling into the same muck they saw me fall into over and over again as I tried to do things my way rather than conform my life to God's Word and will!

Praise God there are no contradictions between His Word and His actions! Jesus Christ came to teach us by example. When we look to Him, we see God in action—the Word made flesh—who invites us to learn from Him. When we keep our eyes on Jesus and take Him into our heart, we will not be led astray.

PRAYER
*Loving Father, when I look at Jesus, I see the fullness of Your Word in human flesh.
Today I will keep my eyes on Him, for He is the way, the truth and the life.*

Journal: Write about a recent time when you looked to Jesus, the Word made flesh, and followed His example.

—Elizabeth Crews

Heart Knowledge

Blessed is the one who reads the words of this prophecy, and blessed are those who
hear it and take to heart what is written in it, because the time is near.
Revelation 1:3

One of the goals of alcohol and drug inpatient treatment is to connect those in early recovery with a 12-step program that will support their continued recovery after they leave the treatment center. To that end, patients are bused to outside meetings several times a week. Of course, treatment facility counselors accompany them on these outings, and being given "meeting duty" was one of my favorite assignments. Listening to the simple, practical, down-to-earth wisdom of men and women with many years of sobriety was food for the soul for this woman who lives in her head much too often! Sayings like "keep it simple," "one day at a time" and "easy does it" grounded and made real the addiction recovery theory I'd studied in textbooks.

One evening, an old gent with more than 50 years of sobriety gave me a simple visual explanation of my difficulty. He talked about the 18-inch drop that must occur before head knowledge becomes heart knowledge—before the words we hear can be taken to heart and made part of our daily practice.

PRAYER
Gracious God, thank You for simple illustrations that give
meaning and substance to spiritual truth. I want to take Your Word
into my heart and make it part of the very fiber of my being as head knowledge
becomes heart knowledge that leads to a new life in You.

Journal: What knowledge about God hasn't yet made the 18-inch drop to your heart? Ask God to knit that truth into your heart in a very practical way.

—Elizabeth Crews

Listening with the Heart

Blessed is the one who reads the words of this prophecy, and blessed are those who hear it and take to heart what is written in it, because the time is near.
Revelation 1:3

There are three key phrases in this Scripture that jump out at me: "reads," "hears" and "takes to heart." Many times we hear and read, but we don't take His Word to heart. I recall that when I came to First Place in July 1997, I "did" First Place with what I had read and heard. I was faithful with my head but not my heart.

That all changed in February 1998, when I attended the First Place conference in New Orleans. I found myself sitting beside and talking with Dr. Dick Couey, who gave me a plan to get me on track. I heard him with my head, but my heart didn't want to listen. He told me that God would love me just like I was—at 310 pounds—or *I* could make the changes. This touched my heart. In the past, every diet I had ever been on involved a pill, a shot, a supplement or some other gimmick to do the work for me. When I failed, I could always blame the diet "whatever." This time I went home and took to heart what the Lord had been telling me in First Place. The secret to my success came when I took the knowledge the Lord had given me and rooted it in the soil of my heart. Thank You, Lord!

PRAYER
Lord, help me realize that my blessing comes not just from head knowledge but also from reading, hearing and taking it to heart.

Journal: In what areas of your life are you faithful with your head but not your heart? Write about what you want the Lord to help you take to heart.

—Beverly Henson

Welcome Jesus Inside

Here I am! I stand at the door and knock. If anyone hears my voice and opens the door,
I will come in and eat with him, and he with me.

REVELATION 3:20

Growing up, I vividly remember the picture hanging in our church depicting Jesus standing outside a big wooden door, knocking. It was explained to me that the door symbolized
my heart and that when Jesus knocked on the door of my heart, I was the only one who
could open it because there was no handle on the outside of the door.

I opened the door of my heart and invited Jesus to come in when I was 12. I remember
the day as if it were yesterday, even though it has been 52 years since that day. For each of us,
there is a time when we must be the one to open the door of our hearts to Jesus. I love the
fact that God gives us the choice to open the door or not.

If you have never asked Jesus to come into your heart, you can do it right now. Simply
tell Him that you know you are a sinner and you believe that Jesus died on the cross for your
sins and rose again after three days. Ask Jesus to come inside and make your life brand-new,
and He will do it. It's really that simple. If you haven't ever done that, I'm praying that you'll
do it today.

PRAYER
Dear Jesus, I'm so glad I opened the door of my heart to You.
Because of You, my life is full of joy and peace.

Journal: Write about the time when you asked Jesus to come into your life, and what He
means to you today.

—Carole Lewis

Will You Answer the Door?

Here I am! I stand at the door and knock. If anyone hears my voice and opens the door,
I will come in and eat with him, and he with me.

Revelation 3:20

It was a blustery night, and I was tired. But I had promised to deliver some supplies to a family in my neighborhood, so I called to let them know I was on my way, loaded up the car and began the five-minute drive to their home. As I pulled up in their driveway, I could see the lights on inside the house, and their dog began to bark. I thoroughly expected that when the dog announced my arrival, they would come out and help me unload the boxes. But no one came, and I began placing the boxes on the front porch. Certainly by the time I was through they would appear!

After unloading the last box, I knocked on the front door. I could hear the TV blaring and people laughing and talking, but no one came to answer the door. I rang the door bell several times. When I tried calling them on my cell phone, the call immediately went to a voicemail system. After about five minutes of trying to make a connection, my Christian charity had dwindled to anger. *How could they treat me like that?* After I went out in the cold for them, they didn't even have the courtesy to answer the door!

That's when I remembered the many times Jesus had stood outside in the cold, knocking on the door of my heart—but I had been too busy to open the door and let Him in.

PRAYER
O Lord, I repent for those times I left You standing outside
the door of my heart because I was too preoccupied with lesser
things to let You in. Please forgive me.

Journal: Write about a time when you left Jesus standing outside the closed door of your heart because you were too busy to hear His voice and invite Him in.

—Elizabeth Crews

He Chose You

Here I am! I stand at the door and knock. If anyone hears my voice and opens the door,
I will come in and eat with him, and he with me.

Revelation 3:20

As a single woman, I can think of no better dinner date than Jesus. I can only imagine how it would feel to sit across the table from Jesus, looking into His eyes and have Him look deeply into my eyes, and have Him really listen to me. I can only imagine how it would be that no matter what size I am, He would be proud to be with me and be seen with me. I can only imagine how it would be to sit across the table from Him and feel like a princess or the homecoming queen I never was. I can only imagine how difficult it would be to leave the table when our meal is over.

The good news is that I don't have to imagine. I am a Blood-bought child of the King who by faith dines with Him every meal. I am His precious princess and bride. I don't have to imagine; all I have to do is open the door and He will come in and dine with me. I can hear His voice now, saying, "Here I am!"

PRAYER
Thank You, Jesus, for knocking on the door of my heart and
choosing me to sit at Your table. I am learning to savor each
moment with You. Thank You, Lord, for first loving me.

Journal: Write the conversation you would have with Jesus if you were sitting across the table from Him.

—Beverly Henson

Only a Prayer Away

Here I am! I stand at the door and knock. If anyone hears my voice and opens the door,
I will come in and eat with him, and he with me.

Revelation 3:20

Many years ago, my husband accepted a job that required a move away from family, friends, church, home and a job I enjoyed. Surely this was not the plan God had for us! Didn't He know we had moved several times in just a few years, and that I wanted to stay put?

Soon after the relocation, we found a wonderful church and made new friends. They didn't replace the ones we had left behind, but God put just the right ones in our path to make us feel welcome and become established in a new town.

Why do we ever doubt that God has our best interests at heart? Even though I missed our family and old friends, we soon found that our two children were in superior schools, and we were able to buy a new house on a wooded lot on a quiet cul-de-sac.

There will be days when everything seems useless and impossible. The temptation to give up will be almost overwhelming. It is in those times of total desperation that we need to call out to the Lord. He will strengthen the hearts of those who call upon Him. The periods of despair will pass; the temptations will subside. However, the Lord's loving support will never pass away.

PRAYER

Heavenly Father, we know that one of the First Place
commitments is prayer. You want us to call on You, whatever the
circumstance. Help us be faithful in prayer. Amen.

Journal: What does it mean to call on the Lord when times are good? When times are rough?

—Judy Dorn

"Jesus with Skin On"

Here I am! I stand at the door and knock. If anyone hears my voice and opens the door,
I will come in and eat with him, and he with me.

REVELATION 3:20

To me, my friend Shari is "Jesus with skin on." She brings Jesus' teachings to life for me. The way she lives reflects Jesus' love, day in and day out. She also challenges me to search my heart, to ask questions, to study God's Word and to find the truth for myself so that my faith has a solid foundation. She models Jesus' teachings and makes it easier for me to understand and apply them in my life.

Jesus is God with skin on. Just as I have learned more about Jesus by spending time with my friend Shari, I can learn more about God by spending time with Jesus. Knowing Jesus is God's way of showing me who God is and how I can live in a way that is pleasing to Him. By having a close relationship with Jesus, I grow in grace and knowledge. But even more important than being God with skin on, Jesus is my Redeemer, the One who came to Earth to save me from my sins so that I might enjoy a loving, personal relationship with Him.

Jesus stands at the door of my heart and knocks, wanting to come in and fellowship with me. Today I will open the door and welcome God with skin on into my heart-home so that I can learn to be Jesus with skin on in the lives of others who have yet to encounter Him.

PRAYER
Holy Father, grant me wisdom and persistence so that I might
apply Your truths in my life and exemplify Your love to others as I become
Jesus with skin to those who need to learn more about You.

Journal: How can you be Jesus with skin on to someone today?

—Susan Johnston

The Bible Is Talking to You!

Do not merely listen to the word, and so deceive yourselves. Do what it says.
J a m e s 1 : 2 2

Many times, when I'm sitting in church listening to the Word of God, I hear it for some-body else. I secretly think, *I hope Susan's here today and hears that! She really needs it.* If you do the same thing, I have two words for you (and for me): Stop it!

God has a word for us every time we hear the Bible read or we read it ourselves. Until we stop listening to the Word for someone else, we will never begin doing what it says. This verse is telling us that we deceive ourselves when we think we don't have the same problems others struggle with. I know that I gossip, complain, criticize and get angry from time to time. By thinking that the Bible is speaking to someone else, I accuse that person of something I am guilty of myself.

In the *Stop It!* book, I wrote about Cindy, who read the Bible and thought it was only speaking about her husband, Chuck. She blamed Chuck for everything wrong in their marriage. Only after learning to hear the Bible for herself was God able to heal her marriage.

PRAYER
Dear Lord, help me stop listening to Your Word and thinking the message is for someone else. Help me listen and do what it says.

Journal: Tell God about the person or persons who need His message when you listen to or read His Word. Ask God to help you stop doing that and start taking to heart the message yourself.

—Carole Lewis

A Listening Problem

Do not merely listen to the word, and so deceive yourselves. Do what it says.

James 1:22

It is so easy for me to confuse listening with hearing. I say I want to hear God's voice, and I make time each day to sit in silence. But listening is not about the ability to use my external ears—it is a matter of listening with ears of the heart. Each day, I must remind myself that the Latin root of the word "listening" is *obedire*, which is also the root word of "obedience." When I say I am listening to God, but I'm not obeying what I hear Him say to me, I am deceiving myself. Jesus put it this way: "Why do you call me 'Lord, Lord,' and do not do what I say?" (Luke 6:46). My problem is not with hearing but with listening. I know what God wants me to do but I just don't do it!

Most often, what I don't do is record my food choices and portions on a consistent and daily basis. After all, I know what I'm eating. "Why should I write it down?" is the excuse I use most often. But obedience is not about selective listening; it's about doing everything God wants me to do. God doesn't want me to be unaware. He wants me to tell myself the truth, which means keeping an accurate CR rather than conveniently forgetting those things that don't quite fit into the boxes. Today, I choose to listen—to obey. I hope that you do too. Blessed is the one who reads the words of this prophecy, and blessed are those who hear it and take to heart what is written in it, because the time is near.

PRAYER

Lord, You continually ask me the question, "Why do you call me 'Lord, Lord' and do not do what I say?" Today I will hear and obey.

Journal: Write about how you hear but don't really listen. Be sure to include what you intend to do about your "inner ear" problem.

—Elizabeth Crews

Don't Just Stand There

Do not merely listen to the word, and so deceive yourselves. Do what it says.

James 1:22

First Place has developed some practical and godly principles to follow, as well as some incredible tools to use. The handy-dandy food journal is one such tool. When I'm discussing filling in the blanks, checking off the little water squares and sharing the practicality of this tool with others, it seems so much simpler than actually getting down to the nitty-gritty of recording my own eating choices. Okay, so I'm being a bit dramatic. Or am I? How can something so simple suddenly become so difficult when it's time for me to pull out my pen and scribble "extra French fries" on the lines across my card?

Sometimes we tend to enjoy talking about accountability, reading about it and planning for it better than actually following through and doing it. When I step backward into a mode of procrastination and even denial by somehow convincing myself that recording the minor details of what I just ate isn't that important, I need to acknowledge the big red flag waving the message that it's time to stop the deceit. Just knowing the truth isn't enough. We must learn to act on the truth. Is it time for you to actually do what your program tells you to do?

PRAYER

Dear Lord, please help me stay on track with my program
by applying the principles and utilizing the tools You have so generously provided.
Thank You, Jesus, for giving me the strength to move forward and accomplish the good
works You have prepared for me to complete this day. In Jesus' name, amen.

Journal: In what ways do you get so busy researching how to live a more balanced life that you fail to actually put into practice what you're learning?

—Carol Van Atta

Out of the Word, Into the World

Do not merely listen to the word, and so deceive yourselves. Do what it says.

James 1:22

Several years ago, I was taking a long-term Bible study whose underlying theme was "Get out of the Word and into the world." The general assumption among the class members was that we would all start leading other Bible study groups, but that was not where I felt called. When I finally applied as a volunteer in my local hospital, I learned that my position would be in the emergency room on Friday evenings. Wow, that was going to be a challenge! I worked full-time in an office. My Friday evenings were usually spent at home with my hubby and a pizza, exhausted and collapsed in front of the TV. But I accepted the challenge and began the training. I learned the technical aspects of the job, but there seemed to be so much more calling to me. I kept thinking about our Lord saying, "Whatever you did for one of the least of these . . . you did for me" (Matthew 25:40).

And there was more. For the past seven years, I have spent nearly every Friday night in the ER doing whatever tasks are required; but more important, I get to spend time with the patients and their families, making them comfortable in nonmedical ways, such as holding their hands and praying with them. I usually continue to pray for them throughout the week. I have received far more than I've ever given. Now I come home after an 18-hour day energized by my evening in the ER.

PRAYER

Lord, show me the areas where You need me to serve. Let me be a doer and put my faith into action. Get me out of the Word and into the world.

Journal: Spend some time talking to Jesus today, asking Him where He wants you to serve others. Then listen for His answer.

—Kathy Geehreng

Do What It Says!

Do not merely listen to the word, and so deceive yourselves. Do what it says.
James 1:22

The last four words of this verse can be used as the daily pep talk I give myself. Well, maybe not daily, but on a regular basis. Why? Because even though I listen to God's Word and His teachings, even when the words are still fresh on my mind, I begin deceiving myself, and my heavenly Father, by not doing what it says. In addition, I am disobedient to the teachings of First Place. I know the Live-It plan—I teach it to others weekly. It is a daily battle in my life to do what I know I need to do. Every day I have to turn every aspect of my life over to God.

I tell my group members that they are not alone in their journey. I experience the same struggles they do. My advice to members is that when they feel they can't make it one more day in First Place, they should just stop, whisper a prayer, listen to the Word hidden in their heart, take a deep breath and do what it says.

PRAYER
Lord, today I want to do more than merely listen to Your words.
My desire is not to deceive You or anyone else with my inaction
but to glorify You by doing what Your Word says.

Journal: Take time today to listen to God's Word and record the Scripture verse. Then express what the verse means to you.

—Betty Lacy

Passing the Test

*As has just been said: "Today, if you hear his voice, do not harden
your hearts as you did in the rebellion."*
Hebrews 3:15

In 1979, my mom and I took the trip of a lifetime. We were part of a choir that toured parts of Europe, and we were privileged to travel to England, Scotland, Ireland and Wales over a 14-day period. We sang 14 concerts, one a day, and met many believers along the way.

Our nearly perfect trip was marred by only one thing. Toward the end, one of the leaders informed us the trip had gone over budget, and each person would need to pay an additional $200. My mom had paid for both of our trips, so that meant an extra $400 for her. She was very unhappy about the additional money, so I offered to pay, but somehow the check never got written.

Twenty years went by. One day, I suddenly remembered what I had said I would do. Oh, how I rationalized! *Good grief,* I thought, *it has been two decades!* I stewed and fumed, but I knew the Holy Spirit was working on me. Would I harden my heart or listen to the Holy Spirit's leading?

Well, I wrote that check 20 years later—for $500. (I owed interest, didn't I?) I tracked down the tour hosts and mailed them the money, along with a letter of apology. They wrote back and thanked me, saying they hadn't even remembered it. But that didn't matter; the test was mine to pass.

PRAYER
*Dear Lord, I want to hear Your voice today. Show me anything
that might cause my heart to be hard toward You.*

Journal: Write about some areas of your life about which God is speaking to you. Is your heart hard, or will you listen?

—Carole Lewis

Don't Dream Your Life Away

As has just been said: "Today, if you hear his voice, do not harden
your hearts as you did in the rebellion."

Hebrews 3:15

When I was a teenager, the Everly Brothers came out with a hit record called "Dream." The song's words spoke about "dreamin' my life away." That type of behavior used to plague me. Today I describe that "dream space" as Some Day Isle. Someday I'll eat right; someday I'll exercise; someday I'll feel better about myself; someday I'll put God in first place. But not today; today I have too many other things to do to get around to doing the things that are truly important to God.

It's easy for me to rationalize my Some Day Isle mentality. It's even easier to give it a socially acceptable name like procrastination. The Bible calls it something else: rebellion stemming from a hard heart! And that's nothing to dream about—or pass off as procrastination!

The solution is given in Hebrews 3:15 (which is a reference to Psalm 95:6-7). Today I am to listen to God's voice and remember that He is the Lord, my Maker. When He tells me what He wants me to do, my answer is to be "Yes, Lord," not "Yes, but." He already knows all the circumstances in my life. He doesn't need my excuses. What He asks is my obedience. Some Day Isle is not the Promised Land, and God does not want me to dream my life away in hard-hearted rebellion.

PRAYER

Lord, I am only fooling myself when I call procrastination "dreaming." You call it rebellion stemming from a hard heart. Today I will listen to Your voice.

Journal: What First Place goal are you dreaming about, while refusing to listen to God? How can you take action today to acknowledge Him as your Maker and your Lord?

—Elizabeth Crews

God Knows What You Need

As has just been said: "Today, if you hear his voice, do not harden
your hearts as you did in the rebellion."
Hebrews 3:15

After retiring from a job I held for several years, I was attending craft classes at a nearby community center. My route to the center was down Highway I-10, past Houston's First Baptist Church. I had been out of church for a while, and each time I passed the church, I felt a strong tug on my heart.

Finally, I listened to God's voice. I had always been a member of a small Baptist church, never one the size of this enormous church. But once inside, I was welcomed, and I started attending Sunday School and church regularly.

One Sunday, the bulletin announced a First Place class. Signing up for my first class was a divine appointment with the Lord. God stepped into my life in a greater way than I ever thought possible. Yes, I lost the weight, but I gained so much more. God opened up something new in my life. I was in His Word more, and for the first time, I was writing prayers in my journal.

First Place has been a part of my life for about 12 years. It has been a glorious journey. My closer walk with the Lord sees me through the bad and the good times. As I look back, I think, *What if I had hardened my heart and not listened to God's voice when He was urging me to attend First Baptist Church?* God knew what I needed, and all I had to do was listen to Him.

PRAYER
Father God, thank You for never giving up on me and for
continually pursuing me until I listen to Your voice. You are a faithful
and loving God. In Jesus' most precious name, amen.

Journal: If you have never written your prayers in a journal, try it and experience the wonder of what God can do in your life.

—Mary Etta Jackson

Press On Today!

As has just been said: "Today, if you hear his voice, do not harden your hearts as you did in the rebellion."
Hebrews 3:15

I came to First Place in July 1997. My top weight was 310 pounds, and my life was out of control in other areas too: My house lacked order; my job lacked order; my relationships lacked order. Every aspect of my life was out of whack.

Deep in my soul, I craved the discipline I once had as a National Class competitive swimmer. Over the years I had totally lost the characteristics that had allowed me to be a winner. I had become lazy and apathetic. Without structure and discipline, the enemy quickly convinced me to quit trying and resign myself to leading a life of defeat.

I remember the first Scripture I learned in First Place: Philippians 3:14, "I press on toward the goal to win the prize for which God has called me heavenward in Christ Jesus." Those two words "press on" became the spiritual logo that gave me the motivation and the inspiration to rebuild my life and reclaim the years the enemy had stolen from me. First Place Scripture memory verses and the First Place Bible studies were the tools the Lord used to help me press on to rebuild—first with small disciplines, then with bigger disciplines.

Today I press on daily to maintain and stay at my goal weight of 150 pounds. I have learned to press on toward the goal that calls me heavenward in Christ Jesus my Lord.

PRAYER
O Lord, give me today the internal drive to press on toward the goal for which You have called me. Thank You for Your protective Spirit as the walls of discipline are rebuilt around my life.

Journal: In what areas of your life are the walls weakest. Ask the Lord to help you press on to reconstruct those flawed walls.

—Beverly Henson

The Protection of the Holy Spirit

*As has just been said: "Today, if you hear his voice, do not harden
your hearts as you did in the rebellion."*

Hebrews 3:15

One of the ways I hear God's voice is awareness of the tactics the enemy uses to sabotage my efforts to press on for the prize. By allowing His Holy Spirit to become a scout for me, I am forewarned about the pitfalls before I step in a hole. This advance warning is very important to my First Place success, because once I fall, I know what will come next: the dreaded "start over again." The enemy loves to keep me in start-over-again mode.

Just a few days ago, I had a chance to see the Holy Spirit's protection in action. My nephew, Ben, started school this year. Every afternoon, I have an after-school snack for him when he gets home. This particular day, my diet was perfect, my workout was over-the-top excellent, and I was planning a weight-training session for the afternoon. Then Ben came in. I went to the fridge to get a little cup of Blue Bell ice cream for him, and that's when the Holy Spirit pointed out to me that the enemy was about to hit me in the taste buds. Ice cream cup in hand, it would have been easy for me to ignore the Spirit's warning. But I have learned to never give up what I want most for what I want right now. I said, "In Jesus' name, no way!" I grabbed Ben's cup and left in the freezer the one the enemy had written my name on.

PRAYER
*Thank You, Holy Spirit, for being my lookout for the tactics of the enemy. Thank You
for being there to show me how to cut him off before he cuts me off.*

Journal: Recall a recent occasion when the Holy Spirit allowed you to hear God's warning voice so that you could press on toward the prize rather than harden your heart in rebellion.

—Beverly Henson

Choose the Life-Giving Path

*Do not be like the horse or the mule, which have no understanding but
must be controlled by bit and bridle or they will not come to you.*

Psalm 32:9

Most of us don't get excited about the thought of obedience. A definition of the word
"obey" is "to comply, to behave, to follow commands or guidance." Not the easiest thing
to do. The apostle Paul expressed this struggle so perfectly in Romans 7:15. He admitted
that he had no idea why he kept messing up—he just did.

Can you relate to that? Is there some behavior in your life that you hate, but still you
keep doing it? A bad habit is like that.

Think about your life for a moment. Do any of the following apply? Overeating is
not good for you, yet a dozen donuts are right in front of you, so you eat the whole box.
Moving around is good for you, yet you settle in on the couch instead of going for a walk.
Spending time each day with the Lord through prayer and Scripture reading is required
if you want to know the Lord better and learn to trust and obey Him; yet when the alarm
goes off, you hit the snooze button—again and again and again. What's the solution?
You've got to *stop it!* You've got to stop wavering between good and evil and choose the
pathway toward which the Lord is directing you.

Our life's calling is to be healthy, whole people who live victoriously and with a
sense of purpose.

PRAYER
*Dear Lord, I don't want to be like the horse or mule in Psalm 32:9.
I want my will to match Your will for my life. Help me, I pray.*

Journal: In what part of your life are you resisting obeying God? Ask God to make you
willing to be willing to change.

—Carole Lewis

Accept His Invitation

Do not be like the horse or the mule, which have no understanding but
must be controlled by bit and bridle or they will not come to you.

Psalm 32:9

Journaling has been part of my daily routine for more than 20 years now, and the pages of my journals contain both my most intimate conversations with God and my most random thoughts. As a persistent journaler, I have learned to pay close attention to the words and phrases that keep showing up on the page, because these words usually contain God's word to me.

One word that keeps popping up lately is "invitation." As I pondered what message God might have for me, it occurred to me that there was a difference between graciously accepting God's invitation to join Him in His work and being like a horse or mule that must be controlled by bit and bridle! So much of my life has been lived in the latter mode. I've said yes to God usually after I have exhausted all other avenues and have come to the painful realization that there's no place left to go except the place where God wanted me to be all along.

Learning to graciously accept God's invitation is also about taking care of my body so that it is fit for His service.

PRAYER
Lord, today I choose to say yes to You by saying no to the
things that keep me from caring for myself so that I am fit for
service and ready to respond when You call.

Journal: Describe a time when you have been like a horse or mule that must be controlled by bit and bridle.

—Elizabeth Crews

Be Committed

Do not be like the horse or the mule, which have no understanding but
must be controlled by bit and bridle or they will not come to you.
Psalm 32:9

The 4-H club had prepared their horses and ponies for the county fair. Our son, Scott, was taking Ted, his dapple-gray pony. Ted had been washed and groomed and was ready to go into the show ring. The judge commanded the kids to walk their entries, and Ted was cooperative. Then the judge told them to trot their ponies. Scott nudged Ted with his heels, but Ted would not trot. The judge told them to canter their ponies; but Ted would not canter. Ted knew how to do these things but would not perform until Scott reluctantly led him by the reins out of the ring after a poor showing.

First Place has set nine commitments for us to follow, and we sometimes think we can ignore some of them, and we remain stubborn in following the program. The outcome is disappointment at the final results.

One of the ladies in our class admitted that she had not taken seriously the filling out of a food record. After not being able to lose any weight or inches for a month, she began to keep track of what she was eating. Suddenly she began losing weight, and she realized the importance of a commitment.

PRAYER
Lord, I ask Your help in following the guidelines and commitments in my everyday life.
Help me not to be so stubborn as to think I can do things my way.

Journal: What commitments are the hardest for you to keep? Why do you have a problem in these areas?

—Bev Schwind

Stubborn!

Do not be like the horse or the mule, which have no understanding but must be controlled by bit and bridle or they will not come to you.

Psalm 32:9

Have you ever gone to the mall and entered on one side of the building but exited on the other side and wondered where your car went? This happened to me one holiday season. It was a cold night, and I walked down several rows of cars only to find an empty space where I was sure I had parked.

My Christmas shopping was nearly finished, and I had made so many gift decisions that my mind was exhausted. But I was sure I knew what door I had come in; I told the officer that someone had stolen my car. I knew right where I had parked it.

I was a bit stubborn when he kindly suggested that perhaps I had come into the mall by a different door. "There are four doors leading out to the parking lot, and it can be confusing," the officer said. I was reluctant to walk with him to the other end of the mall, sure that my tired feet were traveling unneeded steps.

But we headed out the door. There sat my car! "It happens all the time," the officer said as he saw the embarrassed look on my face.

"Thank you" was all I could manage to say.

PRAYER
Lord, forgive me for being stubborn when there are so many times You are trying to direct me a certain way but I don't listen. Thank You for Your guidance.

Journal: Make stubbornness a point of prayer by listing some times when you have made up your mind about a person or a situation and then found that you were wrong.

—Bev Schwind

Learning the Hard Way

Do not be like the horse or the mule, which have no understanding but
must be controlled by bit and bridle or they will not come to you.

PSALM 32:9

"Whoa! Streaker, stop!" I shrieked as the black stallion thundered down the Oregon Coast that fateful day so many summers ago. The feisty beast, with his legs churning beneath me, showed no sign of tiring or of obeying my commands. Not only did the horse refuse to listen, but I, too, had ignored earlier warnings from my mom and an experienced stable hand. Both had cautioned me against riding this now out-of-control animal.

Throughout the years, especially during my First Place journey, this riding experience has been a good reminder that following God should not require a bridle or a bit. Because I am His beloved child, obeying Him should be a joy, not a burden. That includes keeping my body—His temple—pure, healthy and strong through balanced eating and exercise.

High in the saddle on a horse named Streaker, and later from a hospital bed, this rider learned a valuable lesson. Sometimes it's better to just stop and listen before a nasty fall does the stopping for you. Unfortunately, there are times when God reins us in the hard way; but as we begin to put Him first in our lives, we learn to stop resisting and surrender willingly, leaving the bridle and bit behind.

PRAYER
Dear heavenly Father, forgive me the many times when I have
battled against Your loving will for my life. Today, I choose to stop my foolish
attempts to control my life, and I surrender everything to You.

Journal: If you still struggle with stopping the old and putting on the new, you're not alone. Confess your stubbornness right now and pour out your heart to God.

—Carol Van Atta

Permanent Change Is Possible

Take the helmet of salvation and the sword of the Spirit, which is the word of God.
Ephesians 6:17

It's hard to lead a balanced life. We all have areas we fight against. What's your indulgence? What craving calls to you again and again? What pattern causes hurt and harm in your life?

Perhaps it's overeating. You don't think about it—you just do it. When the going gets tough—and that seems to happen most days—you reach for the bag of popcorn or the package of cookies.

Maybe it's anger. You flare up at the slightest provocation—while driving or while talking on the phone to your kids or coworkers. It seems like the slightest spark will ignite a fire within you.

Perhaps your indulgence is shopping. Whenever you're at a store, it seems as though you just can't say no to purchasing something. There's always a good excuse—the store is having a sale or you need to stock up on something.

Is there hope? Is permanent change possible? The answer is a resounding yes! Your Bible has every answer you will ever need tucked inside its pages. Tired of indulging? Then *stop it* with the power of God's Word. Read it when you are tempted to overeat, when you're in danger of losing your temper, when you are tempted to spend too much. Memorize verses that will help you battle against indulging those sinful desires that wage war on your soul.

PRAYER
*Dear Lord, I desperately desire a life of balance. Help me turn to
Your Word today instead of indulging myself.*

Journal: In what ways do you indulge yourself? Look up and record verses from the concordance of your Bible that can help you change.

—Carole Lewis

Flirting with Temptation

Take the helmet of salvation and the sword of the Spirit, which is the word of God.
Ephesians 6:17

The T-shirt slogan read: *Lead me not into temptation—I can find it by myself.* Of course, the comment was meant to be amusing, but the one-liner raises an interesting question: Do we really mean what we say when we ask to be kept from temptation? When I am fearlessly honest with myself, I must admit that I don't use the weapons God has given me to ward off the flaming arrows of the evil one, because temptation promises me way too much fun.

If I were revolted by temptation, if I saw my sins as God sees them, it wouldn't be temptation at all. Rather than being an innocent victim, I am usually a willing volunteer. Now, if temptation brought visible chains to bind me, I might be more inclined to resist the evil one's wiles. But my enemy knows that, so instead, he makes sure temptation comes in the form of food that offers comfort, companionship and cheer. Enticed by an opportunity to indulge my appetite, I dabble, debate and flirt with food rather than standing firm in my faith—and in the process, I invite temptation into my life. I fall prey to temptation because I do not avail myself of the divine weapons God has provided for my defense.

Today I will take up the helmet of salvation and use the sword of the Spirit so that I will not be lured into temptation's web. Following the nine commitments of First Place is a good place to begin the resistance.

PRAYER

Gracious God, You have given me divine weapons to defend myself from the enemy's wiles. Today I resist temptation by standing firm in my faith.

Journal: What temptation do you need to resist by using the divine weapons God has given you for your defense?

—Elizabeth Crews

Making a Stand

Take the helmet of salvation and the sword of the Spirit, which is the word of God.
Ephesians 6:17

"You're such a loser!" "You can't do anything right." "Failure!" The accusatory voice in my head droned on, never missing a beat. If you have ever used food to stuff feelings, you've likely noticed that as you begin to release unhealthy eating patterns, some not-so-comfortable thoughts and feelings emerge from the depths where they may have spent years buried by mounds of apple pie and extra large slices of pizza.

As I began to turn away from food as a quick fix, I quickly discovered other negative thought patterns eager to rear their ugly, mind-tearing philosophies (not to mention that we have an enemy out there who would like nothing more than to see us return to our former state of captivity and dependence on food). I had two choices: One was to return to my old ways in an attempt to hide my age-old emotional aches and pains; the other was to put on my helmet of salvation, pick up the sword of the Spirit and take a battle stance, ready to defend my new way of thinking and living, trusting God to fight for me.

God's Word truly does slice through the lies in our mind, replacing them with His eternal truth. If your thoughts are getting out of control, stop them from escalating. Use your weapons! You'll be glad you did.

PRAYER
*Dear awesome God, today, I commit to putting on the helmet of salvation
and fully utilizing the sword of the Spirit—Your Word—to combat and stop negative
thinking in my life. With You, Lord, all things truly are possible. Amen.*

Journal: Do ever feel as if there's a committee of negative voices shouting in your head? Write down some Scriptures you plan to keep with you at all times, and read them daily whenever you're tempted to think or act contrary to God's truths.

—Carol Van Atta

Claiming Victory

Take the helmet of salvation and the sword of the Spirit, which is the word of God.
EPHESIANS 6:17

Helmets are a necessity for people who ride skateboards or bikes, bat a baseball, work in heavy construction sites, serve in the military—the list goes on. You and I also need to wear helmets, but ours is a spiritual head protector. The head is where our thoughts are formed and doubts arise. It is where dreams are made and destroyed, depending on who protects our thoughts. We need the helmet of salvation, which is God's protection for our thoughts and feelings.

The helmet of salvation protects us from thinking negative thoughts about our goals. We can know without a doubt that God is for us and not against us. The sword, or the Word, is our weapon against all things that would harm us. Jesus used the Word and spoke it aloud when Satan tempted Him. We can do the same thing when we are tempted. We can claim victory over whatever addiction or trial has come our way. Memorizing the Word is our defensive weapon. The Word disciplines us, teaches us and takes away any doubt of who we are in Christ.

Just as people put something on their heads in severe weather, or during activities such as extreme sports, construction work or war, we need to walk out the door with our salvation protecting us and the sword of the Spirit not only declaring what we have read but also verbally declaring it against our enemy.

PRAYER
Remind me, Lord, that You have equipped me with a complete uniform to wear in any situation. Give me boldness to speak out and proclaim Your message.

Journal: List the complete armor God has given you, along with the sword and the helmet. Describe what each piece means as you put it on.

—Bev Schwind

Learning to Starve Sin

Can a man scoop fire into his lap without his clothes being burned?
Can a man walk on hot coals without his feet being scorched?
Proverbs 6:27-28

In my book *Stop It!* I talk about the three reasons we overeat. One of the reasons is that we fail to identify the one food that always gets us going in the wrong direction. My downfall food is anything creamy, like ice cream or cheesecake. It can even be sugar-free pudding that I can whip up quickly and then eat all four servings! For others, it might be salty, crunchy food, such as chips or snack crackers. For others, it might be something like peanut butter. Although peanut butter is good for us, it's also high in calories. If you are a person who begins by eating a spoonful of peanut butter and ends by eating half the jar, then peanut butter is a trigger food for you.

I have found that by staying away from my trigger foods, I have no problem losing weight. Once I start eating those sweet and creamy foods, I make other unhealthy choices as well. Each of us must ask ourselves the same question, *What is holding me back? What is the one thing that keeps me from living the way the Lord intended?*

Which path will you choose today? Are you willing to eliminate whatever leads you back into destructive ways? Are you willing to starve sin so that you can enjoy the banquet God has prepared for you?

PRAYER
Dear Lord, show me the one thing that is keeping me from experiencing victory.
Make me willing to give it up for You.

Journal: Write about the things that cause you to relapse. Ask God to make you aware of when you might be tempted to fall back into old patterns and behaviors.

—Carole Lewis

Full Meal Deal

Can a man scoop fire into his lap without his clothes being burned?
Can a man walk on hot coals without his feet being scorched?
Proverbs 6:27-28

Can I really eat more than allowed on the Live-It plan and expect to lose weight? Can I refuse to make exercise a part of my daily routine and still expect to have a fit-for-the-King's-service body? Can I conveniently forget to keep a daily food diary and expect to remember what I ate that day?

When I began the First Place program, I was silly enough to think that I could keep the commitments that were easy for me and that would be enough to ensure weight loss. If I just prayed enough, read and memorized enough Scripture and spent twice as long on the Bible lessons, then what I did in the physical realm didn't matter. To my dismay, I soon found that the First Place program is not like a smorgasbord deli. I can't take double helpings of the commitments that give me pleasure and ignore those that are rough and hard to digest. One small act of obedience is greater than my most lofty prayers; and obedience asks that I care for my body because it is God's temple, the place where His Holy Spirit resides. First Place is not an a la carte menu. It is a balanced program that addresses all my needs, even those I would like to pretend I don't have.

PRAYER
How foolish I must look to You, Lord, when I think I can do things
my way and reap Your rewards. Thank You for showing me the folly of
my ways through the humorous verses in the book of Proverbs.

Journal: Write about the ways that you are heaping fire in your lap when you don't follow what you need to do to have a balanced and healthy lifestyle.

—Elizabeth Crews

Things *Can Be* Different

Can a man scoop fire into his lap without his clothes being burned?
Can a man walk on hot coals without his feet being scorched?

PROVERBS 6:27-28

While many people desire to be special, my desire has always been to be normal. Beginning in the third grade, I began the struggle with my weight. I remember being so embarrassed when my grandparents had to shop in the chubby section to buy me clothes, while they shopped in the regular sizes to buy things for my sisters. My parents often put me on diets or restricted me from certain foods.

When I moved out of my parents' home, I finally was able to make my own rules. Over the next 20 years, I ate what I wanted and gained weight. Then I would go on a starvation diet to lose the pounds I had gained. Even though my weight discouraged me, I continued to enjoy the freedom of buying what I wanted at the grocery store—all those sweet, sugary desserts. Certainly I would be able to eat just one. *This time would be different*, I would tell myself. Then, time after time, I would fail.

Since I have been part of First Place, doing the Bible studies and memorizing the Scripture verses, I realize that I use sugar to soothe me when I am angry, tired or lonely, rather than turning to Jesus, the One who can heal that pain. Now I know there are certain foods that are irresistible to me, and when I buy those foods, it is like scooping fire into my lap. Without fail, I get burned.

PRAYER
Father God, thank You for loving me just the way I am. Thank You for
showing me how special I am in Your sight. Thank You for reminding me that
I am a unique creation who is loved and adored by You.

Journal: Give thanks to your Creator by writing about how there is no one else on Earth just like you, and why that makes you special.

—Christina Blakeslee

Importance of Accountability

Can a man scoop fire into his lap without his clothes being burned?
Can a man walk on hot coals without his feet being scorched?
PROVERBS 6:27-28

"Mommy! I burned my hand!" my daughter cried in obvious discomfort.

"How did that happen?" I asked, once I'd confirmed the damage wasn't serious. I already had a fairly good idea what had transpired, but I wanted to hear her answer.

She hung her head. "Well, I touched the stove, like you said not to."

How many times have we, as adults, hung our heads after "touching" that sinful something our heavenly Father told us to leave alone?

In First Place, we have learned a number of godly methods to help us keep from getting burned in relation to our eating habits. By following healthy guidelines for eating, exercising and trusting God, we can avoid the scorching heat of failure.

I know for a fact that if I choose to gobble up a whole turkey dinner with dessert, and expect to feel fantastic, with no adverse consequences, I'm lying to myself. That's why we have not only our heavenly Father but also each other to help us stop repeating old, painful patterns. Enlisting others in our quest to become healthier, more God-focused individuals, allows us to experience godly accountability. We can remind each other just how blistering the coals of poor choices feel.

PRAYER

Lord, help me today as I make choices and attempt to live my life according
to Your plan and purpose. Lord, please prompt me through Your people, Your Word
and Your Spirit to turn the other way when I get too close to the heat. Amen.

Journal: What fiery people, places or things are you drawn to? Enlist your group, a friend or trusted family member to help keep you accountable.

—Carol Van Atta

Just a Taste . . .

Can a man scoop fire into his lap without his clothes being burned?
Can a man walk on hot coals without his feet being scorched?

PROVERBS 6:27-28

Can I scoop mounds of food on my plate day after day and not see my body get bigger? I may not see the results the first week, but as time goes on, the number on the scale goes higher and the dress gets tighter. Having an affair may not be detected for some time, but sooner or later there is an unwanted pregnancy or gossip or devastated families. A cashier can't take a few dollars here and there without its being found out eventually. An alcoholic can't take even one drink or it would trigger the desire for more.

I asked one of the women returning to jail where I teach a Bible study, "What happened?" She replied, "I was angry and smoked a marijuana cigarette and was satisfied for a while. Then I took a drink with friends, and soon I was craving the drugs I had sworn never to touch again. I got caught, and I'm glad, because I don't want this kind of life. I realize I can't touch any of my old habits."

If something was harmful for you the first time you experienced it, what makes you thinks it will be okay the next time?

PRAYER
Lord, help me see that anytime I do not abide by the laws and rules
set in place for my welfare, I am asking for trouble.

Journal: What are your triggers for negative behavior? What do you need to guard against the most?

—Bev Schwind

What—and Who—to Avoid

Do not join those who drink too much wine or gorge themselves on meat.
Proverbs 23:20

My friend Elizabeth Crews has provided a wealth of knowledge about addiction. She works as an addictions counselor and often counsels folks who have a relapse problem. These people quickly grasp the principles of recovery, excel within an inpatient treatment program setting and are often role models to fellow patients. But then, for some seemingly unknown reason, they lapse into old habits at a predictable time in their treatment program.

Elizabeth tells me this usually happens when the exterior boundaries of the treatment center are removed and the person has only inner boundaries to resist temptation. In working with these patients, she has learned to quite accurately predict when the relapse will occur. No matter how high their motivation, some people fail to resist the devil by eliminating the people, places and things that can lead them back into old ways.

For those of us who want to lose weight, it may be necessary to stop eating out with friends who support our addiction. Or we might need to stop going to "all you can eat" restaurants. All of us need to build into our lives patterns that do not allow us to be self-indulgent. This is why a First Place group is the answer for so many people. In a group you can find like-minded men and women who share the same problem but who also want to do something positive to change the cycle of addiction.

PRAYER
Dear Lord, show me how to lovingly avoid those who drink too much or gorge themselves on food. Send me friends who desire to give You first place in their lives.

Journal: Write about the people and places that cause you to relapse into old patterns of addictive behavior.

—Carole Lewis

Recognizing Excess as Vice

Do not join those who drink too much wine or gorge themselves on meat.

Proverbs 23:20

When I first went into the alcohol-and-drug-addiction counseling field, I conveniently managed to separate excess drinking from overeating. How silly I must have looked to God, setting myself up as the expert, the one qualified to counsel those trying to overcome an addiction to alcohol and drugs, while I was in the clutches of my own powerful addiction to excess food.

I was also conveniently neglecting the whole counsel of God found in His Word by choosing favorite passages here and there and singling out verses that gave me comfort and assurance. When the pastor challenged the congregation to read the whole Bible in one year, I agreed to be part of that one-year trek through God's Word. What I found when I got to Proverbs 23:20 sent my head reeling! As a champion of civil rights, I had long hung my hat on Galatians 3:28, but Proverbs 23:20 talked about a different kind of nondiscrimination. Not only does God not discriminate based on race, color or ethnic origin, God also does not discriminate between those who drink too much wine and those who gorge themselves on meat. In God's eyes, all excess is vice!

As a matter of fact, it was only when I realized that my gluttony was as offensive to God as the drunkenness of another that I became serious about calling my overeating by its rightful name: gluttony. All change begins with awareness; and awareness tells me that all excess is sin in God's sight.

PRAYER

Father, today I thank You for Your Word that convicts me of sin and comforts me with the assurance of Your unconditional forgiveness and love.

Journal: How have you separated your excess eating from others' sins of excess (such as drunkenness or gambling)? How does that prevent you from telling yourself the truth so that you can change?

—Elizabeth Crews

Stay Right

Do not join those who drink too much wine or gorge themselves on meat.
PROVERBS 23:20

Our society is driven to indulge the desires of the sinful nature—especially overindulging in food and possessions or practicing other negative behaviors. What makes us overindulge? I consider discontentment the culprit—wanting what we don't or can't have, and wanting more and better than we have.

Joni Erikson Tada once defined contentment as the sacrificing of itchy cravings to gain a settled soul. Have you ever had an itch in the middle of your back that you just couldn't reach? No matter how hard you worked to scratch, it just seemed to get stronger, bringing about the urge to scream! I've even wanted to scream when the sweets and snack foods in my pantry continue to call my name until the very last one is gone. Jesus calls my name, too, when I listen closely. He can gratify our soul's desires, and the itchy cravings seem to disappear. No longer are we discontent, for He settles our soul. Contentment is a state of the heart, a soul sufficiency, the peace of God.

Let's remember a good traffic rule on the road of life: When you meet temptation, keep to the right. Jesus is there and ready to direct your path.

PRAYER
*Lord, make me sensitive today to the people and temptations
that trigger my gluttony and overindulgence.*

Journal: Do you have any unhealthy desires in your heart today? Ask Jesus to replace them with the contentment only He can give you.

—Judy Marshall

All In

Do not join those who drink too much wine or gorge themselves on meat.
Proverbs 23:20

In the two years that my wife had been going to First Place, she did well with her weight loss. I had lost 14 pounds during the same time period by just eating the new way she was cooking! We were eating out less and no longer participating in so many food-related events. Sometimes, if I had a taste for something she couldn't eat, I would go out with colleagues at lunch so I wouldn't distract her from her progress.

My wife convinced me that I should join the First Place program too—other men would be there, she told me, and it would be a way for me to take off the last 7 pounds I wanted to lose. I thought, *Why not?* Since the first 14-pound loss had almost been by accident, this would be a breeze.

We just concluded a First Place Bible study, and I am four pounds lighter than when I started. But I gained and lost the same few pounds several times over the course of the study, and I still need to lose three more pounds. So I will be returning for the next session.

As I look back, I realize that God is not pleased with my attitude of eating out of control one week (out with my buddies) because I think I can exert more control the next week (eating healthy with my wife). Living the commitments means that I turn from my old habits about food and choose a new way of living with food—every day.

PRAYER

*Father, making the First Place commitment is making a commitment to You.
And that is a sacred and holy thing. Making light of those commitments
is mockery against You. Lord, I ask for Your grace and mercy and the power
and discernment to learn Your perspective on food.*

Journal: Are there some events in which you can no longer participate because of the overemphasis on food? Are you playing games with God in any other areas of your life?

—Michael D. Smith

Play the Tape to the End

Remember your leaders, who spoke the word of God to you.
Consider the outcome of their way of life and imitate their faith.
Hebrews 13:7

Can you name someone you admire? Does this person always seem to make the right decisions? Do you long to have the peace and joy you see in this person's life? The verse above tells us how to become the person we admire.

You just need to learn to "play the tape to the end." This is what the people you admire have learned to do and what has helped them lead lives of victory and purpose. These people have learned these things:

- God loves me and has good plans for me (see Jeremiah 29:11).
- I must believe God and not doubt (see James 1:6).
- My God is bigger than my problems (see James 1:12).
- When I obey God, I show my love for Him (see John 14:21).

Playing the tape to the end simply means that we realize that God has a purpose for our life, and if we are to achieve His purpose, we must look past the momentary temptation to give in to destructive behavior. When temptation comes, one of the God-given ways of escaping the snare is to stop long enough to picture the end result.

PRAYER
Dear Lord, help me today to look past my present and play the tape to the end. I desire to become like the people I admire most because those people look like You.

Journal: Write about the most destructive behavior now in your life and ask God to heal you of it.

—Carole Lewis

Proof's in the Pudding

Remember your leaders, who spoke the word of God to you.
Consider the outcome of their way of life and imitate their faith.
Hebrews 13:7

"The proof of the pudding is in the eating" was one of my grandmother's favorite sayings. To her, action was more important than words. True to that belief, she consistently practiced what she preached. Perhaps that is why it's so important to me that I model the message of First Place rather than just say empty words that I don't apply to my life.

As a matter of fact, being able to practice what I preach was my greatest concern in starting a First Place group at my church. I was a well-seasoned small-group leader and Bible teacher. Scripture memory was already part of my spiritual discipline, as were Bible Study, Scripture reading, prayer and giving encouragement to others. But when it came to applying the same degree of spiritual discipline to my out-of-control eating, I fell far short of the mark—so far short that unless I could begin to practice loving self-care that reflected my commitment to Jesus Christ, I could not continue to teach in a church setting, let alone lead a First Place group. As hard as I tried to deny the truth of my condition, my oversized body belied my words that Christ was the Lord of my life. A compulsive overeater is never anonymous.

In First Place I have learned that the proof of the pudding is in the eating—and not eating!—of those things that keep me from a right relationship with God.

PRAYER

Sovereign Lord, help me live my First Place profession so that others can see the outcome
of this wonderful way of life and be drawn to You.

Journal: Do your words and your actions match when it comes to self-care? If so, how? If not, why not?

—Elizabeth Crews

Called to Service

Remember your leaders, who spoke the word of God to you.
Consider the outcome of their way of life and imitate their faith.

Hebrews 13:7

"You can't possibly be an introvert" is the response I usually get when the conversation turns to personality type and temperament. When I hear that reply, I just smile to myself, knowing that I am indeed an introvert whose desire to proclaim God's Word of truth is greater than my natural inclination to live a quiet, solitary life. As I have studied personality types and spiritual gifting, I am convinced that the confusion about what it means to be an introvert or extrovert comes from accepting the world's view on what it means to be a leader.

Hebrews 13:7 tells us the truth. A leader is not someone with personal power or charisma. In God's kingdom, leaders are those who speak the Word of God, not those who motivate others with empty words and flattering persuasion. After all, God chose a humble young peasant girl, an introvert who pondered God's truth in her heart, as the original carrier of the Word made flesh who came to dwell among us.

I would much rather meditate on God's Word than bring the message. But God has called me to do both. And I have learned that it is only as I sit in silence, listening to God, that I have a message to speak to others—or the courage to bring it! I can only speak as I allow God to speak to me. I can only lead as I follow the One who calls me into service and fills me with His Word.

PRAYER

O Lord, I can only lead as You lead me. I can only speak Your truth as
You speak it to me. Only as I abide in You will Your words abide in me
so that I can fulfill the plan and purpose You have for my life.

Journal: Talk to God about how He has called you to use your personality and spiritual gifts to lead others to Him.

—Elizabeth Crews

Bringing Glory to God

Remember your leaders, who spoke the word of God to you.
Consider the outcome of their way of life and imitate their faith.
Hebrews 13:7

The fact that the writer of the book of Hebrews chose to remain anonymous gives us an example of what it means to be a servant-leader in the kingdom of God. Through his writing, this unnamed author invites us to consider his way of life and imitate his faith. This side of heaven, we will never know the name of this humble scribe who wrote down the words God gave him without feeling the need to write down his own name.

Why is this subtle lesson so important to me? Because I am called to be a writer who once had grand aspirations of writing the great American novel that would make my name a household word! But God has been very clear with me that fame and fortune are not part of His plan for my life. Yes, I am called to write, but I am also called to humility and a simple life that allows His words to flow though me without my need for recognition getting in the way. Long ago God taught me that it doesn't matter who gets the credit as long as the work is done in a way that brings glory to Him and leads others into His truth.

PRAYER
Lord God Almighty, thank You that You teach me how to live
a life that brings glory and honor to You.

Journal: How has God called you to live a humble, simple life that teaches others and witnesses to His glory in subtle, but powerful, ways?

—Elizabeth Crews

Stop Indulging, Start Thinking

Watch and pray so that you will not fall into temptation.
The spirit is willing, but the body is weak.
Matthew 26:41

In *Stop It!* I talk about the word "trajectory." Picture the curve an object makes as it leaves one location and heads toward another. Our lives have trajectory. The decisions we make today will affect our future. Every choice we make yields a result. When we choose to engage in harmful behaviors, we set in motion events that will produce outcomes somewhere else. What trajectory are you on right now?

Giving in to your impulses creates one set of results. Focusing on the consequences enables you to make better choices that lead to positive results. Your job is to stop indulging and start considering—to start thinking of where every choice will lead.

A wonderful thing about our Lord is that He's able to change the trajectory we are on. No matter what decisions we've made in the past, we are not doomed to destruction in the future. God promises that He will complete the good work He began in us when we commit our lives to Him.

This is why it's so important that we watch and pray. Our spirits may want to do what's right, but our bodies hardly ever do. To change our trajectory, it's imperative that we learn how to take charge of our stubborn bodies. The apostle Paul says that we must make our body our slave so that when we have preached to others, we will not be disqualified for the prize (see 1 Corinthians 9:27).

PRAYER
Dear Lord, my greatest desire is for You to change the trajectory
of my life. Help me learn what it means to watch and pray.
My spirit is willing but my body is weak.

Journal: Write about where you are in your personal trajectory right now. Give God permission to make changes where necessary.

—Carole Lewis

God-Pleasing, Not People-Pleasing

Watch and pray so that you will not fall into temptation.
The spirit is willing, but the body is weak.
Matthew 26:41

Growing up in a home ruled by rage conditioned me to be hypervigilant, always watching for signs that some minor incident was about to trigger a major disturbance. I learned to control my actions based on the anticipated reaction of others, not on my own needs and legitimate wants. If my mother told me I was hungry, I ate, whether my body agreed with her decision or not. If my father told me women were created to keep house and please the men in their life rather than be bright and intelligent, then I accepted that decision rather than risk incurring his wrath. Somewhere along the line, I became so accustomed to yielding my needs and legitimate wants to the out-of-control emotions of others that I couldn't even tell what I needed or how I felt. People pleasing became my way of life. I became someone who always did what others wanted me to do. I buried my true needs deep inside me by stuffing them down with food.

Matthew 26:41 invites me to a different type of hypervigilance: watching and praying so that I will not fall into temptation. Watching and praying invite me to look to God and conform my wants and desires to His Word, rather than fall prey to the temptation to be a people pleaser who meets her own needs by turning to the false comfort of food.

PRAYER
O Lord, the spirit is willing but the flesh is weak. Help me look to
You and not react to the ancient fear of displeasing others.

Journal: Have you been choosing to please others rather than caring for yourself in a way that is pleasing to God? How can watching and praying help you overcome this behavior?

—Elizabeth Crews

Be on Guard!

Watch and pray so that you will not fall into temptation.
The spirit is willing, but the body is weak.
Matthew 26:41

Jesus knew all the temptations that would come to Peter and the other disciples, just as He knows what will come our way in areas in which we are vulnerable. When we are content after eating a good meal, it is easy to sit down and feel our eyes get heavy as we fall asleep. In the same way, temptation leads us to consider the pleasure to be had by indulging the flesh. As we entertain temptation, we let our defenses weaken. Before we realize it, we fall into the temptation. But Jesus tells us to be alert and observant. We are to guard against what is before us. When we know that we are going to a buffet or party where rich foods will be plentiful and sweets too hard to resist, we need to prepare ourselves.

This verse lets me know that it's normal for my body to be weak; but the spirit is willing. If I pray, the Holy Spirit will help me win the battle in those vulnerable areas of my life. We experience victory when we overcome temptation, and we find new strength for the next round.

PRAYER
Lord, I pray I will stay alert and guard my heart against temptations
that come my way. I thank You that You have given me Your Word to equip me.
Help me in my most vulnerable areas.

Journal: Have you fallen asleep while something happened that you could have handled if you had been alert and prayed?

—Bev Schwind

Wrestling with God

Watch and pray so that you will not fall into temptation.
The spirit is willing, but the body is weak.

Matthew 26:41

I had vertigo one Sunday and stayed home rather than drive to church. Things were not right. I was angry. I had suffered an injustice that no one should go through. I had been wronged and wasn't ready to forgive the offender. I tried to watch Pastor Adrian Rogers on TV, only to realize that God was working on my attitude. I turned off the TV and tried to work, but that did not bring relief.

All afternoon, God and I wrestled. He reminded me why I was feeling so bitter today, so I asked the Lord's forgiveness. But we weren't finished yet. The person who had wronged me could not look me in the eye and was not a Christian. It was only after I prayed, asking God to help me forgive the other person that I began to feel any relief. I had wasted the better part of the day in anger and bitterness. Had I sought God's help before getting out of the bed that morning, how much more pleasant the day would have been!

PRAYER
Precious Lord, thank You for being a loving Father who is
quick to reprimand and quick to forgive. Thank You for the relief
that comes from doing things Your way.

Journal: What temptations face you today? Ask God for guidance to enable you to do battle against them and win.

—Betha Jean Cunningham

Scripture Memory Verses

Section One:
Making Wise Choices

Deuteronomy 30:19
Luke 2:52
Joshua 1:7
1 Peter 1:13
1 Kings 3:9
1 Corinthians 6:12
Psalm 127:1
James 3:13
Psalm 20:7
John 3:16

Section Two:
Begin Again

2 Corinthians 5:17
Romans 8:28
Micah 6:8
2 Corinthians 12:9
Philippians 1:6
Colossians 3:23
John 1:16
Philippians 2:10-11
Joshua 1:5
Isaiah 40:31

Section Three:
Living in Grace

2 Corinthians 3:17
Psalm 139:13-14
Galatians 2:21
Hebrews 3:12-13
Romans 3:22-24
John 15:5
Proverbs 18:10
Colossians 2:6-7
Colossians 3:17
Matthew 28:19-20

Section Four:
A New Creation

Romans 6:4
Psalm 37:4
Colossians 3:1-2
Isaiah 41:13
Deuteronomy 20:4
Hebrews 4:16
Ephesians 2:10
Zephaniah 3:17
2 Corinthians 10:5
2 Corinthians 3:18

Section Five:
Healthy Boundaries

John 8:32
Isaiah 59:1
Proverbs 25:28
Psalm 3:3
1 Peter 5:6
Colossians 4:2
Galatians 5:7
Romans 12:11
Proverbs 4:23
Mark 9:7

Section Six:
Choosing Thankfulness

Psalm 136:1
Luke 1:49
Psalm 18:19
John 14:26
Deuteronomy 4:7
Psalm 18:28
Psalm 119:14
Romans 8:32
Hebrews 12:28
Ephesians 5:20

Section Seven:
Celebrating Victory

Psalm 115:1
1 Corinthians 10:31
1 Peter 3:8
Psalm 133:1
Numbers 35:34
Psalm 95:6
Ephesians 5:19
1 Corinthians 15:57
Psalm 126:3
1 Peter 4:7

Section Eight:
Stop It!

Revelation 1:3
Revelation 3:20
James 1:22
Hebrews 3:15
Psalm 32:9
Ephesians 6:17
Proverbs 6:27-28
Proverbs 23:20
Hebrews 13:7
Matthew 26:41

Contributors

Millie Aviles
First Place Member
Manakawkin, New Jersey

PJ Bahr
First Place Member
Rapid City, South Dakota

Molly Bascom
First Place Member
Rockville, Maryland

Christina Blakeslee
First Place Leader
Gaithersburg, Maryland

Janet Boyles
First Place Leader
Morgantown,
West Virginia

Barbara Brown
First Place Member
Taylors, South Carolina

June Chapko
Author, *Making Wise Choices* Bible study
San Antonio, Texas

Jim Clayton
Senior Pastor, Dixie Lee
Baptist Church
Lenoir City, Tennessee

Kathlee Coleman
First Place Leader
Palmdale, California

Pat Cook
First Place Leader
Houston, Texas

Elizabeth Crews
Author, *Healthy Boundaries*
Bible study
Chula Vista, California

Betha Jean Cunningham
First Place Member
San Angelo, Texas

LaWanda Deloach
First Place Member
Meridian, Mississippi

Jack Dorn
First Place Leader
Taylors, South Carolina

Judy L. Dorn
First Place Leader
Taylors, South Carolina

Karen Duffy
First Place Member
Pataskala, Ohio

Susie Duren
First Place Leader
Napavine,
Washington

Kathy Geehreng
First Place
Networking Leader
Gaithersburg,
Maryland

Laura Hartness
First Place Member
Winston-Salem,
North Carolina

Beverly Henson
First Place
Networking Leader
Meridian, Mississippi

Mary Etta Jackson
First Place Leader
Houston, Texas

Susan Johnston
First Place Leader
Winter Park, Florida

Susan Jones
First Place Member
Greenville, South Carolina

Eulalia King
First Place Member and
Worship Leader
Houston, Texas

Janet Kirkhart
First Place
Networking Leader
Mount Orab, Ohio

Betty Lacy
First Place
Networking Leader
Hot Springs, Arkansas

Barb Lee
First Place Leader
Normal, Illinois

Carole Lewis
First Place
National Director
Houston, Texas

Barbara Lukies
First Place Australia
Networking Leader
Farmborough Heights,
New South Wales (Australia)

Judy Marshall
First Place Leader
Gilmer, Texas

Penny Masseau
First Place Leader
Lansing, Michigan

Dee Matthews
First Place Leader
Houston, Texas

Patty Miller
First Place Member
Greer, South Carolina

Denise Munton
Author, *Living in Grace*
Bible study
Houston, Texas

Debbie Norred
First Place Leader
Lynn Haven, Florida

Tammy M. Price
First Place Leader
Myrtle Beach,
South Carolina

Martha Rogers
Author, *Begin Again*
Bible study
Houston, Texas

Bev Schwind
First Place Leader
Fairfield Glade, Tennessee

David Self
Executive Pastor, First
Baptist Church
Houston, Texas

Joni Shaffer
First Place Outlook
Online Leader
Mercersburg, Pennsylvania

Kelly Shearer
First Place Leader
Indianapolis, Indiana

Becky Sims
First Place Member
Hilliard, Ohio

Michael D. Smith
First Place Member
Lyman, South Carolina

Sybil D. Smith
PhD, RN, BC,
First Place Leader
Lyman, South Carolina

Susan Sowell
Author, *A New Creation*
Bible study
Katy, Texas

Sara Toles
First Place Member
Houston, Texas

Becky Turner
First Place Leader
Houston, Texas

Carol Van Atta
First Place Leader
Troutdale, Oregon

Roberta Wasserman
First Place Alumni
Riva, Maryland

Joe Ann Winkler
First Place
Networking Leader
Kansas City, Missouri